FILIP SPRINGER

HISTORY
of a
DISAPPEARANCE

THE STORY OF A
FORGOTTEN POLISH TOWN

*Translated from the Polish
by Sean Gasper Bye*

RESTLESS BOOKS
BROOKLYN, NEW YORK

First published as *Miedzianka: Historia znikania*
by Wydawnictwo Czarne, Warsaw, 2011

First Restless Books paperback edition April 2017

Paperback ISBN: 9781632061157

Library of Congress Control Number: 2016940776

Cover design by Daniel Benneworth-Gray

Printed in the United States of America
Set in Garibaldi by Tetragon, London

1 3 5 7 9 8 6 4 2

Restless Books, Inc.
232 3rd Street, Suite A111
Brooklyn, NY 11215

www.restlessbooks.com
publisher@restlessbooks.com

CONTENTS

HISTORY
of a
DISAPPEARANCE

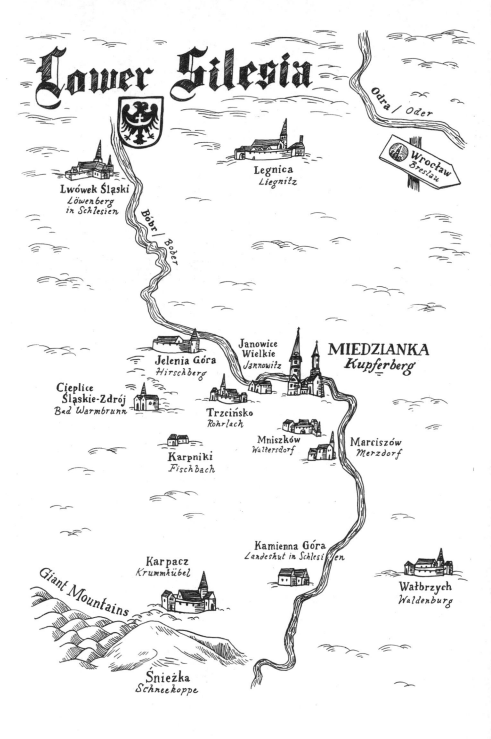

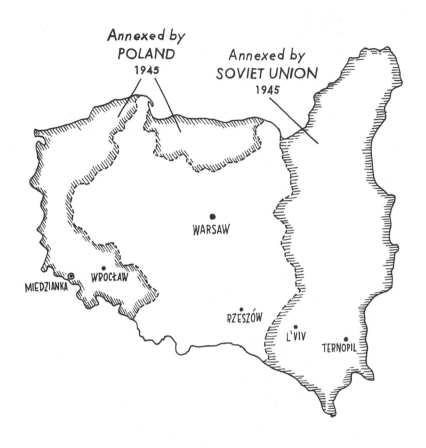

Border changes after World War II

ALL THE RESURRECTIONS

THE GROUND CAVES IN for the first time under the building housing Preus's smithy and Reimann the merchant's. It leaves a crater so large a wagon could fit inside. A crack in the walls has also opened along a row of houses—from Flabe the baker's to Friebe the hairdresser's—caused by the collapse of a mining drift.

One day, the horses plowing Mr. Franzky's field sink into the ground up to their chests and let out such a terrifying howl that those in the immediate vicinity drop what they're doing and race to the field, their faces pale. Only a few are brave enough to come to the animals' aid and rescue them; the rest gaze from a distance at the horses' heads protruding from the earth and the extraordinary, funnel-shaped cavity around them.

*   *   *

The superstitious said this was all because long ago in Kupferberg, a brother killed a brother. The spilling of fraternal blood was said to have brought a curse on the town. The event was commemorated by two stone crosses, placed just beside the road leading to Johannesdorf by the perpetrator himself, according to Silesian custom. The word *Memento* was inscribed on one of them, so that no one would forget. Every time someone looked its way, there it was, sticking up out of the grass. So people learned not to look. *Memento*—remember. As though all the hundreds of years of misfortune that rained down on green Kupferberg were merely a prelude to what would come to pass in this place. *Memento*—a warning that they will pay for a few mistakes for centuries to come. And the account will never be settled.

History never well and truly arrived here, but instead roamed around in the vicinity. To the inhabitants of these few houses built defiantly on the peak of a mountain, though history never found this place in its path, it seemed a beast that knew only how to sow chaos and destruction.

These were brave people. No one faint-hearted could have founded a town in such a spot. Nor could they have challenged nature so audaciously by digging holes into the stone mountainside, hunting for precious metals in the dark. The first of these bravest of men is said to have been Laurentius Angelus—the semi-legendary Silesian master miner, a foreigner from distant Wallonia. In the twelfth century, he reportedly discovered valuable mineral deposits here. Not much more is known of him—perhaps he is merely an agglomeration of the imaginings and stories local miners exchanged on winter evenings. Besides, there were many such stories to fire the imagination: for instance, the one about a silver crossbowman sowing terror among German settlers for mistreating Poles.

What is known for certain is what's in the chronicles. In the early fourteenth century, the landlord of the mountain and its adjoining lands is Albert der Baier de Cuprifodina in Montanis, also known as Albert Bavarus. Perhaps he is the one who quickly makes the region famous for silver mining. In 1370, the settlement then called Cuprifodina is sold by one of Albert's descendants—Heinrich Bavarus—to Clericus Bolcze, a knight at the court of the dukes of Schweidnitz and Jauer. It is he who erects a castle here in a nearby forest, which the Poles will later call Bolczów, and the Germans Bolzenstein.

Later, the demesne and the settlement itself will pass from hand to hand. The local lords are, in turn: starting in 1375, Puta of Častolovic (von Tschastolowitz) and Hannos Wiltberg; after 1397, the von Ylenburg brothers; and after 1398, the brothers Konrad and Reinhard von Boralowicz (Borawecz, Borrwitz). In 1433, the chronicles mention one Hermann von Czettritz, and in 1434 the von Liebenthal brothers. During the Hussite Wars, mining suffers a decline that it will not recover from until the sixteenth century.

In 1512, these estates are purchased by Dippold von Burghaus. He is the first real mining expert in the region, having developed gold extraction and metallurgy in nearby Reichenstein to such an extent that the most powerful mining and metallurgy companies in Europe couldn't wait to sink their teeth in. At its peak, 145 mines are in operation there, though Dippold is beginning to cast around for a new challenge. So he sells the mining rights the duke granted him to the Fugger and Thurzó families. He soon discovers Kupferberg, and knows that here he will repeat his success. Based on a merely superficial examination, he concludes the mountain's interior contains copper first and foremost, in the form of pure ore and pitchblende, but also silver and zinc blende. However, in order for Dippold to get his hands on all these riches, one condition must be met—the settlement must have the status of a Free Mining Town. For three years, Dippold lobbies young King Louis II of Bohemia. Finally, in 1519, he manages to secure the privilege, which endows the landlord of Kupferberg not only with the unrestricted right to conduct any kind of mining works on the grounds of his estate, but also exempts him from the *olbora*—a special tithe paid for the production of copper, lead, iron, and tin. Louis's generosity, or shortsightedness, will be the cause of numerous feuds between the Crown Estate and future landlords of Kupferberg.

Now Dippold can spread his wings: over more than twenty years, nearly 160 mineshafts and drifts are dug in the mountainside. The precious metals extracted are immediately melted down in local forges. Dippold invests the profits in projects like the rebuilding of nearby Castle Bolzenstein, which was destroyed during the Hussite Wars.

Yet the sudden development of mining and Dippold's growing wealth spark resistance among the miners and burghers. They know they could have a larger share of their patron's success, and begin openly to demand one. Dippold knows how to deal with them, though, and meets them halfway. Better to earn a little less than have a revolt of miners and affronted merchants on one's hands—and in the process, risk being thrown from the saddle entirely. He delays for another few years, but when he sees nothing will ease their stubbornness, he hands over one of the forges and a share of the mining profits. All the following landlords of Kupferberg will curse him for making these concessions.

One of these successors is Ludwig Dietz—secretary to King Sigismund the Old of Poland, an Alsatian by descent, and an extraordinarily influential and respected personage in the capital of Kraków. He is a polymath, a diplomat, and an outstandingly enlightened man, as well as a financier. Thanks to his acquaintance with Kraków's all-powerful Jakob Boner, the founder and overseer of the salt mines in Wieliczka and Bochnia, Dietz becomes aware of how precious-metal mining has the potential to multiply his fortune. He also probably dreams of going into business himself, and while on the lookout for a suitable investment, making the most of his acquaintance with the Fugger and Thurzó mining families, his eye lands on Kupferberg. Dippold wishes to divest himself of the property—so at the moment, the prospects seem remarkably promising.

The transaction takes place in 1538. Dietz calculates he will be able to ease the conflicts with the burghers and miners that have plagued Kupferberg's successive landlords, and that the effort will pay for itself through the exploitation of deposits Dippold had yet to tap. After all, Dietz is no amateur and is not buying sight unseen. The experts he's sent to the region have brought him only good news. He does not know he has fallen into exactly the trap that time and time again will contribute to Kupferberg's manifold crises. One characteristic of the local deposits is they display quite surprising quantities of copper, and even silver, in their surface layers, meaning further investigations are always conducted with an exhilaration akin to gold fever. But the results of the sample analyses are overly optimistic and falsely predict great riches hidden within the earth.

Sure enough, Dietz's estimates turn out to be exaggerated—the mining is not as profitable as expected, and the mine workers are constantly demanding a greater share. After barely five years, Dietz sells Kupferberg and its mines and tries the other side of the mountains, in Zuckmantel (today's Zlaté Hory). It seems he has no luck there either, and in 1545 he dies a wealthy man, but not an entirely fulfilled one.

Now Kupferberg finds itself in the hands of the Hellmann brothers. They, however, put their money into exploiting the numerous spoil tips that have come to litter the town over more than two centuries of mining. The brothers provoke astonishment among the miners, and probably outrage as well, when instead of sending them into the drifts, they're ordered to transport spoil from the tips into a valley that a nearby stream runs through. Thanks to hydrometallurgy technology that is advanced for its time, the Hellmanns set about producing blue vitriol in Kupferberg, which is used across Europe for dyeing and tanning. In 1533, the Hellmanns become the leading producers of this material in the Habsburg Empire.

The burghers look down their noses at the new landlords' activities. They derive all their privileges and the small profits these entitle them to from mining. One of the burghers, Valentin Krün, builds himself a house on "Lower Lane" at number 25, a house whose beautifully elaborate portal and sumptuous interior will impress the townspeople and captivate visitors for more than five centuries to come. People say a secret passage runs underground from the house to the mendicant abbey in the lower part of town, then continues all the way to Castle Bolzenstein. Krün anxiously observes the steady demise of one mine after the other, the miners disappearing and, with them, the raw materials he and his comrades have traded, earning their fortunes in the process. But the Hellmanns are doing exceptionally well selling their vitriol on their own.

In 1579, the few local miners are unable to provide the king the requisite amount of ore, and have their property confiscated, halting production in Kupferberg for the first time. The last mines are closed, and those who were still hoping their luck would turn begin to see lean years ahead. It's time to find another occupation.

They don't know the worst is yet to come. At the turn of the new century, Kupferberg begins to hear the beast's first menacing growls. Do the locals, who find it harder and harder to make ends meet, remember the curse? They must gaze uneasily at the stone crosses. *Memento*—remember, perhaps the worst is still ahead of you.

In 1618, armed hordes begin to make their way across Europe, embroiled in what historians will later call the Thirty Years' War. The beast will rage over three decades of terror, desolation, and sorrow. First comes the plague, which takes a deadly toll throughout the region. Kupferberg mourns the deaths of nearly half its inhabitants. The memory of this is still fresh when, on the night of July 18, 1634, awakened by the ringing of bells, the townspeople leave their houses and look westward down the mountaintop in terror. There, against a starry sky, Hirschberg glows with flame. The beast will once again have its due. All of the church towers are burning from incendiary bombs, the bells melting in the heat. A few hours later, all that will remain of the town will be a burned-out shell. Three hundred forty-one houses burn, and the people burn inside them. Their screams can't be heard from Kupferberg, but now the local people await the enemy in terror. At the moment, the enemy is the Croats, fighting on the side of the Habsburgs. They are the ones besieging Hirschberg. When they finally arrive in Kupferberg, the town disappears for the first time. Those who manage to survive the massacre hide out in the thick forest. There, first famine and then disease decimate them, and soon after, an unusually icy winter takes its toll as well. When the Croats withdraw, a few townspeople make their way back to the charred remains of Kupferberg, ready to rebuild.

In May 1641, Field Marshal Lennart Torstenssen becomes commander of the Swedish troops fighting on the side of the Protestant Union against the Catholic Habsburgs. He orders General Königsmarck to take Castle Bolzenstein, which Dippold had made such an effort to reconstruct over a hundred years ago. Those who had managed to withstand the Croats' onslaught must flee once again, this time from the Swedes. A siege commences, during which the Swedish forces burn down nearly all the nearby villages—Johannesdorf, Rohrlach, and Waltersdorf. But if Kupferberg does not disappear for a second time, it is only because they have hardly managed to rebuild it after the Croat invasion.

People attempt to explain these tragic times through recounting legends by the light of hidden campfires. They tell of the heroic duke of Castle Bolzenstein, who, seeing his cause was hopeless, slipped through the fingers of the Protestant butchers by leaping from a castle window into an abyss. For many years his ghost was said to haunt the recesses of the castle, moaning, crying out, and driving away those who dared disturb its peace. Some speak, too, of the funeral cortege that on cloudless nights makes its way between Kupferberg and Johannesdorf: a peculiar one, since its participants have no heads. It usually dissolves in the fog before sunrise.

The Swedes finally seize the castle and hold it for four years. In the meantime, they fight off several attempts by Habsburg forces to recapture the fortress. Finally, the situation on the front has changed so much that there is no longer any point defending it, and so they retreat. However, in keeping with the usual customs of war in that era, they leave a smoking ruin in their wake.

The war not only annihilates the entire town, it also destroys something much more valuable, which has brought joy to the people of Kupferberg for decades: the Habsburgs confiscate the Lutheran residents' church and forbid Protestant worship. For the dozen or so years of the Austrians' most vehement suppression of Lutheranism in Silesia, once again Kupferberg's Protestants will have to take to the forests around the nearby mountains and the ruins of the burned-out castle to obey their preachers' commandments. They don't recover their church until these lands are taken over by the Prussians in 1742. Pastor Fibiger from nearby Rudelstadt writes in his memoirs of this period: "O God! In what times have you commanded us to live! Come, good spirit, save this poor nation. See how much havoc and ruin lies about it! Silesia is in mourning and weeps over her bitter fate."*

The conclusion of the war doesn't bring an end to the plagues afflicting the town. After years of disasters, now no one believes in chance. There is no resurrecting the once-flourishing mines. The people are starving and try their luck with farming and breeding animals. But they are condemned to failure: the ground here is infertile and the climate harsh. Chroniclers record that in August 1693, an enormous quantity of snow falls on the entire area, and many puddles are covered in a thin layer of ice. Soon afterward, locusts appear in the town and nearby villages "in terrible quantities." Prayers commence in the churches for "the lifting of this curse and of the Hand of God." In the years to come, entirely unprecedented winters strike the town—in 1708, 105 people freeze to death in the area, and a further 185 elderly people and children die of dysentery and the pox.

Yet the townspeople are used to picking themselves up after each of these failures and catastrophes. When someone dreams up brave, fantastical plans running far into the future, they always say "*Wenn die Zeit erlaubte...*"—if time allows. They know the past too well. Walking once again along the road to Johannesdorf, they avert their gazes from the stone crosses, but they remember the *Memento* and the growls of the beast lying in wait beyond the mountains.

---

* I know the pastor's memoirs secondhand; Dora Puschmann cites them in her manuscript *Chronik über Kupferberg*.

Johann Martin Stulpe knows all this too, and arrives in Kupferberg in November 1724 firmly resolved to instill a modicum of hope in the townspeople's tormented souls. He was born in 1686 in Wartenberg to a poor cobbler's family, who were nevertheless so pious they prepared no fewer than two of their sons for the priesthood (the older Johann and the younger Michael). From a very young age, Johann distinguished himself through his diligent studies—first in elementary school in his hometown, then in secondary school in Liegnitz, finally at the university in Breslau, where he graduated in 1710 with a master's degree in liberal arts as well as a bachelor's in theology. He was ordained three years later, and began his service in the neighboring parishes. After years of wandering, and in recognition of his service, he was finally named priest of the languishing and desperate parish of Kupferberg. In 1725, despite meager resources, he embarked on the long and dangerous journey to Rome, to ask Pope Benedict XIII for permission to found the Confraternity of the Sacred Heart in Kupferberg. The Pope granted his assent.

So begins an almost thirty-year stay in the town by a priest who will be remembered here for the next two centuries. It does not get off to a good start, however. In 1727, Stulpe spends his own savings to completely renovate the church, which is dilapidated as a result of war and recent decades of neglect. However, the faithful cannot enjoy the sight of the church for long. One freezing January night in 1728, a great fire once again reduces the church as well as a considerable portion of the town to ruins. The townspeople must get back on their feet again. They rebuild the church over five years, and construct a parochial school as well.

Thanks to the scrupulous records Father Stulpe keeps, we know that over the next two decades he delivers 2,551 homilies, celebrates 2,392 Solemn Masses, and as many as 10,077 Low Masses. He performs 744 baptisms (of 374 boys and 370 girls). In the cemetery located at the rear of the triangular market square, he sends 768 worthy citizens on their final journey. He also blesses 265 couples who decide to take the sacrament of marriage there, inside the welcoming church. Yet what gives Johann Martin Stulpe the most joy are the annual church fair and the patron saint's feast day, which are always held on the third Sunday after Easter. Then, the town teems with hundreds of pilgrims from all over the region, and the membership roll of Stulpe's brotherhood burgeons with new entries. The priest is unaware that in the distant future, this custom of gathering the faithful in Kupferberg on every third Sunday after Easter will be one of the few pieces of evidence the town existed at all.

The beast awakens once again in 1740 in the mind of King Frederick the Great of Prussia, who decides to seize Silesia back from the Austrian Habsburgs, and green Kupferberg along with it. The subsequent wars over this territory will last over twenty years. In the fall of 1744, the Habsburgs' Imperial Army imposes a tribute on the townspeople, on pain of pacification. The price is ten thousand guldens in cash, thirty pairs of shoes, twenty draft horses, three hundred portions of oats, six hundred portions of hay, and eight hundred loaves of bread, which are to be provided to the Austrians within twenty-four hours. There are barely a thousand people in the town and they all know full well that they won't manage to fulfill these obligations. So they gaze sadly at the nearby forests, sensing that from there they will once again watch their town disappear. But their parish priest Johann Martin Stulpe unexpectedly comes to their rescue. Disregarding all orders to the contrary, he sets off for Schömberg, where Colonel Franquini—the commander of the Austrian forces—is stationed. He secures an exemption from some of the tribute as well as permission to provide much of it in longer than twenty-four hours. Kupferberg is saved. The beast slinks off with its tail between its legs. It will return in a few years for the latest conflict over Silesia, from which the Prussians will emerge victorious. This time Kupferberg will no longer have anyone to save it: on January 26, 1753, Father Stulpe, beloved by the townspeople, meets a sudden death. He is buried, according to his wishes, at the foot of the altar he himself built.

Meanwhile, every now and again new owners and investors come to town, lured by what lies on the surface and attempting to tunnel into the mountain, seeking their fortune. These also include charlatans and swindlers, for instance a certain Herzer who, wanting to prove to the new King, Frederick the Great, that there are promising cobalt deposits in the local mines, ships this valuable material all the way from Saxony and "mines" it once again. So Frederick pays a pretty penny for a survey that is meant to lead to profitable, regular mining, but finally discovers it is all a giant hoax. Perhaps that's what brings him to the town in person in 1766. Tipped off that he is about to be exposed, Herzer makes a run for it, and his capture and exemplary punishment mean mining in the hillside has once more died a death. All subsequent attempts to extract riches hidden beneath the earth here will end in varying degrees of disappointment—a feeling Kupferberg already knows all too well.

For a while, the town sees potential in weaving, especially since a new type of spinning wheel installed in the mills of the Old World has been producing remarkable results. But fairly quickly what had seemed a wonderful innovation turns out to be a curse: manufacturing linen becomes easier, but the market does not grow. In 1725, nearly half of the hitherto prosperous weaving families in the town lose their livelihoods due to a decline in spinning work. Kupferberg begins emptying out: in 1785, the town has barely 796 people, the majority of whom are living from hand to mouth. Soon it will get even worse—industrial spinning mills will open in nearby Merzdorf, and the remaining handful of weavers in Kupferberg will lose their livelihoods completely.

Soon the beast of history will once again have its way with this cursed place on the mountaintop, though this time it will be kinder. In August 1813, Prussian partisans under the command of Major Bolstern von Boltenstern arrive in town. They're starving, but they keep their distance. They're hunting for small French divisions speeding northward to reach the field of one of Napoleon's bloodiest battles. On August 26, on the banks of the Katzbach River, Napoleon's forces under the command of Marshal Jacques MacDonald are vanquished by the Prussians and their Russian allies, who leave four thousand of their own dead and fifteen thousand French corpses behind them. The people of Kupferberg do not learn of the allies' victory until afterward—during the battle they can hear only menacing rumbles and booms from over the mountains. They are glad that this time the town has survived.

But they don't have long to wait for the next disaster. On the evening of October 12, 1824, at number 84, the wife of Mansche, the white-leather maker, roasts a flitch of pork so fiercely it catches fire. First the flames spread through the house, and once they've reached the outside, they quickly make an ally of an unseasonably strong wind. The fire rages through the whole town for several hours, burning down sixty-seven houses, both churches and the schools attached to them, as well as the hospital and the town hall along with nearly its entire archive. The headquarters of the Royal Mining Office of the Duchy of Schweidnitz and Jauer also burn, and barns filled with harvests and winter supplies go up in flames. The pastor of the nearby town of Alt Kamnitz, who is visiting Kupferberg, is amazed to witness the scale of the tragedy:

> The construction methods and the condition of the buildings, which were entirely wooden, facilitated the spread of the flames. They engulfed both sections of the town with great speed. A harsh, southerly wind bore the raging fire toward the Catholic church, the schools beside it—both Catholic and Lutheran—and also toward Johannesdorf, where the flames had already begun spreading to the part of the town nearest Kupferberg. Once the fire had reached the Fechtergasse, having destroyed everything in its path, the wind changed from southerly to easterly and bore the same destruction and annihilation to the lower part of the town. Faster and faster, the flames swept through everything around, so violently they seemed to be mocking the collective efforts of hundreds of people rushing from near and far near to rein in this frenzy.

For some time, they succeeded in protecting the Lutheran church in the center of town, the main part of which still defied the surging sea of flames, but even it was forced to surrender to the fire's devastating effects.[*]

In the course of a single night, 140 families—503 people—lose everything they have. They are left with no roofs over their heads or any idea where to spend the next night. Amid the still-smoldering ruins of the lower part of the town and the charred grass on its outer edge there stand only the two stone crosses. *Memento*. Remember. But it's hard to say if, at that tragic time, anyone thinks of the curse.

Two days after the fatal evening, Countess Friederike von Reden of Buchwald arrives in town. In her memoirs she writes:

> I approach that sad vision, the like of which I have never beheld; I cannot understand what I am seeing, I feel petrified. In the manor house, which has survived completely intact surrounded by nothing but ruins, I was received by Anton and Count Gustav Matuschka. They led me directly into the center of a small group of people—a committee made up of Anton, two clergymen, the mining tithe collectors, the mayor, and an official, who asked me to take part in supporting the reconstruction of the town. We determined how to distribute the aid funds and that the money for reconstruction must be placed on deposit.[†]

---

[*]   Dora Puschmann quotes the words of this pastor.
[†]   I know of the Countess's account from the same source.

The countess is heartbroken at the sight of the town disappearing once again. She visits the townspeople, comforts the healthy, and shows concern for the wounded. Then she goes to the market in Bad Warmbrunn and buys what seems most necessary in the cold days of October for people who have lost everything: sixty-one pairs of boots and twelve pairs of children's shoes, everything the cobblers of Bad Warmbrunn can sell her that day. The countess puts the entire staff of her family estate to work knitting warm woolen clothes for the fire victims.

The town yet again pulls itself to its feet. Two years after the fire, on November 12, 1826, Pastor Christian Schreck can proudly consecrate a new Protestant church. He gives a beautiful speech at the ceremony, and next orders it printed and sold among the townspeople and visitors. He donates the funds this raises to the Catholic parish, which takes another three years to rebuild its church. The designer is none other than Karl Friedrich Schinkel, architect of the Altes Museum in Berlin. Each new building is constructed with all kinds of rules and fire safety regulations in mind. No one here wants to see the churches burn again.

In 1840, 677 people live in the town and only nine call themselves miners. Despite this, prospectors are constantly arriving here, wanting to seek their fortune in the mountain's interior. A series of arrivals from Upper Silesia fail to have any luck: Mr. Tiel-Winklers, Mr. Rosentiel, Messrs. Sarsten and Grundman. The latter two's treasure-hunting ends with the spectacular detonation of a gunpowder tower, along with the machine room serving one of the shafts. However, this doesn't deter the Schönfelder brothers—Richard, Hermann and Robert—who decide to try their luck in 1880. After a few years without much to show for it, and with large losses besides, they sell Kupferberg's mine to Mr. Arend, a Jew from Berlin. Yet again the mineshafts are dedicated and the workers march with torches through the early morning in the hope the ceremonial inauguration of the mine will bring them good luck and wealth. Mining goes on a few years, new shafts are even built, but once again the deposits do not bring the expected profits.

Only now there is no time to perfect the extraction and introduce new technology. The beast is starting to become restless, and once again rears its head. On June 28, 1914, Gavrilo Princip shoots Franz Ferdinand and his wife, and the world the people of Kupferberg have known disintegrates before their eyes.

However, the Great War makes no incursion into Kupferberg— it takes a different route. None of the fronts even graze the town— yet they bear away more than a dozen of its sons and fathers. When the cannons fall silent, a memorial will be placed on the triangular market square in remembrance of their spilled blood.

The townspeople are hardy. Within five years of the war's end they once again march in procession before the mine building, once again miners' lamps burn, once again standards wave. A large portrait of Saint Barbara painted by the mining assessor's brother, Mr. Fitzner, glistens on one of the mineshafts. Pastor Helmut Eberlein and Father Johannes Kaufmann jointly explain to the faithful that only ardent prayer will bring them mercy and safety as they work.

Now engineers from the Giesche Erben company are overseeing the extraction. This firm owns a significant share of the mines and forges in Upper Silesia, as well as an even larger share of Kattowitz. The people of Kupferberg listen hopefully for news from that region—they learn, among other things, of the beautiful and comfortable garden cities the company is building for its workers. But the dreams of Kupferberg's last sixty miners are considerably more modest. They have no desire for luxurious housing projects or narrow-gauge railroads transporting them to the gates of the mine for free. They wish only for the shafts opened by Giesche Erben to offer up so much raw material that no one here need worry about tomorrow any longer.

So it's certainly not that the prayers urged by Pastor Eberlein and Father Kaufmann are insufficiently ardent, rather they are simply ineffective. Nor does the Giesche Erben engineers' experience suffice. It was easy for them to restart the mines in Kupferberg and it is even easier to decide to close them for good. These few mines and handful of miners do not amount to a particularly important line on the company's balance sheet. First the Toni shaft is shut down—soon after, in 1927, the final shaft, Adler, is closed. From now on, the miners will only be able to gaze nostalgically at its carcass, visible from nearly every house in town.

* * *

Yet the town's mining past will not be forgotten. Kupferberg stands at the peak of a mountain riddled with holes. For whole centuries, tunnels have been bored into the interior, which now—unsecured—are beginning to cave in and endanger what stands above. The shoring in the old drifts rots, and now no one with any sense will go in to assess the state of the damage and future risks. Securing the old shafts is therefore out of the question.

The pipeline bringing water all the way from near Ochsenkopf Mountain breaks increasingly frequently. The town authorities wrack their brains for the cause—it soon turns out small rock bursts and landslides are causing the pipes to breach.

One day, the horses plowing Mr. Franzky's field sink into the ground up to their chests and let out such a terrifying howl that those in the immediate vicinity drop what they're doing and race to the field, their faces pale. Only a few are brave enough to come to the animals' aid and rescue them; the rest gaze from a distance at the horses' heads protruding from the earth and the extraordinary, funnel-shaped cavity around them.

But the ground caves in for the first time under the building housing Preus's smithy and Reimann the merchant's. It leaves a crater so large a wagon could fit inside. A crack in the walls has also opened along a row of houses—from Flabe the baker's to Friebe the hairdresser's—caused by the collapse of a mining drift. This crack is only the beginning.

THE BOTTLE

I GOT THE BOTTLE STOPPER from Zbigniew Pawęska at the end of our conversation. The whole time he'd been playing with it, turning it over in his fingers, delicately tapping it on the tabletop—right next to the microphone, so I had to wonder if he wasn't doing it on purpose. Finally, he said it was for me, and I feigned surprise and for a moment tried politely to refuse. I asked him where he'd gotten it.

"I just have it," he said. Then he assured me right away that for him it was no sacrifice or offering: "I'll find myself another one just like it."

And so the stopper. Too old to treat as ordinary trash, too modern to consider a museum piece. A porcelain lump with a red enamel inscription: KUPFERBERGER BRAUEREI. G. FRANZKY. No date, nothing else. The o-ring is already ruined, same with the wire bail, the remains of which are still inside the hole that runs through the middle.

For a moment I give in to the urge to fantasize, to invent history. I do my best to resist, and the feeling passes on its own. The stopper remains a stopper, dug out of the earth; it won't tell me anything other than what I know anyway. There was a brewery, there was Georg Franzky, there was beer. Nothing more—and all in the past tense. I carry the stopper in my pocket, sort of like a good-luck charm. Although why would it bring me good luck? I even work out a way to thread my key ring through it, making the two of us inseparable.

Then I find a bottle. And once more that presumptuous symbolism, which I struggle to resist. A whisper of history, as though green Kupferberg, a town which no longer exists, is mocking me and flinging trash at me, with which I am meant to patch together a history. Attempting to understand, this is all I can get my hands on—first a porcelain bottle stopper, and now a bottle from Franzky's brewery. And so you could say I have a full set (though to add insult to injury, the bottleneck is broken in a way that prevents me from celebrating the rite of fitting the two together and getting ridiculously excited about it).

The stopper and the bottle—nothing more. If I'd walked through the freshly plowed fields, I'd certainly have found a few pieces of broken plates. But they wouldn't have meant anything either—that sort of archaeology is pointless, because when it's over you still have to imagine anyway, as you sit on the bus from Jelenia Góra, staring through the window and wondering: Did Franzky walk past this bottle, did he hold it, who bought it, who drank the beer (Beier at number 10, or Casper at number 6)? Did it go to their head, maybe they got into a scuffle, maybe they got beat up themselves? Did they drink for Dutch courage? Because they were bored? Because they had to? From thirst? From joy or sorrow? Or maybe they just drank?

The bottle lay in the leaves next to Ueberschaer's tomb. Maybe he brought it there himself, when his wooden lodge still stood here? Or maybe by the people who laid him in his grave and hung his spiked Prussian helmet and sword on the brick wall just over the coffin? They covered it all up with a reinforced concrete slab, and then, instead of carving his date of death, they drank his health and unhurriedly made their way back toward the town. "Poor Ueberschaer," they thought, "why did he do it?"

Or maybe it wasn't like that at all. Maybe the bottle ended up there because someone decided it was the perfect place to throw away the trash left in every house once the Germans had gone. After all, they weren't able to clean up after themselves.

Now it has no meaning, because all the sentimentality, all my adoration for these two objects, is a result of what's above and beyond them, of what I know about the town. But this is all that's remained of the town, of green Kupferberg, so that's how I justify getting excited at being a home-grown archaeologist.

KUPFERBERGER GOLD

"YOU'LL GET THE NEXT LITTLE MONKEY," promises Max Sintenis, and his eyes flash in the dark. To peer through the dark and into Sintenis's mischievous eyes, young Georg Franzky has to stand on tippy-toe and reach up high, holding the bottle of blessed gold liquid. The operation is risky, because the window of the jail holding Max the troublemaker is too high for the boy's modest capacities. Success depends on the dexterous fingertips of Max, who after all has never failed to hold onto a full bottle, nor will he this time.

There is another risk too. Max Sintenis—a ne'er-do-well, reveler, and carouser—is in jail precisely because under the influence of some drink or other he has once again shocked and embarrassed the townspeople of green Kupferberg. Bringing beer to such an individual would surely be met with the reproach of one's neighbors and Mayor Smude, and most certainly with a plain old whipping from father as well. Yet the promise of owning his own monkey is too alluring for Georg to be deterred. Besides, they have repeated this ritual fairly frequently, so the boy has some experience. First, obscene songs emanate from the home of the Sintenis brothers, only one of which is repeatable. It begins: "If you had one more mother-in-law..." Then Max's sonorous baritone moves outside and, no longer muffled by the walls of his study, echoes through the streets. Next comes the policeman's whistle or the irritated voice of Mayor Smude, which at such times tends to be limited to an ordinary: "Max, you ass!" The Mayor then summons the policeman to drag the drunken singer by his coat to the cell in the rear of the poorhouse. There he will have until morning to sober up and reflect on his shameful behavior. He manages neither the one nor the other.

Contributing to this educational failure is Georg Franzky himself, son of the brewer Ewald Franzky, grandson of Wilhelm and Ernestine. For over forty years now, the Franzky clan has been bolstering the town's good name by providing the region's taverns and restaurants both far and near with a drink known, not without reason, as Kupferberger Gold.

The secret to the success of the local beer, at least according to Ewald Franzky, lies in the perfect water gushing from the interior of the mountain whose peak the town stands on. An article by Professor Liebreich even appears in *Der Wanderer im Riesengebirge*, the local newspaper published in Hirschberg, on the curative properties of the water bursting from the local Julian Spring. "The content of arsoric acid, unadulterated by other strongly interactive salts, defines this water quite specifically as a mineral water containing arsenic, whose properties render it easy to digest. The content of 1.66 milligrams per liter of water is exactly the appropriate amount to ingest, and such a dosage, even consumed over the long term, is not excessive."

In turn, another water expert, Professor Wilhelm Windlich, after repeatedly testing the local water intake, dares to come forward with the bold claim that the water in Kupferberg is just as good as that of the famous Pilsner Urquell spring. The reason for its perfection is said to be layers of veined marble; the water seeping through it sheds undesirable carbon dioxide and becomes soft.

One way or the other, it's to this water, as well as to the impeccable cleanliness of the brewing equipment, that Kupferberger Gold owes its unique, slightly bitter flavor. The brewery where this marvelous drink is made lies in the lower part of town, at the crossroads on the way to Jannowitz.* It's built of beautiful clinker brick, and behind it stands the brewer's villa in all its glory, with servants' quarters and a carriage house. Little Georg knows every nook and cranny; besides that, he knows how to get inside the brewery where the beer is bottled, how to sneak a cold bottle out, and then stand on tippy-toe to get the bottle to Max Sintenis's dexterous fingers. He never gets caught stealing.

Georg can't help it—he's seven years old and adores both Sintenis brothers with a boyish passion. He loves the younger, Max, for the pleasure he gives the boy by spinning tales behind the bars

---

* Starting in the mid-nineteenth century, the old name Johannesdorf is replaced with a new one—Jannowitz im Riesengebirge. The name Jannowitz is already in use in a travel guide to the area from 1845. Yet the local people will keep saying "Johannesdorf," even into the mid-twentieth century. In some memoirs written by Germans the official name is also rejected. However, in this book the official names are used, except in quotes.

of the jail. He tells of distant lands—the deserts of Persia and Central Asia, the green jungles of Africa and the churning waves of the oceans. The stories also include amazing and hair-raising adventures, and monkeys too of course, specimens of which Max has supposedly collected. Truth be told, Georg has never seen Max bring a monkey back from his trips; he doesn't even remember Max being away from Kupferberg for very long, but for him, hearing of these faraway lands is reward enough. Anyway, if little Georg Franzky were to accept all the monkeys Max promised him, there's no way the villa behind the brewery could fit them all.

But then there is the other Sintenis brother—Paul, one year older than Max. He's the exact opposite of Max and the real inspiration for his incredible, drunken stories. Paul is a botanist and spends more time traveling than in his study in Kupferberg, which is packed full of plant specimens and collections. On his first trip, he heads for the Romanian region of Dobruja, then keeps venturing further—to Greece, Turkey, Armenia, Turkmenistan, Persia, and even distant Puerto Rico. From each of these places, he brings back hundreds or even thousands of plant specimens. They include, for instance, a specific species of knotgrass, brought back from distant Sakhalin. The plant takes root perfectly in Kupferberg's harsh climate and for many years to come will be an identifying characteristic of the town. During one of his expeditions to northeastern Turkey, Paul Sintenis makes an arduous eight-thousand-foot climb just so he can find out from the local peasants what unknown plants occur at such an altitude. The effort pays off—his discovery goes down in the history of botany as *Tulipa sintenisii*.

No wonder, then, that each time Paul returns to his hometown, it becomes an event. His expanding private botanical garden is a stand-in for the distant lands of which his younger brother tells tales with such passion and conviction. Georg Franzky especially looks forward to his return. Taking advantage of his father Ewald's close relationship with both Sinteises, he has the rare pleasure of calling from time to time at Paul's house and observing him at work. Each such visit is a journey into the unknown. The rooms of his study smell of tobacco smoke, boxes of dried butterflies are stacked up on the work surfaces, the glass eyes of taxidermy animals peer at the boy from inside the cabinets. All this is the domain of a huge angora cat and three squawking parrots, which roam the entire house freely. Paul cheerfully initiates the boy into the mysteries of the naturalist's trade, showing him plant and animal specimens—and under the microscope the boy discovers a world he hadn't known before. The great botanist addresses the young explorer as "curator," which for the boy is a particular source of pride.

Paul's loyal, and usually rather silent, companion—a Turk by the name of Fuss—also inspires Georg's admiration and respect. His unusual goatee and requisite fez add color to the botanist's already vibrant character. They met in Constantinople, and Paul was immediately convinced their acquaintance would be beneficial. Fuss is actually the son of an Austrian woman and a German man; he was merely raised in Turkey in the Oriental fashion. As a result, he has a suitable education and, most importantly, he speaks German, Greek, Arabic, and Turkish. During each of Paul's expeditions, Fuss is his interpreter and assistant; he quickly acquires an essential knowledge of botany and is even able to support Paul in his field of research. In one of the photos that hung for a long time in Ewald Franzky's study, Paul Sintenis, Fuss, and a German consul warmly embrace one another with a Persian city in the background. In old age, Fuss will settle in the town, where he will be tormented by recurrences of malaria for many years. Because his illness is so severe, he has his own glasses and beer mugs in the Franzky family's tavern. But the vexations of old age drive him to morphine addiction, which brings him an untimely death.

Max's stories and Paul's achievements fire the imagination of young Georg Franzky, who dreams of equally distant and no less incredible journeys. The wide world begins right at the train station in Jannowitz. It's not even a twenty-minute walk from Kupferberg. All he has to do is pass the brewery and the two stone crosses, one of which still bears traces of a faded inscription: *Memento*. Then he only has to walk through the birch forest. Or rather run through, because there are far too many mysterious and terrifying sounds emanating from that green thicket for the young boy.

But at the train station it's possible to relax and get on a train that will reach Breslau or Görlitz in two hours, and Berlin itself in barely five. However, if you choose a train going the opposite direction, in just over a quarter of an hour it will arrive in Hirschberg. Georg loves riding that route. There, the tracks meander through the mountains and time and again bound across the river on vaulted bridges. There's a perfect view of Kupferberg's two church towers from near Merzdorf. But the boy most enjoys the moments when the whole train is engulfed in darkness, in the tunnel carved into the foot of the mountain. Grandma Ernestine has told little Georg a story about this place. On September 9, 1865, at the western entrance of that tunnel near the village of Rohrlach, some tables were set up and lit with lanterns. The occasion for this peculiar gathering was the ceremonial opening of the Breslau–Hirschberg line. A folk band played for the guests, including Ernestine Franzky and her then-husband Wilhelm Bach, and of course Kupferberger Gold flowed freely. After speeches from the railroad representatives and the lord of the manor, Count Wilhelm of the House of Stolberg-Wernigerode, all those gathered marched through the tunnel, lighting the way with torches. And so the railroad connected Jannowitz and nearby Kupferberg to the rest of the world.

His train journeys lead Georg Franzky to somewhat peculiar reflections. As an altar boy in the Catholic church, the boy learns of the brave journeys of Father Johann Martin Stulpe, who nearly two centuries before made his way to Rome to ask the Pope for a brief founding the Archconfraternity of the Sacred Heart of Jesus in Kupferberg. Little Georg Franzky finds it impossible to imagine that the courageous priest setting out on this journey was unable to take the train.

Nearly everyone in the village remembers Father Stulpe, especially on every third Sunday after Easter, when the roads from Jannowitz, Rudelstadt, and Waltersdorf bring absolute crowds of believers here for the church festival. The taverns fill up with them just after morning Mass, which, according to long-standing custom, is celebrated at five in the morning. The

altar boys train especially hard for these celebrations, beginning their study of the Latin Mass a month beforehand under
the stern eye of Cantor Vogt, who apart from his pedagogical
skills is also a talented musician, gracing church services with
his organ playing.

So Georg is thrilled to assist in the Mass. Yet by the time he's
ten, his zeal is also accompanied by a certain impatience, and
he sneaks peeks at the green meadows and forests. Georg knows
he's needed out there: the seeds Paul Sintenis planted in his mind
are beginning to sprout and bear their first fruits. It happens
they have fallen on fertile ground—a naturalist's passion begins
to develop in the boy. An old mine worker, Mr. Bergmann, lives
next door to the Franzkys. When the Toni shaft is operating at
full capacity, Bergmann spends more than twelve hours a day
there, tending the mine's steam engine. But his passion is for
animals, especially birds. In his house near the cemetery he has
aviaries full of winged, singing creatures. For a while, he also
has a fox on a chain hanging around near the house, but one
night, under unclear circumstances, it disappears, along with
the chain. (The shadow of suspicion falls on a Gypsy caravan
that left town in a hurry that very night.) Little Georg drops by
from time to time and Mr. Bergmann regales him with his avian
passions; he also introduces him to Hermann Gärtner, a wiry
but exceptionally warmhearted stonemason, who has developed
a specialty in the difficult technique of catching birds on perches
smeared with sticky birdlime. He supplies birds to all the breed-
ers and ornithology enthusiasts in the area. Yet there is one
problem Gärtner has been unable to overcome. He lost his leg

in a fatal accident, and for several years has propped himself up on a wooden prosthesis.

Trapping birds with birdlime is a difficult art. To keep a high success rate, Hermann Gärtner creates special watering holes in the forest and the meadows, which birds of a particular species accustom themselves to over an entire summer. He takes care that in these places no leaves or other off-putting contaminants fall into the water. When the animals have gotten comfortable with one of these places, the hunt begins. For this, Mr. Gärtner prepares glue from a base of flaxseed oil and spreads it on rods, which he places right at the edge of the water, where a winged guest might want to take advantage of it. Most often this ruse draws in robins, who, as soon as they're stuck to the perch, raise the alarm with an utterly desperate screech. Yet the glue does not imprison them forever. Here the lame Hermann Gärtner's role ends and the young and nimble Georg Franzky's begins. Instructed appropriately, Georg dashes out of his hiding place and nabs the twittering prisoner. After removing the bird from the trap, he places it in a special bag, which he proudly presents to Gärtner, who will just then be hobbling his way toward him.

After a few months of training at this task, Georg Franzky becomes so proficient at bird trapping that old Hermann Gärtner entrusts him with the birdlime and devotes himself only to establishing and tending new locations. Georg sometimes brings the birds he's caught home, and his mother, who finds her son's new passion concerning, immediately releases some of them. On more than one occasion, a catch unleashes chaos in Mr. and Mrs. Franzky's household. This happens with a nutcracker Georg traps one autumn. It's so unruly that the boy only manages to get it unstuck with a great deal of effort once he's home. But he ends up paying for it with several painful pecks.

Aside from these various pleasures and amusements, as the son of a brewer, little Georg Franzky also has chores he must carry out scrupulously. Most often he's summoned to help when his mother and grandmother can't keep up with serving customers in the tavern next to the brewery. This is the case during the annual spring church festival, as well as four times a year during the town fairs, especially during the fall fair, when Ewald Franzky erects a sturdy stall on the market square in the upper part of town to sell beer, hot drinks, and seeds roasted in kerosene ovens. The boy's job is to go back and forth between the brewery and the marketplace, bringing clean mugs and hot water. Speed is of the essence, especially for the latter. Fall in Kupferberg is cold and windy, so sometimes if the boy is too slow bringing the water up the hill, it will simply no longer be hot.

However, Georg Franzky's most important duty is his education, for his parents decide to send him to school in Potsdam once he is old enough. Before long, the two modest train platforms and the tidy station house in Jannowitz come to hold special significance for him. From now on, they will always evoke memories of tender goodbyes heralding the start of the school year and warmhearted welcomes marking its close and the beginning of his long-awaited summer vacation.

With every summer he spends in the town, Georg Franzky is curious to note certain changes taking place here. The population of miners—still fairly large when the Schönfelder family ran the mine—dwindles every year. As the miners vanish, so too do their peculiar customs. The pit traditions are revived once a year; his mother tells him that's when elderly men march through the streets in their miners' dress uniforms. Despite this obvious change, Kupferberg is becoming more beautiful, for the Association of Municipal Beautification for the Tourist Movement has been founded here. Lines of leafy trees, dwarfish pines, and red hawthorns stretch along the Fechtergasse, the Feuergasse, the Hochgasse, and the Niedergasse. The smallest town in Prussia, a status Kupferberg proudly claims, begins attracting visitors on rest cures. After all, it stands on a hill, the view all around is breathtaking, and the air is pure and crisp. Kupferberg advertises in Berlin newspapers, and local entrepreneurs have to purchase appropriate stationery and envelopes with information encouraging people to visit. While without the necessary treatment facilities or a sanatorium, Kupferberg is unable to obtain the status of a health resort, cheap and comfortable lodging nevertheless quickly springs up, and it's rare for the town not to have at least a few health tourists.

For Georg, his summers in the town are also a chance to develop his passion for the natural world. One summer, he befriends the great hunting enthusiast Heinrich Betterman, an apprentice in Reimann's smithy. Now an adolescent, Georg supports Mr. Betterman just like he used to support Hermann Gärtner when he was a child, for Betterman was also crippled as the result of an unfortunate accident at work. It happened while repairing a waterwheel in the wood pulp mill in Bergmühle belonging to Count Stolberg-Wernigerode—someone accidentally released water onto the wheel, causing Betterman the smith's arm to be crushed and, as a result, amputated. But he is not abandoned to his tragic fate, since old Count Wilhelm is moved to hire the crippled workman, employing him as his forester. This is Heinrich Betterman's salvation, and so he enthusiastically teaches himself to write left-handed and does the rounds of the Count's estate early every morning. It is on these hunting rounds that Georg Franzky accompanies him. Georg is an invaluable assistant to old Betterman, since the front-loading hunting rifle they use requires two functioning hands. Reloading is Georg's job. Then, after handing the shotgun to the one-armed hunter, the boy takes a few steps away to observe both the target and the shooter. For many years, Georg retains the unforgettable image of Heinrich Betterman enveloped in clouds of gunpowder smoke. Their joint hunting expeditions make them an inseparable team, and—most importantly—a successful one. Georg's skill and dexterity mean the hunter's sharp eye need never wait for a loaded shotgun. It's thanks to this collaboration that several times over his hunting career Betterman boasts in town of a doublet: felling two partridges with a single shot. Unfortunately his numerous attempts to hunt down the goshawk wreaking havoc among the townspeople's pet pigeons do not succeed.

The boy's family watches with concern as his passion for hunting develops. They have already had one tragic hunting death. A distant relative on Georg's mother's side was struggling through some bushes with a loaded shotgun when he caught the trigger on a branch. The shotgun went off, wounding him in the chest. The man could not be saved. Georg Franzky has no intention of repeating his relative's mistake and reassures his mother that he's almost obsessively careful while hunting. But even that does not protect him from mistakes, and one occurs during a winter fox-hunt. It's this form of solo hunting that has most captured Georg's heart; he sits for hours in moonlight, hidden at the edge of the forest, and imitating the sound of mice squeaking. On one of these late-night outings, he falls just before shooting at a target peeking out from behind a tree. He scrambles to his feet, not noticing one barrel is clogged with snow, and fires twice. The first shot fells the fox, but the second causes the barrel to explode. It's a close call, but everything is all right in the end. Georg decides not to breathe a word of his momentary lapse in judgment either at home or to his dear friend, the merchant Georg Gotter. It was with Gotter that he entered his first hunting competitions back in high school. Though Georg Franzky is only a helper and assistant to Heinrich Betterman, he soon becomes an equal hunting partner to Gotter, who is only slightly his elder. They practice their aim on the outskirts of the village, shooting nutcrackers and squirrels, and before long they are invited to Rohnau to hunt. Both are practically bursting with pride as they set off on that first hunting expedition, even though they return empty-handed.

Things change when Count Wilhelm zu Stolberg-Wernigerode grants Mr. Gotter permission to take over one of the hunting areas near Kupferberg. He knows it like the back of his hand, every cluster of trees and every fawn, so he only shoots those that are sufficiently mature. The two Georgs usually return happy from these hunting trips, each carrying his take in their hunting packs. Franzky takes a liking to smaller game, especially foxes; Gotter prefers the drawn-out tracking and stalking of deer. Many admire the plentiful antlers he hangs in his apartment, which sits over a store in the market square (at numbers 93–94). Pride of place goes to a beautiful twelve-pointer—Gotter the merchant's most cherished hunting trophy.

In 1904, after finishing his education and performing his mandatory military service, Georg Franzky returns to Kupferberg permanently. Now he is a trained brewer, but his father Ewald Franzky manages to keep on top of things perfectly well for another three years. So Georg finds a job in the town hall as a local official. He so enjoys the confidence of Mayor Schnabel that he's continually entrusted with greater responsibilities. However, he doesn't always carry out his duties to the letter. Once he even forgets a wedding scheduled for a certain animal trainer. While the young couple waits outside the town hall for the ceremony to start, Georg is amusing himself shooting small game near the old gunpowder tower. When he realizes he's forgotten what he has to do, he rushes back down in a few minutes and, slightly winded, conducts the modest ceremony.

He too makes up his mind to get married. He's now twenty-six and has fairly good career prospects. Not much is known about the woman who claims his heart. Most likely she's a local named Anna. The wedding, therefore, takes place in Kupferberg. It is certain, however, that the marriage is officiated by Mayor Schnabel himself, while the church service is led by the priest of the local Catholic church, Johannes Kaufmann. This fact is worth noting because Kaufmann is an uncommon character and will leave as much of a mark on the town's history as Father Stulpe did. It is Johannes Kaufmann who reveals Kupferberg's charms to the world—he writes the first travel guides to the region, boasting of the trails and monuments of the Falcon, Giant, and Leaden Mountains, and their benefits to health. Father Kaufmann also meticulously gathers knowledge about the town's ancient past, and is the first to lay hands on the most archaic sources mentioning Kupferberg.

But Georg's idyll does not last long. First, Paul Sintenis, his great friend and above all his teacher and mentor, dies in 1907. The great naturalist is buried in Kupferberg's cemetery, while his collection, in accordance with his will, goes to the Museum of Natural History in Görlitz. Years later it will be divided up—a share of the specimens will remain there, others will be sold to museums all over Germany, and even to Lund in Sweden. During the Second World War, a significant portion of Sintenis's collections will be incinerated in fires from bombs falling on the capital of the Third Reich.

Shortly after Georg's wedding, his father Ewald also falls gravely ill. So the time has come to leave his work in the town hall and take up the family business. And there is much to look after. The brewery is the largest industrial facility in town, with fourteen people permanently employed there, carefully overseeing the brewing process. Georg has the necessary training, having observed his father for years, so he's not a novice; he also has an idea of how to develop and streamline production. As long ago as two years before Georg was born, his father introduced techniques that revolutionized the production of local beer. In 1876, a steam motor was introduced in the brewery, which led to the production of Bavarian-style beer. The Franzkys all agree that if you're not developing, in practice you're going backward, and so before long, Georg hires the master brewer Hermann Hütter, who will oversee production until the late 1930s. Soon, modern steam-heated brew kettles and electric lighting are introduced as well. The workers no longer wash the bottles and barrels by hand, for Georg has machines installed to do it for them. In addition, a malt house is opened—freeing the brewery from dependency on malt supplies from elsewhere. Yet the largest improvement the brewery's new owner introduces is the refrigerator. Until now, low temperatures have been achieved in the brewery's cellars using large blocks of ice, acquired every winter from the brewery pond and a similar reservoir in Jannowitz. This makes Kupferberger Gold perfectly thirst-quenching in the scorching summer heat. Now a modern machine keeps the bottles frosty.

Georg Franzky doesn't have to worry much about the market for his beer. If he doesn't change the recipe or the water supply, customers of the town's four taverns will still gladly drink it. A tavern operates right next to the brewery, run by his father's siblings—Aunt Josephine and Uncle Franz. The tavern lures customers with its cool interior and its beer garden, where they can peacefully take in the small-town hustle and bustle. Those making the most of this include officials from the local government, several of whose departments are housed upstairs in the tavern building itself. The brewery's proximity and family connections mean its workers are obliged to drink there. Every year, this is where Georg Franzky kicks off the spring beer festival by cracking open the first keg of March.

Besides that, the stylish Ratskeller restaurant and wine tavern, owned by Max Bräuer, is at number 95 on the market square. It's easy to find—the first floor of the building is overgrown with ivy, and above, it boasts decorations and an elaborate gothic-lettered sign. Inside, under arched vaults, a dozen or so tables await their customers. The thick walls keep things comfortably cool here even on roasting July days. A magnificent tile stove standing in the center warms revelers in the harshest winters, when Kupferberger Gold is served slightly heated, in gigantic lidded beer steins.

Each week, the singing society holds rehearsals in the Ratskeller; the town council's community meetings and debates take place here as well. At these meetings, the councilors do their best to embody the wisdom of the motto hanging over the entrance portal:

DRUNKENNESS IS THE COUNCILMAN'S VITAL DUTY,
A DRY LAMP OFFERS NO LIGHT.

Each week, local notables also take seats in the banquet hall, to play the traditional round of skat. Georg Franzky probably joins them too; local officials come, and so do Gotter the merchant and the restaurant owner Max Bräuer. They don't come alone—their wives are seated at an adjacent table to share the latest gossip. They wrinkle their noses and glare menacingly in their husbands' directions when, merry with wine from Bräuer's cellar or with Franzky's beer, the men start singing "If You Had One More Mother-in-Law." Every now and again the gentlemen get a notion to play truly childish pranks, and so one evening, using one of the swords hanging from the wine tavern wall, they manage to fish a bottle of choice alcohol out from behind a metal grille, where Mr. Bräuer had been saving it for a special occasion. But once they've drunk the bottle they politely add it to the bill for the evening's entertainment. At the next skat party, the expensive vintages will be secured not only with the steel grate, but also an impenetrable wire net.

Bräuer's wine tavern is also equipped with a washroom with bathtubs, which all the townspeople are able to use. This pleasure costs them just under one mark.

Just above the market square, nearly at the very peak of the mountain, at the intersection of the roads leading to Merzdorf, Rudelstadt, and Waltersdorf, stands the Schwarzer Adler tavern (the Black Eagle), where Martin Lachmann plays the saxophone every Sunday in a large hall with a stage. Each couple must pay him ten pfennigs a dance. On the remaining days, guilds of artisans living here use the space for their meetings, and a traveling movie theater also holds screenings. The inn offers over a dozen rooms, and guests especially love visiting the garden and the glass-walled conservatory, whose windows reveal an exquisite view of the Leaden Mountains.

An entirely different atmosphere prevails at the tavern run by Joseph Kaszynski and his wife Katharina. This inn is located inside an inconspicuous-looking building on the road from Kupferberg to Rudelstadt. The tavern's interior is a particular joy for out-of-towners, as murals in all three banquet halls display the history of the surrounding territory, starting with the legendary ruler of the Giant Mountains—Rübezahl. Here, too, dances are held nearly every Sunday evening. The Kaszynskis' tavern is also famous for throwing carnival parties, each one with a theme. Year after year, the people of Kupferberg let their hair down at the Coachmen's Ball, the Household Servants' Ball, or the Underwear Ball.

Georg Franzky's brewery supplies beer not only to the taverns of Kupferberg, but to inns and taverns all over the region. They include the beautiful Rosenbaude hostel across the river, the mountain hostel not far from Fischbach, and taverns in Waltersdorf, Rohrlach, and Rudelstadt. So every day, horse carts filled to the brim with barrels and clinking with green bottles set off from Kupferberg on the road down the hill to provide the inhabitants of the region with the best beer in the Giant Mountains. Business will go on as long as streams of the precious beverage keep flowing from the little brewery's tanks.

While Georg does not need to concern himself with the production process—the brewing master Hütter minds it with the diligence required—they keep having more trouble with the leaky aqueduct bringing water to the town and the brewery. The now-late Ewald Franzky sued the town, demanding damages for the interruption of water supplies to the brewery, since the halt in production caused his company serious losses. Georg Franzky takes charge of this problem too—and although he may count the local powers that be among his friends, he insists they resolve the matter of the water supply.

Meanwhile, the wooden aqueduct is constantly springing leaks due to landslides and rock bursts accompanying the collapse of underground drifts and corridors. When that happens, sirens reverberate throughout town, signaling it is forbidden for the townspeople to draw water. Then everyone holds their breath, and Carl Lukaschek, the electrical and hydraulic expert the town has put in charge of maintaining the aqueduct, lets out a swear word, fires up his Opel, and sets off in search of yet another leak. Many times he's spent an entire day pinpointing the unlucky spot, while in the meantime Kupferberg suffers a complete drought. Other times, Lukaschek's expedition comes to naught, and the water flow into the municipal reservoirs resumes just as suddenly as it was interrupted. For several years both the townspeople and the local authorities wrack their brains for the cause of these strange events. The explanation is found by chance when a local, suffering one night from insomnia, spots a farmer in the fields around Waltersdorf packing rags into one of the inspection chambers of the aqueduct, redirecting water meant for the town into his own fields. So these chambers are sealed and secured with an appropriate mechanism that makes them impossible to open. From now on the only concern will "merely" be mining damage.

After repeated negotiations with local officials, Georg Franzky finally gives up and decides to build his own aqueduct, which will supply the brewery with water from beneath Sandy Mountain. Work begins in 1912. The investment is inexpensive and grants the brewery a certain degree of autonomy, yet the water problems never stop for good, and now and then the town's mining heritage continues to rear its ugly head.

In 1914, Georg Franzky wins the annual shooting tournament and becomes a master marksman. This would be unremarkable if not for the fact that he will hold the title for the next five years, and certainly not for want of competition in tournaments to come. But that June is the last month the old world exists: Franz Ferdinand perishes at the hand of an assassin in Sarajevo, and a war breaks out that will summon the sons of Kupferberg to its fronts, where five will fall and one will forever be considered missing. Meanwhile, in Bräuer's restaurant, pride of place on the wall will go to a steel helmet taken from the head of a British soldier. Ernst Küttner from Jannowitz was said to have taken it during the Battle of Arras in October 1914. A flag hanging in the dining room, from a German warship that fought in the naval battle of Tsingtao in distant China, also serves as a memento of the war's turmoil.

Five killed, one missing in action, a British helmet and a flag as full of holes as Swiss cheese—that is Kupferberg's wartime balance sheet. Compared with over seven million German victims and over thirty-seven million killed on all the fronts of the Great War, that is perhaps not so high a price. Although obviously tragic, such an outcome does not seem convincing evidence that one of the bloodiest and most brutal conflicts in the history of the world has just taken place beyond the surrounding mountains. It goes without saying that the people of Kupferberg are affected by Germany's requisite efforts to arm itself—there are temporary shortages of supplies, military drills are introduced in government offices, the reservists hold more frequent exercises, mothers and wives tremble for those fighting in the Kaiser's name. Yet compared to the tragedies of thousands of European cities and towns, as well as the millions displaced and killed, those who find themselves waiting the war out in Kupferberg can say they've had quite some luck. Occupied with everyday troubles, it probably doesn't occur to them that the cost of their peace will be deferred for many years. It will turn out that the modest memorial they erect on the square to the heroes of the First World War is an inadequate offering: Here, the beast has yet to claim its due.

Much more menacing are the results of the wartime turmoil all Germans feel as soon as the last shots fall silent. Hyperinflation starts running amok across the whole country; it's so colossal employers pay salaries twice a day, so people are able to buy anything at all with the money they've received. Suffice it to say that by the early twenties, the price of bread in Breslau has reached 240 million marks per loaf—and of course is constantly rising.

Also forced to deal with these economic problems are the merchants and businessmen of Kupferberg. They are too numerous to list—in this respect, Kupferberg is fairly self-sufficient. The townspeople have a plumber, an electrician, a metalworker, and a stove-fitter on hand. What the merchants aren't able to supply is produced locally. Mrs. Trenkler sews shirts, Mrs. Assmann and Mrs. Alex make bed linens, Mr. Reuhs runs a damask-weaving mill, and Mrs. Bräuer, Max's wife, sells butter and eggs. Townspeople without their own businesses to run find work in Kupferberg's industrial facilities. These are: two masonry factories—Zeidler & Wimmel, and Schlesische Granitstein AG—and a large farm belonging to Count Stolberg-Wernigerode, plus a wood-pulp mill on the river in Bergmühle. The cellulose produced there supplies the paper factory in Jannowitz, where people from Kupferberg also work, producing goods such as extremely thin tissue paper for export to China.

August Schiedeck's slaughterhouse stands in the upper part of town at number 41, while his meat stall near the market square is run by the Raupach family. The townspeople buy baked goods and cakes at the master baker Wilhelm Flabe's at number 10; just next door, at number 8, Georg Fischer sells vegetables and tropical fruit. At Gustav Reimann's at number 70, you can stock up on colonial goods. It's right next to this store that the ground caved in. The pharmacist Kurt Haenisch and his brother Ulrich keep the town supplied with medicine. They run their own pharmacy on the square at number 90.

The townspeople get their hair cut at the semi-itinerant master barber Adolf Friebe's. For Friebe, it isn't enough to live and serve customers in his shop at number 103—in addition to that, he travels on foot to Rudelstadt, Rohrlach, and even Fischbach, equipped with the necessary accoutrements and offering his services to the people in these villages. Perhaps he has the shoes he destroys on these journeys repaired at the Wagner-Kaiser-Exner cobbler's workshop. "Perhaps" because he could equally well have been served by the Wahn-Drescher shoemaker's, located in the upper part of town. That said, it is almost certain the mountain-hiking barber orders his pants and jackets from his relative—the tailor Hermann Friebe.

Aside from the brewery, Albert Schütz also runs a distillery here, providing outstanding-quality vodka and liqueurs. Soon Maximilian von Glyschinsky's mineral water and sparkling lemonade business will also begin to flourish.

Kupferberg has its own post office and two branches of trust companies. A preschool operates in the town (located in one room of the tavern near the brewery); there are also two parochial schools, which in the future will be unified into a single public school. When the other residents of the town follow the lead of Carl Lukaschek—the master electrician driving around in his Opel—and cars arrive on the streets, a Shell gas station is also built at the back of the Black Eagle tavern.

Yet the people of Kupferberg do not live for work alone. They spend their free time on activities organized by the many associations and unions. One that cannot pass without mention is the Men's Gymnastics Union, run by Georg Franzky's loyal friend, the passionate hunter Georg Gotter. Despite its name, the union has three sections—a men's, led by Gotter, a women's, with Käthe Lukaschek, and a youth section. In poor weather their exercises on the high bar, parallel bars, and pommel horse are held in the welcoming interior of the Black Eagle tavern. But the gymnasts from Kupferberg dream of a real open-air practice field. Finally, they build one for themselves by the road leading to a slightly peripheral neighborhood of the village of Adlersruh. Here, the young gymnasts stage demonstrations, cheered on by crowds of onlookers.

Those with no taste for acrobatics on the balance beam choose the remarkably social and exceptionally enjoyable Men's Singers Union—directed by the tailor Hermann Friebe—or the People's Dramatic Stage run by the retired actor Paul Schulze. The latter does not content himself with just acting, for he is also a fire sergeant and a member of the Kupferberg Volunteer Fire Department. The fire alarm wails every first Saturday of the month at six in the morning; then he and over a dozen other men tear off to the fire station standing near Schütz's distillery. There they hold firefighting exercises, after which the whole brotherhood makes their way to the tavern, where over a cool mug of Kupferberger Gold they discuss the experience they've just gained. The firefighters from Kupferberg enjoy an exemplary reputation; there's even a story in Jannowitz about how the courageous fire sergeants from the town on the mountaintop, unable to wait for their carthorses to arrive, grabbed the wagon pole themselves and pulled the cistern and the fire hoses to the neighboring town, thus saving the possessions of one of Jannowitz's townspeople. There is, unfortunately, no mention in this story of how the cart was pulled back up the mountain after the fire was put out, although the return must have given the heroic firemen more trouble than the wild dash downhill.

Georg Franzky also joins in on community activities. As a reservist and a member of the Military Association, he participates in all the national and military celebrations; he also oversees bearing war veterans to the cemetery with the necessary pomp, and ensures their burials are accompanied by the obligatory honorary salute. After a military defeat and in the midst of an economic crisis, it is hard for the townspeople—as for all those who have outlived the Empire and are now citizens of the Republic—to find their footing in this new reality. In Europe they are "those evil people." So, whether consciously or not, they treat tending to the memory of their heroes as a collective therapy for the difficult period of transition.

Many who struggle to return to normal in this new reality come to the town to recover their health and to rest. Both the locals and their visitors agree it's most beautiful here in fall. Then, the mists rising from the river valleys allow those lucky enough to wake up in Kupferberg to feast their eyes on a vision of the town protruding, island-like, from a sea of fog. Father Johannes Kaufmann extols this sight in his travel guides, which are now renowned throughout the country. Within a few years, Kupferberg becomes famous as the smallest town in Germany, a quiet, enchanting place, and above all a rather cheap one. Getting there is now much easier than it's ever been before. In June 1920, the electrification of the Niedersalzbrunn–Hirschberg rail line is finally finished, and now, elegant red electric train cars begin running here, meaning one can get from Jannowitz to the airport in Hirschberg in less than twenty minutes. There, in turn, regular Lufthansa flights come in and out, connecting the city to Berlin, Breslau, and Leipzig. Meanwhile, taxis run between the train station in Jannowitz and the market square in Kupferberg, so it's no wonder the town is occasionally inundated with visitors on rest cures.

The region changes too. People hope the growing number of visitors will allow them to escape the economic doldrums. Even Waltersdorf, which locals always said was on the edge of the world, has as many as seven different inns. For his part, Count Stolberg-Wernigerode has renovated some of the ruins of Bolzenstein Castle specifically for the tourists—which is what they're now called. A pleasant inn situated there is a favorite destination for hikes.

Georg Franzky is pleased to see all these changes, even more so because his family life is flourishing too—soon his youngest child will be born. In his heart of hearts, Georg dreams of a daughter.

After the wartime turmoil, the country is having a hard time getting back on its feet, but Georg's business, despite the constant water problems, is doing exceptionally well. His beer is renowned; now it is transported greater distances by car—to Goldberg, Schönau an der Katzbach, and even to Löwenberg. The brewery is an increasingly popular destination for pilgrimages of beer connoisseurs, hoping to sample this choice golden beverage in its place of origin. Following the now nearly century-old tradition of Georg's aunt, Josephine Franzky, he serves them chilled beer in the summer and slightly warmed beer in the winter.

The tavern by the brewery is besieged with customers in the winter months, especially on Saturdays and Sundays, for there is yet another reason Kupferberg is famous all over the region. The road leading from here to Jannowitz turns out to be the best natural tobogganing track winter sport lovers could imagine. While it's possible to ski in almost any direction from here, and ice skaters turn pirouettes on the pond near the brewery, it's the steep downhill road to Jannowitz that appeals to tobogganers. There, a six-person bobsled team—famous throughout the Falcon Mountains and belonging to Bernhard Becker, a landscape architect from Jannowitz—holds its training sessions. The pilot is Kurt Mende. Behind him sits Johannes Ritzka, then Georg Grabs (a chimney sweep from Kupferberg), then Hermann Hirsch (also a citizen of the town), then finally Eric Nolte hurriedly clambers into the back. They usually push the sled off with a joyful cheer near the Black Eagle tavern, taking a running leap onboard and flying down the ice-covered road, first through the market square, then past the brewery. Next they pass the two stone crosses protruding from the snow right at the edge of town, and then they can hurtle more than a mile down, as far as the yard of Kluger's hotel in Jannowitz. After properly fortifying themselves at the restaurant there, they set off on the road back, pulling the 220-pound sled behind them. On the way they pass shrieking children, zipping after them on their own sleds. The young sportsmen leave the sled by the brewery and go inside for a mug of warm beer, which fortifies their courage ahead of the next wild descent.

Make no mistake—life in Kupferberg is not easy, but the townspeople have learned to make up for daily hardships with small pleasures. The only harbinger of worse times to come is the death of Father Johannes Kaufmann, who is buried in the church graveyard in Jannowitz on November 16, 1926. Despite the rumors decades later, there is no hint that this might be an unnatural death at the hand of a Protestant assassin. There is an abundance of evidence for the peaceful, or at least neutral, coexistence of representatives of both faiths. However, the death of the priest who made such a key contribution to popularizing positive aspects of the town casts a pall over the people of Kupferberg. No one takes the closing of the last of the Adler mineshafts as a bad omen. Of course the handful of miners regret it, but the mines here have been closed many times—everyone is used to it.

However, dark clouds are rising and gathering far away, not just beyond the mountains surrounding the town, but beyond the great ocean, in America. October 24, 1929 goes down in history as Black Thursday, the beginning of the Great Depression, which will soon consume the whole world.

But before the first significant echoes of the economic depression manage to reach Kupferberg, winter comes and the townspeople endure their own small tragedy.

It's a freezing, starry night on December 29, 1929. The snow crunches under the shoes of the chimney sweeps Georg Grabs and Josef Stenzl, as they walk silently through sleeping Kupferberg. Near the Black Eagle tavern, Georg takes a child's sled off his back and places it on the ground. They pull up their collars and draw their fur hats down over their ears. Georg sits in front and Josef behind him. They set off downhill, toward Jannowitz. They have an urgent job there that cannot be delayed. No one knows why less than a quarter-mile further along, they run off the road and into a tree. The ball on a steel cord used for cleaning, and which Georg is tied to, smashes into his body, damaging his spleen and liver. A horrifying cry tears through the night from dying Grabs, the twenty-two-year-old chimney sweep from Kupferberg and member of the famous bobsled team. That cry awakens the people living in the houses nearby, probably here and there a lamp is lit, perhaps Georg Franzky races to the window of his yellow villa, his heart in his throat.

And from the surrounding trees, a flock of crows takes wing.

DADDY ISN'T THERE

"IT WAS RIGHT BEFORE THE WAR, and we'd put all the poverty and deprivation of the Great Depression behind us. The whole economy was doing better, hardly anyone was unemployed, they'd get jobs building the Autobahn or could get permits to work abroad. The craftspeople in town got plenty of commissions. It wasn't until the draft came in and Germany started openly rearming that I found out the mayor was required to report to the police on local people's political views."*

"They would hold roll calls at school where we all had to stand for an hour with one arm held out in a Nazi salute. Usually it was Mr. Wendler organizing these things, not so often the other teachers."

---

* The first, third, fourth, and fifth quotes in this chapter come from the manuscript *Chronik über Kupferberg* by Dora Puschmann, while the remainder come from interviews I conducted with Germans.

"In school they also told us under no circumstances were we to sled down the main road to Jannowitz."

"I was still in school when the refugees started arriving from the East: Mr. Stolpe and his family, who'd lived in Posen province, and Mr. Rose and his wife, from Russian Ukraine. They could tell us plenty about the persecution German citizens suffered in Poland and the Soviet Union. But other than that, before World War II broke out, life in Kupferberg went on harmoniously."

"For years and years, Wilhelm Ducksch—who ran a leather workshop out of our building—could barely make ends meet and on several occasions he ended up almost bankrupt. In 1935, a large order came in related to the reconstitution of the air force. One room in the attic of a tavern wasn't enough for Ducksch anymore, so he had to move his whole operation to Petersdorf. Over there he could come into his own, though nobody in Kupferberg could buy his perfect briefcases or leather goods anymore."

"In 1938, many young men from Kupferberg were drafted into the Wehrmacht and took part in the annexation of Austria, the Sudetenland, and Bohemia. A year on, we had high hopes the march to Poland wouldn't lead to war. But it turned out our hopes were in vain."

"The first man from Kupferberg to fall on the field of battle in Poland was Alfons Müller, the son of Müller the cantor. The longer the war raged, the less often we got to see our young men—they only came home on leave occasionally. But they didn't tell us what was going on at the front."

"It just meant my father was gone for a long time. That was how it began, and I actually never saw him again afterward. So, for me, the outbreak of war meant nothing but my father's disappearance. I didn't even know where he'd gone or what he was doing there.

"That was our whole war. The one way it manifested itself was that there were just women, children, and old people left in town."

"Before the war we already had a few youth organizations in Kupferberg and the villages nearby. Each one had different types of uniforms. As we got closer to war, you'd see fewer of those uniforms and more of the brown Hitler Youth shirts. But no one would ever think of complaining about the Nazis. That would get you thrown in prison, or at least beaten up. So everyone kept their mouths shut."

"Some people in Kupferberg were always doom and gloom, they were sure Hitler would take us to war. How right they were! The first men were called up just as soon as the draft was introduced. Next they held the extended autumn maneuvers. The atmosphere in the village council kept getting tenser, because they weren't hiring anyone new but they were being absolutely inundated with work. Now they had to insist that some of the townspeople confirm their Aryan status."

"The only sign of war in town was how hard it was getting supplies, especially food. In summer we'd go through the forest gathering mushrooms, berries, and, by the end of the war, even pigweed. But the trips for bread were worst of all. I was a little older by then, so I could handle them better than the other children. But every time my mother sent me to get bread, it meant an entire day going from village to village. First you had to go around Kupferberg asking if there was bread to buy. If there was none, you'd go to Jannowitz. There I'd usually hear I could buy bread in Rohrlach, which was a two-and-a-half mile walk along the Bober River. Every so often I'd have to go all the way from Rorhlach to Fischbach, and wouldn't manage to buy a couple loaves until I got there. Then to top it all off I'd have to go back to town. A trip like that usually took me all day."

"We combined waste from the paper mill with crushed brick and rock, and formed cinder blocks from the mixture, which was used to build three small houses on the outskirts of town. The houses were supposed to be reserved for refugees, who we expected to arrive at any moment. I was only a few years old when they ordered me to help build them."

"That was my last stay in the Rosengarten hostel before the Germans were driven out of Silesia. It was fall of 1944 when I hiked out there with one of my girlfriends. We sat down under a tree on the way and ate some apples. It was all peaceful and quiet, there wasn't even the slightest breeze. After a moment, a weasel came running toward us and for a little while we got to watch it going about its business, paying us no mind. Then we set off home. Looking at Johannesdorf sinking into the dark and Kupferberg high above it, Leni almost shouted for joy. She said it was so beautiful there, she had never seen anything so wonderful before. We never went to Rosengarten again after that."

"The best nettles grew not far from Mr. Franzky's brewery. You'd stew them with garlic in a covered pot, sometimes with onions as well. And every now and again we'd manage to get hold of a few potatoes—Mom would parboil them, and then slice them and brown them on the stove. We'd eat them along with the stewed nettles and found it all really delicious. I remember at those dinners we'd always promise ourselves next time we'd have baked potatoes with butter too. But we never got the chance."

"A tank stopped for a while behind the Lutheran church at the very top of the hill. The soldiers got out of it and said every child who brought them two eggs could sit in the tank for a bit. I ran home for the eggs and I got to sit in the tank. That was at the start of the war."

"The whole war long we didn't hear a single shot fired in town. Now and again a rumble or a boom would come from over the mountains, but then our mother would say a storm was probably coming.

"Simply put, we didn't know about the war. But then we saw the Russians and everything changed."

O LORD, MAKE NO TARRYING

Make haste, O God, to deliver me; make haste to help me, O LORD.
Let them be ashamed and confounded that seek after my soul: let them
be turned backward and put to confusion, that desire my hurt.
Let them be turned back for a reward of their shame that say, Aha, aha.
Let all those that seek thee rejoice and be glad in thee: and let such as
love thy salvation say continually, Let God be magnified.
But I am poor and needy: make haste unto me, O God: thou art my help
and my deliverer; O LORD, make no tarrying.

PSALM 70, KING JAMES VERSION

SUMMER

They don't leave their houses, but peer out from behind drawn
curtains. Not out of disbelief, it's too late for that. Perhaps out of
shame. Shame? Now? Life seems to be carrying on in its rhythm.
No one says a word, everyone listens. In a moment they'll look
out. They won't believe what they see.

They were already listening when the boys came marching
from the direction of Jannowitz. The powerful, measured step of
hobnail boots. Pounding them on the pavement. Singing songs.

No one knew what to expect. Housewives stood at their stoves (it was dinner time), men were coming home from work, little kids were frolicking in the streets, a heat wave had condensed over beautiful and green Kupferberg. But its teenage sons had decided this would be a day everyone here would remember. Or maybe it wasn't them? Would they have thought this up on their own? Did someone think it up for them? Who?

And so they come, passing the two stone crosses—one with the inscription: *Memento*, "remember." They don't remember. They are looking to the future. They come. For a while, people still gaze at them, not yet beckoning their children inside. They will before long. They'll slam their doors shut and stand at their windows. They'll watch.

The boys enter the town, not slowing their march, they pass the brewery, then the tavern, climbing the hill and marching onto the square, their temples dripping with sweat. Black shorts, mustard-brown shirts, handkerchiefs tied around their necks with leather rings. Armbands. Knives at their belts.

Maybe they'll keep going? Pass through the town and march into the fields, to practice marching lockstep in different formations. Maybe they'll just salute by the monument on the square then go off home (the ones from Jannowitz will have to make their own way; they'll run carefree down the road or dash through the fields to the riverbank and dive in with a shout).

They stop in front of the parish priest's house and form up in a row. Their commander steps into the middle holding a megaphone, a tin tube he begins to speak through. The priest is home, but does not come out.

Is he listening? Certainly. What does he hear?

The town stands stock-still. People stand at their windows watching, or go out to the back garden, not wanting to see anything. But they listen. The leader's voice carries over the Niedergasse, the Hochgasse, the Feuergasse, the Fechtergasse. Every now and then they also hear the group chanting slogans. They stand there, shouting, and singing a little. The afternoon is hot, there is the smell of lilacs, the shrubs are in bloom, the cherries will be ripe soon.

Nothing else happens. They could have thrown a stone or led the priest outside. Or hit him in the face.

Maybe the people standing watching this in their homes and behind their curtains think, "there's no way they could punch Father Rother in the face." But an hour ago they still thought there was no way the boys could march to the presbytery, line up in a row, and vilify a clergyman, call him a dog, a thief, a scrounger.

"Our Father Rother? The one who renovated the church and drives that rattling car of his around all the villages in the parish?" they think, shaking their heads. Everyone here respects the Father. You don't insult a respected person, you take your hat off to a respected person on the street, you welcome them into your home, you bow and scrape.

Father Rother is thinking too. He's been thinking, sometimes he's even said something out loud. The boys never came. They would meet in the Black Eagle. They'd give talks, show movies. When there were movies, there would be crowds too. They would salute heroes at the monument, at night they would march with torches, they sang, they saluted. Boots, knives, shorts, knee socks, a dead look in their eyes, gazing straight ahead and marching. They never came close, they always marched on past.

Now they've come, they're standing in an even row. The Gläser brothers are there: Kurt was once a drum major in the Gymnastics Association band, and Erich was in the Scharnhorst Youth. Now they're here. There are no more gymnasts, no more youth organizations, no more St. George's scouts. Only the mustard-brown shirts and those knives. There is the Party and the Hitler Youth. They stand, sing, and look in the windows. As tough as leather, as hard as Krupp steel (that's what the Führer says about them). Do they see the priest? They don't, but they know full well he's listening.

And the priest? What does he feel that sweltering summer afternoon in 1936, when for the first time in the history of the town a Hitler Youth squad stands at his windows as their commander insults him through a large tin tube? Father Rother is an old man now and has seen his fair share. But nothing like this before. He knows something has changed in the town this day, a line has been crossed and no one, not even Father Rother, knows what will come next, what these boys outside could go on to do. Nothing great happened today, but at the same time something awful has taken place. So Rother is afraid. The beast has come, it is in the town once again. It had been gone for so long!

The Gläser brothers really are standing in that grim row before the presbytery. They couldn't not be there. And the less they want to, the more they must. There's no Hitler Youth in Kupferberg, but membership is increasingly compulsory. Anyway, all the other youth organizations are gone now. They willingly closed themselves down. That's the official version. Of the unofficial version, not a word is spoken. So Kurt and Erich don their shorts and mustard-brown shirts and march down the road to Jannowitz for meetings, just as they did today. But at the time they didn't know they would end up returning to Kupferberg on this shameful mission. When their commander informs them of their task, do they protest? It's hard to imagine—they know what the consequences would be. So they march uphill, doing their best to keep in step, and they sing songs. When they enter the town, Erich wants to disappear, sink into the earth. Yet he stands ramrod-stiff before the presbytery and obediently repeats the slogans and chants. On the inside, he's curled up into a ball. He loves Father Rother, he even used to assist at Mass in his church. Besides, Father Rother has never done anything bad to anyone. So Erich doesn't understand at all why, as of today, the priest is an enemy. Once the whole hellish experience is over and Erich has grown old, he'll write in a letter to his friend that never before or since has he felt such embarrassment and shame as he did standing before the presbytery.

WINTER

It started innocently enough. Few of the townspeople thought Hitler's rise to power would bring misery on the whole of Germany. Probably no one at all foresaw that misery spilling out over almost the entire world. People's lives have improved rather quickly. Now business-owners in Kupferberg are getting government commissions and everyone is producing to meet the army's needs. The quarries in Jannowitz, which employ a large number of the town's inhabitants, are also stepping up their output. Word is the blocks crafted in the stonemasons' workshops beside the train station are going all the way to Berlin, where they're being used to build the Führer's new Reich Chancellery. The unemployed are being hired for jobs the government has initiated. The nearly seven hundred inhabitants of Kupferberg quickly forget the years of poverty during the Great Depression.

Disconcerting rumblings periodically reach the town. The first set of changes is made in the local administration. The office of Mayor vanishes, and a Town Leader arrives. Among his duties is reporting all the townspeople's temperaments and political sympathies to Party representatives. Particularly vital is ascertaining the mood among the workers—the greatest danger is a Red Plague. Communism masks itself behind labor unions, only to suddenly transmute into squads of anarchist terrorists, intent on obliterating the Führer's great deeds. Therefore, they must be destroyed quickly.

The parochial schools are closed down and the children are required to attend the new public school. It's located in the old Catholic school building and is run by cantor Müller. One day he brings to class a flag they've never seen before. The black stripe represents the German nation; the white one, the white Aryan race; and the red one, National Socialism, he explains. The flag will hang in the classroom—it will hang there every day, unlike the old black, red, and gold flag, which the cantor only hung up on Constitution Day. Starting in January of the next year, each class will begin and end with the Nazi salute.

Now the Germans are, as Rudolf Hess puts it, "the most modern democracy in the world, built on the confidence of the majority." Confidence in the Führer. This confidence has to be confirmed accordingly, so new officials also have the duty of maintaining lists and documentation confirming citizens' Aryan blood. Each inhabitant of green Kupferberg must go to the police station and fill out the proper declaration. On this basis they will be given a new identity document. If they have pure Aryan blood, the document will be brown (some say Brownshirt-colored). If even a drop of Jewish blood flows in their veins, their document will be yellow, and they themselves will be put in the special register of Jews.

FALL

A year before the Hitler Youth's loathsome roll call in front of Father Rother's house, Hugo Ueberschaer, a retired police lieutenant from the faraway Silesian village of Pless, arrives in town. He decides to leave Silesia and hole up in the mountains right at the moment when the so-called Nuremberg Laws are coming into force in Germany. Now people are openly dividing themselves into these superior and inferior categories. The beast is running wild. First the Party dispensed with its political enemies, now it is tackling race enemies. Perhaps Ueberschaer hopes the beast won't catch him here, that great History will pass him over. Or maybe now he's so tired he's simply seeking a quiet nook where he can spend his old age and die at peace with life. One way or the other, he finds what he's looking for in Kupferberg, at least to begin with. He rents out the beautiful house at number 25 on the square, the one Krün the merchant built five centuries ago, and from which a secret passage was said to run all the way to Castle Bolzenstein. Yet Hugo Ueberschaer does not dwell long in the sanctuary of these ancient walls. Perhaps the hustle and bustle of the town and the noise of endlessly shrieking youngsters on the square irritate him. Or perhaps he merely seeks solitude? On the outskirts of town, on the old road leading to Waltersdorf, he finds himself a run-down hunting lodge and decides to renovate it. The lodge is in a fairy-tale setting. To get there, you have to leave the square, cross next to the cemetery and the school, and then go beyond the last few houses. Then the road begins to meander gently along the mountainside. After a ten-minute walk, Hugo Ueberschaer reaches his rather luxurious hideaway.

The view that unfolds in every direction from there is enough to cheer even the lowest malcontent. Far below one can see the main road to Waltersdorf, while by looking the other way and lifting the gaze slightly, a panorama of the Falcon Mountains comes into view. Though there are many beautiful spots here, a more beautiful one than this would be hard to find.

The lodge itself is built of wood, but it stands on a raised stone foundation. Inside, it contains two large rooms and an attic. Ueberschaer installs a wardrobe painted with folk designs, cleans the house up, and makes some minor repairs. In the attic, he decides to install a spacious library, and bit by bit he transfers his collection from the house in town. It soon turns out there is not enough space in the attic, meaning the first floor becomes piled up with books as well.

So early every morning, no matter the weather, Hugo Ueberschaer sets out from number 25 and heads for Mr. Flabe's bakery. He also stops at Reimann the merchant's, then finally embarks on his daily ramble. He walks in an unhurried, dignified manner, with a slight limp. He's made friends fairly quickly with the people of Kupferberg, and now he greets them with a nod of the head and a smile as they poke their heads out of their stores, saying, *"Guten Tag, Herr Oberst."* Yes, a retired policeman is able to enjoy the respect and kindness of his neighbors.

Karl Heinz Friebe is one of those waiting somewhat longingly for the elderly gentleman to appear on the steeply sloping street. The boy is three years old when nearly all the men vanish from the town, including his father. The draft has just been reintroduced in the Reich, and Heinrich Friebe is called up. Only children, women, and the elderly remain in Kupferberg. Hugo Ueberschaer sets himself apart with his gravity, gentility, and the general esteem people hold him in. He is certainly someone to admire. And Little Karl Heinz admires him with all his heart.

SPRING

The Greater German Reich is so great because it has just increased in size by the addition of Austria, which from now on is called Ostmark. Apparently over 99 percent of Austrians were in favor of joining in the Führer's great work. Some of the soldiers entering Austria are sons of Kupferberg. In letters, they report the whole operation has run peacefully. Their worried mothers can breathe a sigh of relief.

But not for long. The beast's rumbling approach is increasingly audible, coming this time from the south, over the mountains. In the fall, military columns make their way from Breslau to the Sudeten mountain passes—when the Führer gives the signal, they are to spring to the aid of the Germans living in Czechoslovakia. In border towns on the far side of the mountains, demonstrations, riots, and protests are ever more frequent, with people singing "Deutschland über Alles" and giving the Nazi salute. On September 29, the leaders of Europe sign a document that will go down in history as the Shame of Munich and German forces enter the Sudetenland. So the beast is now just beyond the mountains.

Precisely—beyond the mountains. A person standing in this green town would feel sure the whole world is beyond the mountains from here. You can go up Chaussy Hill and take in an impressive vista of the Giant Mountains, the Falcon Mountains and the Leaden Mountains. Everything important happens on the other side of them. Austria has ceased to exist somewhere beyond the mountains, Czechoslovakia is dismantled beyond the mountains, and Kristallnacht has struck the world beyond the mountains as well. In Hirschberg, twelve miles away, on the night of November 9, 1938, 146 Jews fear for their lives as their synagogue burns, their cemetery is destroyed, and Jewish stores are plundered. Synagogues go up in flames in almost every city and town—in Breslau, Brückenberg, Gottesberg, Striegau, and Trebnitz. Across the Reich, ninety-one Jews die at Nazi hands, and thirty thousand are arrested and sent to camps whose existence no one speaks of openly—though they have already started operating.

There are almost no Jews in Kupferberg. But there are some who must account for their Jewish ancestors: half-Jews, quarter-Jews. One of them is Haenisch the pharmacist. He and his son will come to pay for their partly Jewish blood. But on that infamous night, the people of the village sleep soundly. The greater story is happening beyond the mountains.

Yet Karl Heinz Friebe has no concept of any of this, and even though as they speak the beast is beginning to rage somewhere far away, his only concern is whether today he will see *Oberstleutnant* Ueberschaer marching to his hideaway. He is there, too, on September 1, 1939, keeping an eye out as he does every day. Neither he, nor the old policeman, nor Flabe the baker, nor Reimann the merchant, nor even little Karl Heinz's mother has any idea that day is the start of their personal tragedy, and the first beginning of the end of green Kupferberg—for there are still a few beginnings of the end yet to come.

FALL

Mr. Ewald Nieke the schoolmaster and Woike the cantor disappear. Mr. Wendler takes their place—he has a penchant for holding sports practice in a gym in the attic of the school. There, a parquet floor has been laid down, so only children with athletic shoes participate. In Karl Heinz Friebe's class, some of the the children have no shoes at all, so most gym classes take place, at best, in socks. The children don't like Mr. Wendler much, but this is also because he is much more zealous than his predecessors about holding roll calls where they must hold their arms extended toward the Reich flag.

That fall, soldiers come to the town and remove the bells from the steeple of the Catholic church, as well as the clock mechanism. The hands on the clock face stop for good and never move again. Karl Heinz observes this with curiosity; later on, Mr. Wendler explains to him in class that it will all be melted down to make German guns.

The clock is not really needed anymore—since war broke out, people have measured time a different way. The rhythm of their days is marked by the arrival in town of the mailwoman, Ida Klein. Although she looks inconspicuous, Ida arouses simultaneous dread and hope, for no one knows what she's carrying in her bag, who will receive letters today, and what those letters will contain. Perhaps the latest news from sons and fathers—this is met with joy, and quickly checking to see when the letters were sent. Sometimes no letters come—this is met with concern, though people tell themselves this means nothing yet. But there are also letters from commanders. These are what the women of Kupferberg fear the most. Those letters come five times to the Rüffers at number 11. Ida Klein knocks at the door of the Seifert, Schmidt, and Kriese families three times, and the Fischers and Mr. and Mrs. Rose twice. In the fall of 1941, Ida Klein also knocks at Mr. and Mrs. Friebe's door. The letter she brings consists of the brief notification that their beloved father and husband Heinrich has given his life for the Fatherland. He gave it in the Soviet Union, where the Fatherland and its Führer bade him go. The Reich will be forever grateful to him.

Karl Heinz doesn't know his childhood has just ended. His father's death is part of the Führer's greater plan. Now the brave

German nation will also do battle in the East, and the Soviet Union will become its greatest enemy. Yet the burden of this effort, undertaken in the summer of 1941, will also fall on the shoulders of the people of Kupferberg. Not just because many of them will lose their lives there (Fischer, Friebe, Kriese, Hain, Hartmann, Kosmaly, the Rose brothers, the Schmidt brothers, the younger Rüffer, and Seifert). When the Eastern Front is opened, Kupferberg begins experiencing shortages. And in most Silesian villages like this one, refugees are arriving from German cities where Allied bombings are increasingly frequent. But the bombers can't reach Silesia—it's out of their range—so it's fairly safe here for the time being. But people are also getting poorer.

Karl Heinz Friebe is now the only man in this family, and an exceptionally important task has been entrusted to him: obtaining milk. To fulfill this duty, every few days the boy rises before dawn and sets off for Jannowitz. There, he somewhat hopelessly does the rounds of the local farmers. This does not usually lead to the intended result and little Karl must walk farther, through Rosenbaude all the way to Seiffersdorf. For a seven-year-old, this is an almost two-hour trek through the mountains. The effort does not always pay off, for Seiffersdorf is suffering shortages of milk and other goods just like Kupferberg. So that means little Karl Heinz must walk to Kauffung. By then he will be so tired his haggard appearance will soften the heart of some farmer, who will sell him a little milk. From there back to Kupferberg will be a six-mile hike. If he manages to catch a car heading toward home, he can arrive before nightfall. But that isn't always possible. These expeditions are especially arduous in winter, when Karl Heinz must press on through deep snow in search of milk. Thank goodness at that time of year he can sled down to Jannowitz, and he eagerly makes the most of that meager portion of wildness and joy. He takes the old road there—the main one running past the brewery and the two stone crosses is closed for sledding. Only cars are allowed on it, but there are not so many of those (fuel is getting scarcer), so it remains empty. Meaning at any given moment, a military convoy might come rolling along it.

SPRING

Mr. Wendler disappears. Young Miss Franzky takes his place. She lives in the yellow two-story villa near the brewery and is the daughter of its owner, old Georg Franzky. It's not long since she graduated from high school, but helping hands are needed all over town, and so she is entrusted with teaching the children. Everyone greets the decision with joy—the Franzky family enjoys great respect in Kupferberg, and Mr. Wendler was never well liked here. People will only think warmly of him two years later, when he turns up dead somewhere on the Hungarian-Romanian border.

Gisela! Gisela Franzky! Karl Heinz Friebe loves her with a love as great as a seven-year-old's love for his teacher can be. Little Karl does absolutely everything for Gisela; in the evenings he pores over his book in hope the next day her brown eyes will give a glimmer of acknowledgment, and maybe even approval. After school, little Karl Heinz hides in the bushes and waits until Gisela leaves school. This is when the young teacher abandons all the seriousness and sternness she is forced to maintain in front of the children. She looks around intently to see if anyone is watching, and next she does what she herself forbids her students to do—she squeezes under the fence and races through the meadow, taking a shortcut home.

One day, when as usual the boy is hiding in the bushes near the cemetery (where he has the best view of the school and the meadow), instead of seeing Gisela, he spies a black car stopped in the road, and two soldiers with strange crackling devices walking around what remains of the Adler mineshaft. Karl Heinz Friebe decides not to budge from his hiding place. If he knew what he was looking at, he would certainly observe much more closely. But he doesn't know. He finds out years later, but by then it will be too late.

However, these observations lead him to confide in his grand-mother. She lives on the Hochgasse, right beside the Lutheran church. The boy likes to walk along there, he often plans his route so he can pass, slightly awestruck, along the avenue of Swedish whitebeams leading to the double doors of the church. When the boy's grandmother learns what he saw, she merely places a finger to her lips. Best not to see, best not to know.

SUMMER

Father Rother disappears. Someone overheard a BBC radio trans-mission coming from the presbytery. Or maybe they heard nothing at all, they just wanted to point a finger? Or they had no choice? Regardless, when a Gestapo car parks in front of the presbytery, everyone knows they won't see Father Rother ever again.

A few months after this event, Gisela Franzky arrives at school in tears. Karl quickly manages to work out what has made her upset—news gets around here exceptionally quickly. It's a small town, people are suspicious of one another, the authorities are keeping their eye on everyone. Everybody knows everything, especially about those who have already found themselves under scrutiny. A series of setbacks for the previously undefeated Reich have meant there's a certain palpable nervousness in town. Government radio is still reporting the Germans are not retreating, only regrouping to previously determined positions more amenable to counterattack. But those brave enough to secretly listen to *Feindsender*—transmissions broadcast by the Allies— know the Reich's situation is increasingly desperate. Old Georg Franzky is one of these brave listeners. Yet his lack of faith in Goebbels's propaganda costs him a great deal, for the Gestapo catches him red-handed listening to Swiss radio, and he is taken away to Hirschberg. This is why Gisela is so upset. Under interrogation, Georg Franzky is beaten severely. After a speedy trial, he is sentenced to eighteen months' imprisonment. Gisela, and all the townspeople, know this could be tantamount to a life sentence. "Radio criminals" are enemies of the nation, and the government combats them with absolute ruthlessness. Kupferberg is shaken. Now that the priest and Mr. Frankzy have been taken away, not a single person in the town can feel safe.

The pharmacist Kurt Haenisch absolutely does not feel safe either: he is half-Jewish, and so one of few in the town with a yellow government ID. He constantly encounters unpleasantness from Party members. If there were another pharmacy in the town, his family would have certainly been driven out of here before 1939. Pragmatism, and perhaps personal connections and sympathy as well, trump ideology. Yet the Haenisches' Jewish roots don't prevent their two sons enlisting in the *Volkssturm*, the last intake of draftees into the German army, a real popular movement made up of people from the so-called "final category." The older boy, Ulrich, trusts the Führer unreservedly. When they return home from the front on short stays of leave, he greets his father with a Nazi salute. Perhaps Ulrich's zeal in showing his love for Hitler is the Haenisch family's salvation.

WINTER

The situation beyond the mountains is getting worse. By 1944, the Soviet counteroffensive has reached the Vistula River. It stops there, though not for long. On January 12, 1945, at five in the morning, "Stalin's organs" begin to play on the banks of the Vistula. A thousand Katyusha rockets give the Red Army the signal to attack. It won't stop until it reaches Berlin. Over the next few days, panic breaks out in the furthest-flung eastern provinces of the Reich. Since mid-January, hundreds of thousands of refugees from Upper Silesia—mainly women and children—have already been heading west. On January 20, all across Breslau the civilian population is ordered to abandon the city immediately. The scene on the streets is like Dante's *Inferno*. There's not space on the trains for everyone, so thousands set off on foot in sub-zero temperatures.

Helena Szczepańska is also among the refugees. She's eight years old and the youngest of five siblings. Until now, she and her mother have lived in Niklasfähre, on the border of Upper and Lower Silesia. Thanks to their German ancestry—and despite their *de facto* Polish ethnicity—they are evacuated along with the other Germans. They stop for a day when they reach Schurgast, and then walk westward for almost two weeks. On February 1, 1945, they reach a small town on top of a hill—Kupferberg. Helena will remember this place well, for during their almost three-week trek through Silesia, Kupferberg is the only place she and her family get to sleep in a heated building. Everywhere else they sleep in barns, sheds, cellars, and God knows where else.

Starting in early 1945, a post operates in the Black Eagle tavern giving out hot meals and tea for refugees from the East. Before long, Kupferberg's population has grown to nearly a thousand. The authorities estimate there are almost twenty thousand refugees in the region around Hirschberg. Watching them, young Karl Heinz Friebe wonders if he, his mother, and little sister will share the same fate. The feeling of hunger hasn't left him for some months, and the supplies they'd prepared that summer are slowly running out. Bread, milk, and sugar are getting harder to find. It's true the authorities have issued ration cards, but they're no use, because finding anything to buy with them borders on a miracle.

The townspeople and the refugees generally believe even a trek over the ringing frost is better than falling into the Communists' clutches. People can remember the films and photos shot by German soldiers in the East Prussian village of Nemmersdorf in the fall of 1944, just after retaking it from the Soviets in a ferocious battle. This is how one of the soldiers who marched into Nemmersdorf described what he saw in the pages of the German press: "At the first farm, there was a hay wagon off the left side of the road. Four naked women were nailed to it by their hands, in a pose of crucifixion. Two naked women were nailed to the door of the barn, also in a pose of crucifixion. All in all, we found seventy women and children, and one old man, seventy-four years old. They were all dead. You could see they'd been tortured horrifically, except a few who had been shot in the back of the head. Even babies had been killed, their skulls smashed in. The bodies of all the women, including girls from eight to twelve years old, showed signs of rape. Even an old, blind woman wasn't spared."

No wonder news of the Russians' approach makes people desperate to escape. The ones who can no longer flee resolve to commit suicide. There are hundreds of these cases in the towns and villages of the Reich. Entire villages and hamlets hang themselves. Entire families hang themselves; mothers kill their children and then take their own lives. They don't know that, although the Red Army has committed unimaginable crimes in Nemmersdorf and other places, the descriptions in German propaganda are strongly exaggerated. The authorities are trying to induce panic in the nation, terror of the savage hordes from Asia. You don't negotiate with a horde; with a horde you fight to your last breath, because falling into the clutches of barbarians from the East is a fate worse than death.

When routine bombardment of Breslau begins in early February, in Kupferberg the decision to evacuate is made. Karl Heinz Friebe dresses warmly and makes sure his little sister is equally bundled up. A blizzard is raging outside. They take the remaining food from the house, as well as their most essential possessions; they don't know where they're going. They clean the house, lock it behind them, and pocket the key. They know the first section of the route perfectly. They have to leave the house, pass the brewery and then the two stone crosses, which at this time of year barely peek out over the snowbanks. They take the road down toward Jannowitz. If it weren't for the war, there they'd get on a train and go wherever their hearts desired—but at the station, they're shocked to discover the trains aren't stopping there, just slowing down a little only to speed up again a moment later and rush southward. The fountain has also vanished from the front of the station; a deep crater now lies in its place, and the walls of the surrounding houses are pockmarked with rounds from machine guns. Karl Heinz Friebe looks at all this and doesn't understand what the little fountain in Jannowitz had to do with the war going on beyond the mountains.

The refugees don't get onto a train but instead into military trucks waiting at the station. They spend the next few hours packed together, trying to withstand the deadly cold forcing its way through the canvas roof. Finally, just before dusk, they reach Gablonz and are quartered in the gymnasium of the local public school. For more than a week, every morning they will pack up their possessions and wait for their transport westward to depart. They know their destination; everyone here says there's nowhere safe anymore, but the least dangerous place is Dresden. That's exactly where most trains and columns of refugees from Silesia are being directed.

So they wait patiently. Every now and then another family will disappear from the gymnasium where they've ended up living, and new ones will arrive in their place. A large share of the nearly six hundred thousand refugees passes through Gablonz. The ones who've stood eye-to-eye with Red Army soldiers have terrible stories to tell. One of the refugees will later write in his memoirs:

> The terrifying news magnified our fear. We heard blood-curdling stories about young men and old people being murdered, women being raped regardless of age, nursing mothers having their breasts cut off, pregnant women having their wombs cut open and the still-unborn fetuses ripped out, deep wells being filled with the bodies of living people, eyes getting poked out with bayonets, tongues being cut out, crowds of Germans being burned alive in barns or houses, militiamen being driven into captivity by powerful tanks and armored cars charging them from behind, and many other stories that would make your hair stand on end.*

Yes—compared with all the horrors talked about in the school gymnasium in Gablonz, the thought of escaping to Dresden is a true comfort.

Finally it's their turn. They head out the afternoon of February 13. They have almost a hundred miles to cross, but the train they get on stops constantly, because there are already Soviet planes about and there's a danger they'll bomb the tracks. But the refugees

---

* Zygmunt Dulczewski and Andrzej Kwilecki, *Pamiętniki osadników Ziem Odzyskanych* [Memoirs of the Settlers of the Recovered Lands] (Poznań: Wydawnictwo Poznańskie, 1963).

are moving. They leave Kupferberg, and their fear, behind them somewhere. Supposedly it's safer in the west. They're going farther from home, but farther from danger too. Dresden isn't far now, almost within reach. But when night falls, the whole convoy stops completely; they turn out the lights and everything is enveloped in darkness. In the air they can hear a terrifying hum growing louder and louder, as though a giant swarm of bees was waking from its winter sleep. Karl Heinz Friebe presses his nose against the frost-covered window of the train. The other passengers do the same. They look up to the sky, but can't make anything out. After a moment, they see the first flashes far to the west: one, a second, a third. Soon they won't be able to count them anymore; the flashes transform into a golden glow taking up almost the entire horizon. There's a rumble from afar, but it's muffled enough inside the train that they can still hear the children crying. They would be able to hear whispered conversations too, but no one speaks. They all stand and watch. It's the night of February 13, 1945, and right now several hundred Allied planes are carrying out the carpet-bombing of Dresden. Over the next two days, they will turn the city into a heap of rubble and take the lives of twenty-five thousand people. Those who managed to get onto the earlier trains leaving Gablonz will also be among the dead. The train from which Karl Heinz Friebe is watching the glow in the west has stopped ten miles from the city, because it was one of the last to leave.

They can't go to Dresden. That city is gone, so where to now? Breslau is under siege, just like Posen, Thorn, Danzig, and Königsberg. They head south, slowly. They come to Gablonz again; there's chaos and weeping at the station. They don't get off there. The train will go somewhere, a train has to move, the train will take them away from there. They're on the road the next few days; Karl Heinz Friebe loses count, he's hungry and cold. It's quiet on the train. They're in Bohemia; they're getting as far as the border of what used to be Austria. Suddenly an alarm sounds: there are Soviet planes in the air and people are fleeing the train. It's winter, there's snow and a town in the distance. They run; the planes are getting closer. Karl holds his sister with one hand and his mother with the other. His greatest fear is losing one of them. The planes fly low overhead and fire their machine guns. First they shoot at the train, then they turn around and fly over the town. People scatter in all directions. They run up to the first houses they see—there are walls and cellars, they can hide there! But no. The whole town closes its doors to them. No one lets them in. They can pound their fists, they can shout and weep, but they can't go in. They can only lie curled up against a wall and hope the planes shoot at the people lying in the street. Once they've flown off, the grown-ups lead the children away, and then pile up the corpses in one place. The train will be able to move on.

They travel this way for three weeks—Bohemia, the Sudetenland, Silesia. Finally, at the beginning of March, they reach Hirschberg, where they also meet those who survived the bombing of Dresden. They don't want to hear their stories; they're going up the mountain—returning home. Lomnitz, Schildau, Boberstein, Rohrlach, Jannowitz. On the way, Karl Heinz asks the farmers if perhaps they have a little milk to sell. Finally, the two stone crosses, the brewery building, the key from the pocket. Home.

SPRING

Columns of skeletons appear in the area. It's the evacuation of a sub-camp of Gross-Rosen. They come from Hirschberg, Bad Warmbrunn, and Landeshut (where after a day's march they end up back where they started and the SS men fly into a rage). In Bolkenhain, they undergo selection first. A prisoner from that camp later testifies he saw living people thrown into ditches with lime, and the *Lagerführer* personally kill some prisoners with poison injections.

Kupferberg is out of the way; maybe if the women's camp in Merzdorf were evacuated, the four hundred women would pass through the town on their grim march. But that camp operates right to the end, until the Russians liberate it.

Bolkenhain is thirteen miles from Kupferberg, Hirschberg is a little closer. It's eleven miles to Landeshut and barely six to Merzdorf. That's not beyond the mountains anymore. That's here.

There are other camps here too, small factories, individual farms where French, Belgian, and Polish prisoners work. They've been brought in throughout the war. They were meant to work for the Reich and be glad they were alive. Now it's said they can't wait for the Russians to come, so they can point out who treated them the worst.

The Nazis disappear too. One night, in a panic, they load up a van, gather up all their documents, and head out of Kupferberg toward Bohemia. The mayor of the town is among them; they're all Nazi Party members. After a few days, they return beaten up, with no van, shabby and resigned. The ring of encirclement has long since closed. There's no escape; the only thing to do is wait.

Explosions can already be heard in every direction; planes appear more and more frequently in the sky. Once they find out the Russians have captured the German airport, no one looks at the symbols on the planes' wings anymore; they all just go straight into the cellar and wait. Yet not one bomb falls on Kupferberg. A plane is shot down and falls on the rail bridge just beyond Jannowitz, meaning the route to Hirschberg is cut off too. The townspeople are constantly being thrown into panic by word the Russians are coming: one more town will join the ghost of Nemmersdorf. As February turns to March, the Germans successfully retake Striegau from the Russians. The streets there are covered with the corpses of civilians who didn't manage to evacuate.

Helena Plüschke, one of the inhabitants of Striegau, later recalls when the Russians captured the town:

A Russian patrol bursts into the house. They chase out the women and girls. They catch them all, street by street, and take them to the school. There, it's hell on Earth! The nightmares still linger in my mind: drunken soldiers, a gun in one hand, a torch in the other—on the hunt. German women are their main prey. Women from Striegau and nearby are held in schoolrooms for entire days, imprisoned and tortured. In overcrowded rooms, their tormentors select their victims. If anyone resists, they drag her down the corridor by her hair to the "slaughterhouse." Every two or three hours, a special team appears to pick out women for the officers' quarters [...]. Those who return from there are mental, and sometimes physical, wrecks. I am a victim once again. Luckily, I manage to protect my eleven-year-old daughter. I wrap her in old rags and hide her behind a pile of junk. The torture begins by asking whether I am a Nazi. My denial is answered with a powerful blow to the face and then a whipping. They hold a pistol to my head and force me to drink; ironically, it's German rye vodka. It doesn't take long before I'm engulfed by drunken intoxication. Whatever they've done to me I don't feel until the next day. Now I've completely lost my will to live, and I'm finished. I throw up a few times, and then lie apathetically among the other women who've met the same fate.

Since the Nazis have fled, Richard Fürle becomes the mayor. (He doesn't know he'll be the last in the history of Kupferberg.) When the news of Hitler's death reaches the townspeople on April 30, a meeting is held in the Black Eagle tavern. The mayor appeals for everyone to stay calm and reasonable until the war ends, and he abolishes the requirement for them to greet one another with the Nazi salute. When he returns to his office, an officer of the Waffen SS division currently stationed in Kupferberg is already waiting for him there. The officer accuses Fürle of treason, and puts a pistol on his desk.

"Mr. Mayor, I think you ought to carry out the sentence yourself. Otherwise, I will be forced to do so."

"If you do as you intend, you can be sure you will not leave here alive," answers the mayor.

The officer looks out the window. By now a considerable crowd of townspeople has gathered in front of the mayor's office. After a moment's silence, the officer takes the pistol off the desk and leaves. Soon the SS men abandon Kupferberg.

On May 9 at about five in the afternoon, the first Russian motorcycle patrol rides into Hirschberg. They're shot by the one SS post in the town, making up the sum total of shots fired in defense of Kupferberg. That same day, Karl Heinz Friebe, walking on the road to Rudelstadt, spots the first Russian soldier. The boy stands stock-still; the soldier would probably have done the same, if he weren't completely drunk and barely able to stay on his feet. So here they are! Karl runs toward the town and prays the soldier won't shoot him. A moment later, all the inhabitants of Kupferberg are sitting in their cellars, shaking with fear. They'll spend almost twenty-four hours down there, because the Russians won't enter the town until the next day. They drive up the road from Rudelstadt and Merzdorf in tanks. They evict the inhabitants of a house at the bend in the road right next to the brewery, and set up their headquarters there. That's where the Germans are to come and hand in any guns they have, and any radio receivers too. The ghost of Nemmersdorf claims its first victim: in the cellar of the Black Eagle tavern, the first young woman hangs herself.

SUMMER—FALL

If anyone has to leave the house, now young Karl Heinz Friebe does it. He's relatively safe—he's a little boy. Because of the rapes taking place in Kupferberg, several more women have already hanged themselves. In the hamlet of Kreuzweise, a few minutes down the road, the Russians burst into one farm worker's home and raped her for so long she died of exhaustion. The women don't go outside; they cover their heads with headscarves and do their best not to look anyone in the eye.

In truth no one is safe. The Russians come into Kurt Haenisch's pharmacy and demand rectified spirit from his laboratory. The pharmacist refuses and explains that without it he won't be able to prepare any medicines or dress any wounds, of which there are plenty, after all. They drive him off in a car and beat him. He returns a week later. He dies a few days after that.

For similar reasons, a railroad worker from Jannowitz and the merchant Seidel are shot, and the Russians beat Mr. Gehde unconscious with truncheons. He dies a few days later as a result of an abscess in his brain.

The first Polish policemen and soldiers arrive in town. They don't maintain order—their appearance causes even more chaos and fear. Their orders are clear:

> Treat the Germans as they have treated us. Many have already forgotten how they have treated our children, wives, and old people. The Czechs proved capable of forcing the Germans to flee their territory. We must be tough and decisive in performing our duty so that the Teutonic vermin don't just hide in their houses, but run away from us on their own, and once they're back in their own country thank God they made it out alive. Let us not forget that Germans will always be Germans. As you perform your duty, do not request, but command.[*]

---

[*] Order from the Second Polish Army Command, June 24, 1945

It's enough for the Poles to show up in Kaszynski's tavern for yet another tragedy to take place. They don't think the German owner greets them with the proper respect. So they beat him unconscious, then tie him by his legs to a motorcycle and drag him through the whole town, and then farther, past the brewery and the two crosses all the way to Jannowitz.

Anyone who falls under suspicion of Nazism is also at risk of being killed. In May, Georg Franzky, the brewery owner, comes back to Kupferberg. The joy at his return doesn't last long, though, for his sudden appearance catches the attention of the Polish police. Suspecting him of fighting for Nazi partisans, they order him to hand over the gun he's allegedly hiding in his garden. Franzky explains he has no gun and digs up his entire garden before the Poles' very eyes. When he doesn't find anything, they beat him unconscious. Miraculously, he survives.

Count Christian Friedrich zu Stolberg-Wernigerode is also suspected of Nazism. It's not enough that he's a capitalist and a bourgeois; on top of that, during the war he had two forced laborers from France working on his farm. The Poles take the Count away and detain him for five weeks in Hirschberg. Two other townspeople die on his account—Mr. Beiwe and Mr. Maiborn. He himself is saved by a Polish doctor, who tends to his injuries, but the Count never fully recovers.

Karl Heinz Friebe already knows from official announcements posted around Kupferberg that he is no longer German, but merely *a* German, a member of an ethnic minority in a new country. He doesn't know that, in the terminology of the new government, he, his mother, and all the elderly people in the town are "undesirable elements" with no "productive capacity." Such elements must be disposed of as quickly as possible.

Soon Karl Heinz Friebe also finds out Kupferberg is no longer Kupferberg. Its new name is Miedziana Góra. Jannowitz becomes Janowice, Rudelstadt is Ciechanowice, Merzdorf is Marciszów, and Waltersdorf is Mniszków. In addition, Hirschberg is now Jelenia Góra and Bad Warmbrunn is Cieplice. Breslau is now called Wrocław, and Görlitz is Zgorzelec. Karl Heinz Friebe doesn't know how to pronounce any of these names. Only Berlin has stayed Berlin, though some people say there is no Berlin anymore.

Other rumors crop up too. Apparently no one knows whether the whole area will even end up inside Poland's borders. There's a chance Kupferberg will be Kupferberg again and will be taken over by the British or American occupation zone, or it could become Czechoslovakia. In July 1945, German posters appear in the town:

> *Labor is the only cure for poverty,*
> *Work is the only source of bread,*
> *Don't complain!*
> *Don't lose heart!*
> *Approach the new task*
> *With new strength,*
> *Be ready to admit your mistakes bravely,*
> *And to take a new path honestly.*
> *The times demand it of you,*
> *Be prepared!*

Despite the rumors, it quickly becomes clear that the days of Karl Heinz Friebe and his countrymen in the town are numbered, as they are in all the towns in Lower Silesia. On July 11, Major Smirnov, the military commandant of Jelenia Góra, meets with the German population:

> I'm holding this meeting to warn you all that you're going to be deported from here. The area around Jelenia Góra is already being resettled; Jelenia Góra and Warmbrunn will be resettled on July 14 and 15. That's why I'm warning you in advance, because the Poles don't know about it yet. If they did, they would already be looting and plundering.
>
> The deportation will happen in a normal and orderly fashion, not the way the Poles do it. They come at midnight, give you twenty minutes, and only let you take forty-five pounds with you. I'm letting you take not just forty-five pounds, but more—as much as you can carry.
>
> [...] As long as I'm here, I won't let the Poles do any harm. Whenever I've heard the Poles are looting I've come out to stop them, even in the middle of the night. I don't allow that sort of thing.
>
> [...] I think you all understand, because I've said enough, even too much, because I'm sure there are no Poles here. If one of the Poles were here I wouldn't have told you so much.*

---

* Daniel Boćkowski, ed., *Niemcy w Polsce 1945–1950: wybór dokumentów* [The Germans in Poland, 1945–1950: Selected Documents], vol. 4 (Warsaw, Wydawnictwo Neriton, 2000), 134. Stenographic records from a meeting organized for the resettled German population by the military commander of Jelenia Góra, Major Smirnov. No one knows how a translation of these minutes found itself in Polish hands.

The expulsions do indeed go ahead, but not as quickly as Major Smirnov predicted. In fact, no one knows how to deport hundreds of thousands of people and their possessions from such a large area so rapidly, especially since the first thing the Russians did was to dismantle the electrification on the railroad from Jelenia Góra to Wałbrzych and export the equipment to the East. Now, once again, only steam trains can run there.

At the moment no one even knows how many Germans there are. The population records scrupulously maintained by German local officials aren't much use, because thousands of people were stranded there during the evacuation of the east to Lower Silesia. So they're all required to register in the towns and municipalities. There, their names are added to the repatriation lists. From July onward, all Germans without exception are also required to wear a white band on their right arm.

Karl Heinz Friebe's mother tears up one of their sheets and cuts three armbands out of it, neatly hemming the edges. The boys ask how long they'll have to wear them, but no one in the town knows.

WINTER—SUMMER

More and more Poles are arriving and taking houses over. Once they've picked out a specific building, the police go in and order the German living there to move into the attic or the cellar. As per regulations, the former owners are assigned to the first round of repatriation. Only those Germans working in the paper mill in Janowice or in the linen factory in Marciszów are protected from this fate. There's a shortage of specialists across Lower Silesia, so

German experts who know how to keep production levels up are worth their weight in gold. Notices are nailed to the doors of their houses; they can stay here the longest.

Right from the beginning the Poles try to work the local soil and begin farming. The new authorities encourage them, for people are arriving all over the region and the granaries are half-empty after the war. But the new farmers don't know the particulars of the harsh climate here, or the history of the fields. They don't know what's been grown on them before, so they can't tell what they should plant now. They don't ask the Germans, though. When the Germans offer to help, they just get told not to interfere, because they'll be gone soon anyway.

So now there's winter and hunger. The supplies of nettles and pigweed Mama gathered up ran out long ago, though there are still preserves made from fruit secretly gathered from their own orchards. Karl Heinz Friebe doesn't even go out for milk. The more enterprising Poles have taken away the Germans' cows, and now milk is even harder to get. They can't buy anything in the stores either, because the new government has introduced an exchange rate that's detrimental to the Germans. They can only pay in marks, because they can be punished for possession of Polish złotys.

The ongoing deportation of German families doesn't proceed without problems. For example, so Waltersdorf can truly merit the Polish name Mniszków, the population of the entire village is summoned to leave the town three separate times. Three times someone pounds on the door at midnight, three times they find out they'll leave their homes at dawn. Three times they carefully pack and weigh each of their bundles so they're not over forty-five pounds. Three times they set off on the long road to Jelenia Góra. There they find out it's not their turn yet, and they're to return home.

Those who leave in winter have it the worst. The transports heading out of Lower Silesia are rarely heated. There are no stoves in the railroad cars, not every train has an assigned doctor, and there are problems with food supplies. The deportees aren't always able to bring food with them; often they lose it at the station during the baggage inspection. There are stories of death trains going around. One of those is a train that leaves Wrocław in the winter of 1946. There are 1,543 people on it, of whom one-third are children and young people. The Poles don't allow the travelers to bring straw onto the train for bedding; they also don't check the stoves. In the course of the six-day journey in sub-zero temperatures, the Germans are only given hot coffee four times, and bread just once. Meanwhile, several (four or five) pregnant women give birth; in these conditions the babies have no hope of survival. A Breslau resident, Dr. Loch, tries to provide medical assistance. During the journey he has a heart attack; despite this, he does his best to help everyone in need, but there's little he can do. In total, 32 people freeze to death en route. Another 298 go straight from the train to the hospital when they arrive in the West. Altogether, over the next few weeks another 58 of the train's passengers die as a result of the night-marish journey.* A dramatic appeal reaches the British military mission in Kaławsk: "Incidents of mistreatment of Germans are

---

* Ibid., vol. 4, pp. 285–288.

increasing, and the main perpetrators appear to be railroad policemen."*

Some are afraid to leave Miedziana Góra, others are afraid to stay. Some still hope everything will work out somehow. The owner of the water bottling plant, Max von Glyschinsky, doesn't want to leave his factory; the gravedigger Neumann doesn't want to leave his graveyard; the Blümke sisters don't have anyone in the West.

Hugo Ueberschaer doesn't want to go either. He says you can't transplant old trees. Besides, he doesn't have any reason to go west. He's already prepared everything for his departure here. So he puts on his dress uniform and takes his own life. They put him in the crypt he built himself; they cover the coffin with a reinforced concrete plaque, on which he'd carved the following inscription with his own hand:

HUGO UEBERSCHAER

BORN DEC 19, 1870 IN PLESS

DIED ....

PSALM 70

R.I.P.

---

* Letter from Colonel Carroll, dated May 14, 1946, to the Polish Committee of the Red Cross Representative in Berlin, on the subject of incidents of abuse during the deportation of the German population (Archive of New Records, Ministry of Recovered Lands, 73, book 85). The majority of complaints against the Polish authorities went through the British Mission in Kaławsk (today's Lubliniec).

Only the date of death is missing. Maybe he put off the decision day after day? The people who bury the old policeman put the date on the plaque. From here, he'll have a beautiful view of the whole of the Sokole Mountains.

SUMMER AGAIN

Finally, it's the Friebe family's turn too. They pack their bundles, clean the house, lock the door, and leave the key on the doorframe. They won't return. It's June 1946. There's a scent of lilacs, and the cherries will be ripe soon. They walk away from their house and past the brewery. Then the two stone crosses. Jannowitz, Rohrlach, Boberstein, Schildau, Lomnitz, Hirschberg station—Jelenia Góra station. They wait at the station. One day, two days, a week. Their bags are inspected: no valuables can leave Poland. But they have no valuables.

They wait again. It rains.

The train is fitted with cattle cars; there are fifty-five of them, and thirty-five people are loaded into each one. Hold Mama's hand so you won't get lost. Karl quickly works out an entire town, even two, can fit in one train. They could pack all of Kupferberg into train cars and send it all west. But the town will stay. Only they will disappear.

The train stops outside Marciszów. Karl Heinz Friebe goes up to the door of the car and looks at the two church towers, the one with a broken clock, for the last time. Water pours in through the leaky roof of the train car.

They ride through Jawor and Legnica to Kaławsk. Here they learn they're going to the British occupation zone. They're glad. Now for delousing; they're ordered to undress and wash. Then they get back on the train. Soon comes the border, the bridge over the Oder River, and the new Germany beyond it. The riverbank is all white: people are taking off their armbands and throwing them out of the train. Mrs. Friebe does the same with Karl's. The boy watches for a long time as the scrap of white linen floats on the wind.

THEY WENT AWAY

"WE CAME TO JANOWICE in the summer of '45, so we were some of the first Poles here. We were really frightened to make the journey. Everywhere we heard there were werewolves hiding in the woods, meaning German partisans, and that they would kill Poles on sight. But there were also gangs of looters and thieves in the area who'd come from Central and Eastern Poland, and they'd attack anyone and shoot them all, they didn't care if you were German, Russian, or Polish. Lots of people died that way around here.

"Back then, the majority of the people living in Janowice and Miedzianka* were still Germans. They didn't want to leave and thought everything would work out somehow. But my parents told me this was going to be Poland now. When I mentioned that to

---

* Officially, for the first few months of 1945, the town was called Miedziana Góra, which was a literal translation of the German name. Yet townspeople remembering those times often use the modern name.

my German playmates, we had a huge fight about it. We argued all the time anyway, but in spite of that I have good memories of them. After a few months with them I learned basic German and for a while I suppose I spoke better German than Polish.

"I don't remember any adult Germans from that time at all, a few at most. And I have absolutely no memory of their women, as though there weren't any at all. They were probably staying in their homes, and I never went into any of the Germans' houses. I don't know whether I didn't want to go in or they never let me in. I only saw the inside of the German houses once the Germans were gone.

"Once September arrived, I went to school, where most of the teachers and students were already Polish. The Germans didn't want to go to our school, so they were still on vacation then and we were all really jealous of them for that.

"They went away in the fall and didn't say goodbye to anyone. As the days went by I simply had fewer German playmates, and the ones who were left didn't want to say what had happened to the ones who were gone. We also never knew in advance who would leave, and I remember being really sad that my friends were disappearing without saying goodbye. I'd made very good friends with some of them. If any of the Germans cried when they left, I don't remember it.

"Furniture, china, and paintings got left behind in the German houses. No one had confiscated any of that from them, and we never understood why they didn't want any of it anymore, because everything was perfectly good. Sometimes fights broke out among the Poles over this stuff, which kept the police pretty busy. Anyway, the government took the most valuable items, and what happened to them afterward, I don't know.

"In the summer, some soldiers and policemen got into an argument over some of the valuables. That was in Janowice, on the banks of the Bóbr River, beside an oak tree. My father didn't want to tell me what they were fighting over, and we didn't find out until afterward that the police had had to shoot one of the soldiers there to get the whole gang to shut up and cool off.

"Later, when there were fewer and fewer Germans, what they left behind was administered on behalf of the township by this old man who was half-Jewish, half-German, and half-Polish—Tennenbaum. I guess during the war he was some kind of *Volksdeutsch*, because there's no way a Jew could have lived through the whole war among the Germans. When a Polish family moved into an ex-German house, he was the one who went along with the township commission and valued the individual items. And if someone wanted to and had enough money, they could get their hands on a piano or a cuckoo clock for a fraction of what it was worth. But back then people had no money, so they told Tennenbaum only to value the essentials, like the bed, chairs, stools, and tables. And everything else in the house would get left out in the yard. And these pianos, cuckoo clocks, or slightly fancy dressers would stand in the fields until they'd dried out completely and would fall apart into scrap wood. When winter came, people burned the wood in their stoves."

PHOTOGRAPHS I

IN NEARLY EVERY ISSUE of *Schlesische Bergwacht*, a German will write *unser schönes Hirschberg* ("our beautiful Hirschberg"), or something of that nature. Then, when they come to Trzcińsko, Janowice, or Miedzianka, they climb out of their spacious Mercedes ("can someone tell me how it is that we won the war, but it's their retirees who come here driving Mercedes?") and then that *unser* or *mein* slips out in front of the Poles, and it makes things somewhat awkward. People here aren't stupid, they know what's what. And maybe they don't catch every word, but they can make out *mein* and *unser* right away.

Afterward the locals say, "We know what they're up to coming here." After all, they know that as they were leaving, the Germans left all their valuables hidden here: gold, jewelry, and money.

I look at the photos sent to the editors of *Schlesische Bergwacht*. Each village, even the smallest ones, get their own item. Predominantly they're photos from get-togethers and reunions of former neighbors. Older women with requisite platinum perms pose, usually half-smiling, alongside their gray-haired and slightly overweight spouses. Also included are pictures from an era when speaking the phrase *unser schönes Kupferberg* aloud would offend no one.

"Kindergarten Kupferberg 1936." I imagine the torment of a photographer having to tame this diminutive pack of nearly thirty children, getting them all to look at him at the same time. He probably tried employing cunning rather than harsh words— but his efforts were unsuccessful, and the result is that only few children are looking directly at the camera, while the rest are fooling around. Some of his little models stand with their backs completely turned, occupied with their own, surely extremely important, matters. The two teachers standing in the background wear bemused expressions. One is still half-heartedly scolding a troublemaker. Only the elder of the two is serious, obediently facing the photographer. All four give the impression that long experience has taught them to give up trying to control these screaming creatures, and that simply grouping all the children into a relatively compact space counts as a success. The tiny gang ripples and vibrates, and the photographer is unable to fit all of them into the frame—two children on the right side are cut off by the edge of the picture. It's too bad, because at that moment the two of them were looking straight at the photographer and smiling.

It looks like early spring. The kids are wearing jackets and sweaters, some of them have thick wool caps on their heads, jauntily cocked at all angles or slipping down over their eyes. The light is soft and dispersed, the photographer has selected the proper exposure, but the details have been lost through repeated reproduction. The children in light-colored clothing now almost merge into the background and the texture of the paper.

This is a picture of a boisterous, fun-filled rabble, of carefree spirits and joy. It's something of a chilly spring, it's something of the yearning to now venture outside jacket-free, even though the weather is still too cold for that. Yet such power of expression lies hidden in many of these squirming, riotous figures that you can't take your eyes off them.

A few issues later I come across a photograph from the school in Kammerswaldau (today's Kromnów), about ten miles from Miedzianka. It's obvious at first glance these children are older, and there are nearly as many of them as the preschoolers from the town on the mountaintop. They could even be the same children, only a few years later. Now they stand obediently in four lines and everyone without exception looks into the camera. Right in the middle of the frame stands an already gray-haired teacher in suit jacket and tie. Out of everyone in the picture, he seems to have the most playful expression, as though amused by the serious-ness of the students standing around him. Only two girls at his sides have permitted themselves a gesture of familiarity, and are rather shyly holding his hands. It appears to be summer, though one of the cooler days. Everyone but the teacher is dressed lightly and, it must be said, rather modestly. Only two boys in the first row are wearing shoes; the rest stretch out their bare, dirty feet toward the camera.

Two photographs taken almost at the same time—at the start of the 1930s. Perhaps even the same photographer took them. The carefree rowdiness of the preschoolers versus the seriousness of the slightly older elementary school students. In the second picture, a boy in dark clothes catches my eye. He's placed his hands on his knees in the manner of all well-behaved schoolchildren. Like the others, he looks into the camera. He's got his legs stretched out the farthest in front of him; maybe he was the tallest. His bare feet nearly reach the lower edge of the frame. I look at him and think to myself that if I'd had gold, jewelry, and money, I'd have bought the kid some shoes.

WESTWARD, OR ALL THE DEATHS OF BARBARA WÓJCIK

THE FIRST DEATH

Her father has decided her life is meaningless. Forty-odd years old, he takes a pillow and walks toward her crib. The crib stands by the window—through the window is a scene of desperate poverty. Her father says:

"There's no future for this child."

Her mother lies weeping on the bed, and doesn't have the strength to hold him back. She can only look and scream. She screams louder than she's ever screamed in her life. Their neighbor comes running.

This time, Barbara Wójcik won't die.

COMRADE STANISŁAW

Order #1 from Stanisław Piaskowski, plenipotentiary of the government of the Republic of Poland in the Lower Silesia region, April 2, 1945:

We go as pioneers of the Polish way of life, as avengers for centuries of injustice inflicted on the Slavic peoples and tribes at German hands. So I will demand that you show unconditional obedience to my directives, carry out ministerial orders rigorously and punctually, and keep in mind that with every step, in every place, and with every action, we are a Slavic Nation with an ancient and unspoiled culture. [...] Until specific orders are given, it is essential to behave amicably toward persons of Slavic origin who surrendered to Germanization, though without making any future commitments.

JÓZEF

He doesn't feel like an avenger. Maybe a little like a pioneer. He's going because they've ordered him to. He's frightened to death, because everyone says the west is "wild." He, Józef Ostrowski, age twenty-seven, is to bring order to it.

The war is barely over, but the hustlers have arrived in Kalisz. At that time, Józef was working in a toy factory, perhaps not the most difficult work, but poorly paid. He already had a woman and her kid from a previous marriage to maintain. Some strangers offered him a job in the Polish police. You had to be healthy and wish to serve Poland. Józef was healthy.

Training took place in Gdańsk—it wasn't actually an academy, just a few weeks of exercises, a little shooting, and some instructive lectures. Then they were supposed to go out into the field: they were the authorities now. Not everyone got uniforms. He didn't know they were sending him west, he thought they'd train him and send him to Kalisz. They took a different tack.

"Comrade Ostrowski," they said, "you're going to Lower Silesia," and he remembered that "Wild West." All over the new Poland, people were saying it was peaceful everywhere but there. That's where they had German partisans hiding in the woods, shooting whomever they came across, because they had nothing left to lose. They weren't even fleeing to Germany, since their Reich was gone. They'd just dug in and were going to stick it out until every last one of them was shot dead. But they wouldn't go down easily. To make matters worse, all kinds of unsavory characters, gangsters, and riffraff were being drawn to Lower Silesia like moths to a flame. Stories were going around the country of the treasure and riches the Germans were leaving behind. Everyone wanted a piece of the action.

He gets off the train in Janowice Wielkie, where they're already expecting him. It's the summer of 1945. On the way, they explain the situation. They drive around the area. There are still plenty of Germans, most of whom don't leave their houses. Some have locked up their homes to protect what they've got left. They barricade the doors from the inside with strong wooden beams. No one goes in, no one goes out, and it will be a disaster if anything catches fire. Now and then, something does. A few people sometimes get it into their heads to find out what the Germans have got hidden under the floorboards or in the attic. They haul them out of their houses and go digging around. If they can't find anything, they fly into a rage. They set the house on fire, then move on to the next one.

They drive to the town on the mountaintop. Ostrowski meets Wypschlak, the new mayor. The old man is just getting ready to leave. The Nazis have been gone from here for a while—they fled as the front approached.

"What is this town called?"

"Miedziana Góra, Comrade, but you can call it Miedzianka for short."

BRONEK

The train has forty-four cars and is running on moonshine. When it shudders to a halt out in the open, people leave their cars to go up front to the locomotive and negotiate. Then they poke around in their bundles and pull out a bottle.

"This is the last one," they say, and the train starts moving once more. In another couple of hours, it'll stop running yet again.

The last car is the love car. It has compartments, the compartments have comfortable fold-out beds, and in these beds, young people taste forbidden fruit. Above them, Bronek Hac lies on his stomach, peering down through holes in the roof. For him, the road westward will be the road to adulthood. Even if right now it seems less of a road than a modest dirt track.

There are a few rules on the train—most important of all, you are required to relieve yourself into buckets. Relieving yourself out of the train is dangerous. Do not empty the buckets unless they are already full. No one empties them. They've been on the move like this for two weeks. Bronek wonders what it will be like if they keep on for two more. He's afraid the moonshine will run out, they'll come to a halt in the middle of nowhere and be stuck there forever.

They've reached Sambir, nearly fifty miles from L'viv. Before long they'll reach the new Polish-Soviet border, and there are more and more soldiers on either side of the train, some with dogs. Bronek remembers seeing the same ones when they invaded nearby Boryslav. The first time they came was in 1939. They took away the teachers, local officials, and railroad workers, none of whom were ever seen again. Then the Russians retreated, and the Germans came. They were more afraid of nationalist Ukrainian insurgents than of the Poles. Later, the air raids began. His uncle was killed in a refinery fire in Drohobych. Bronek was assigned to a forced labor battalion—he was lucky, they ordered him to work in a turning shop, a long way from digging trenches under the hail of gunfire and bombs. Maybe that's why he survived?

Then the Russians came again, but different ones this time, who ordered them to pack their things. They grabbed whatever was in arm's reach and went to the train station. There, they waited two weeks for transportation. They used their bundles to mark off little spaces for themselves, each space holding a single family. Someone was playing the concertina when forty-three cattle cars—and one car for love—rolled up to the platform. They hung out Polish flags, threw their bundles onboard, and were off.

Now Bronek learns why they needed the full buckets. The border is crawling with soldiers, everyone is armed, and the train is rolling slowly along a double file of Russian thugs. The new Poland isn't far now. So they bid the old one goodbye by dumping the buckets out in their red, Commie faces. The soldiers swear and leap out of the way, and the dogs bark menacingly. The train roars with laughter, but no one shoots at them for pouring shit all over their Soviet brothers.

Once again they stop somewhere. The old men go up to the locomotive and the young men run to the love car. Space is limited and many want to get in. A priest hurries after them. But when he sees what the fuss is about, he seizes a bottle and heads for the locomotive too. Then the railroad men uncouple the love car—now forty three cars will go west, and the one for love will get left out in the open somewhere. Some people leap out, yanking up their shorts, and sprint after the departing train. They catch up to it two days later. They have to be restrained from giving the priest a friendly thrashing.

After four weeks they reach Bytom, outside Katowice. A mother spots chimneys on the horizon—where there are chimneys, there ought to be work. But there's no work in Bytom—there is seventy miles along in Prudnik, but in linen-making. They don't know anything about that, so they keep moving. In late November, they reach Wałbrzych. They train won't go any further. They'll stay here.

It's different here from the East: there are mines and factories running everywhere. It's easy to find work, and they take over apartments the Germans left behind. Bronek goes to high school and develops a fascination with chemistry. His teachers urge him to apply to college in Wrocław after he graduates. Industry requires chemists, it's a profession with a future. He applies for technical chemistry, but comes a few points short on his exams.

He has just enough to get into the geology program—so Bronek becomes a geologist.

It is 1953 when Bronisław Hac, a third-year geology student, gets off a bus in Miedzianka and goes to the office of the closed mine. There, he's given a carbide lamp, the key to his room, and the task of mapping the tangle of closed former mining tunnels. As soon as he enters the first one, he realizes the town will soon disappear. He will wonder for the rest of his life why that had to be so. He asks that question to every Russian he meets.

THE SECOND DEATH

Basia Wójcik is meant to die the second time up against the wall of a house in the village of Windyki, seventy miles northwest of Warsaw. This time her life is meaningless because German soldiers wish it so. It's 1940. They arrive in the village and line everyone up against walls. Those unfit for work are unfit for anything. One of those is a lame woman with a little girl clinging to her skirt. That little girl is Basia. What use do the Germans have for a lame woman with a child? They tell her to stand aside, then lead them to an abandoned house. Everyone knows what will happen next.

Basia decides she is going to fight for her life. Just as her mother did a few years ago, she starts to scream. She doesn't scream in hopelessness—she screams at the Germans. One of them finally opens the door and lets her go. But her mother is to stay. Basia refuses to leave, she starts crying, she won't go without her mother. They're up against the wall facing soldiers with dogs. The air is filled with barking, screaming, and weeping. Then, finally, comes relief. The Germans let them both go. They can live a little longer.

MIŚKA AND STASZEK

Miśka only wanted some apples from her own orchard. But they sent their dogs to chase her away, and she's heading back to the train station empty-handed. She's hungry and angry. She just wanted a few apples. She didn't want to see strange people bustling around her house, strange children running around in the yard, a strange dog sitting in the doghouse. It all looks the same, only the faces are different. Miśka didn't want to see that, and didn't want to ask anyone for something that already belonged to her. But she was hungry, so she had to.

It's 1945, in the Galician village of Buchach, near Ternopil. For three weeks she, her sister, and dozens of other people from nearby towns have been packed up and waiting in the main hall of the small station for a train that might be able to take them west. They're not even a few miles, a few hundred yards, or even a few steps from their houses. But they can't go home and wait like ordinary human beings. Out there, beyond the train station, it's not Poland anymore—out there is Ukraine.

Michalina Pławiak, known as Miśka, is nineteen and has only bad memories of that train station. Not long ago, she was climbing into a cattle car in tears, and the Germans slammed the heavy double doors behind her. Her whole life, she will never forget that sound—it was dull and heavy, like the blow of a hammer. Her sister, brother, and mother were in there with her.

They were meant to go west for labor. She was rescued from the transport by a Polish railroad man, who agreed to look after Miśka and her sister until the war was over. Her mother and brother went west.

The railroad man took them to Radymno, near Przemyśl. She was in one house, her sister in another. They wanted to stay together and decided to return home. It's over 120 miles from Radymno to Buchach as the crow flies. They mostly walked at night, hiding in barns and eating whatever they could beg from farmers. It was Ukrainians they feared most of all, and they heard frightening stories about them. Miśka's shoes fell apart, and she reached home barefoot. When they saw their ramshackle house, they wept for joy.

Until the end of the war they farmed on their own, with their neighbors helping out. They don't know what happened to their mother, but Staszek has been in touch. When it was all over, he set off for home, but stopped near Kalisz in central Poland. He wrote asking them to come, saying he had a house and jobs for them. But they'd already been informed of their imminent deportation from Soviet Ukraine, so they were leaving anyway.

Finally, the train arrives and they can go. They ride for two weeks—the train stops constantly, and when it does people climb out into the fields or walk to a village to look for food. Everyone already ate through their supplies at the train station, so now they're going hungry. Sometimes the train sets off unexpectedly, and there's the sight of a crowd of people racing over the fields toward the tracks. The bravest ones stand in front of the locomotive and wait until the stragglers have climbed aboard, then they keep moving.

The train stops for the last time in Wrocław, where Staszek is already waiting for them. And their mother is with him! With red hair! She was working in a munitions factory and the chemicals turned her hair red. Staszek is skinny as a rail, he says if not for a German friend, he'd have died of hunger.

"He always left a couple slices of bread in one of the factory machines for me and would go away so I could eat."

First they go to a place near Kalisz, but Staszek already has his eye on something else. Around Jelenia Góra, entire villages lie empty because their German populations have been deported.

"They've left houses behind with running water, electricity, all the furniture inside, dishes on the table, even food in the pantries. And every settler gets a field, we'll be able to farm."

Staszek goes first. He'll scope it out, get the lay of the land, then send for them later. Miśka doesn't want to go—she's gotten herself a boyfriend here, Władek Łuczak. He's a local and owns a farm. Things are starting to look up. But Staszek says that down there they're opening up mines where they're paying so well no one will think it's worth plowing fields. Władek wants to give it a try, and Miśka agrees to go with him. After all, they can always come back.

They get off the train at Janowice station. They ask for Miedzianka. They have to walk up the hill, past the wooden signpost. The road turns sharply right, and after a moment they see the church steeples and the first buildings through the trees. They pass the two stone crosses, then the brewery. The houses here are tidy, brick, and two or even three stories high. Flowers grow in front of each one, and red hawthorns are blossoming in the squares. There are orchards behind the houses. Miśka is glad: in the fall, there will be apples.

THE THIRD DEATH

The third time Barbara Wójcik's life loses its meaning is when she and her mother fall ill with typhus. But before that, the Germans kill her father, and then a grenade explodes in her brother's hand while he's trying to defuse it. When the war is over, little remains of Windyki (a few run-down houses, mined fields, and burned-out barns filled with soldiers' corpses). Even less remains of her life. Then her mother dies, and Barbara is left with nothing at all. She, however, is not permitted to die—though then, for the very first time, she wonders why not.

STEFAN AND HELENA

Stefan Spiż was meant to be discharged on September 20, but war broke out on the first, and the whole plan was shot to hell. That said, if not for the war, Stefan wouldn't have been wounded, wouldn't have been captured, and wouldn't have been sent to work in Germany—and then who knows how his life would have turned out. For all he knows, it might have been awful.

First came the train, and the landscape drifting slowly from west to east. They traveled a few days—not everyone was sure where from, and no one knew where to. On the front, Stefan had taken a bullet through the hand, but only one hand, so he was deemed fit for work. They put him on the train and sent him west. That was all they knew—they were going west.

He was frightened and sorrowful, most of all when they passed Szulec. The train was approaching Kalisz when he saw his own fields and the houses of his village in the distance. He immediately recognized these places which he so cared for. Right then, something tightened inside him—for although he would be fine in the end, at that moment he had no idea. He didn't even know whether they would shoot him the next day.

But they didn't shoot him. They brought Stefan to Rötz and marched him into a brewery.

"This is where you'll work," they said.

At first he did everything—take this out, bring that in, sweep. They treated him well, he had nothing negative to say about them. Then it occurred to someone to train him to move up, and they found a different person to clean. Stefan spoke German, which made training him easier. And there was a shortage of men here, since they'd all been taken to the front. The Germans took the same approach to everything—war, government, marriage, even beer: most important of all was *Ordnung*—order. The hose had to be wound in an even circle, the tanks glistening, the floor clean enough to eat off of. If there was order in the brewery, the beer would be good. It was a mess, the beer would be ruined.

So if not for the war, Stefan Spiż wouldn't have learned to brew beer. That's the first thing, but secondly and most importantly, he wouldn't have met beautiful Helena. And if he hadn't met her, everything would have been pointless—the war would have been the war, his work just work, and his exile a miserable exile.

Helena is tough, and that is probably what impresses him the most. They deported her from near Rzeszów, now she lives in Bernried, a couple miles from Rötz. There, she tends to the children of a wealthy farmer's wife, treating them strictly, and she also helps out at the farm and the restaurant. That's how she knows Stefan. Whenever they have to ship beer to Bernried, Stefan volunteers—though the Germans aren't stupid and have already figured out what's going on. Yes, Helena is the true light of his life, and the true light of Bernried. She impresses everyone there, and although she's Polish, some of them even fear her.

When American troops enter the town, they're drawn to her like moths to a flame. This suits nearly everyone: the Americans, because they live in hope, which in difficult times is as good as medicine; and the Germans, because Helena would defend them against the Americans and later the Russians, and doesn't let them touch a hair on their heads. Meanwhile, Helena knows just how to use their infatuation for her material gain. One soldier comes to her swearing to love her to the end of her days, begging her to accompany him to America, and giving her gifts of chocolate and cigarettes. Helena doesn't say no, but she doesn't say yes. She leaves the chocolate for herself and the farmwife's children. The cigarettes are for Stefan. For several months now, the light of Bernried has shone for him and him alone.

They set off for Poland before summer is out. She hurries home, near Rzeszów, while he wants to go to Szulec to see if anything is left of the village. They promise each other this is not the end,

but merely the beginning. That same year, Stefan hears specialists are needed in the western territories, including brewers. The
Germans left behind a large number of breweries and now they
need to be started up again. He finds a job in Lwówek Śląski, in a
facility overseeing several smaller ones across the region. He writes
immediately to Helena: "Come." They marry a year later, and soon
Stefan is made brewmaster of a small plant in a mountain town.
They set off, and their truck climbs to the top of the mountain,
squealing relentlessly. They pass the sign reading *Miedziunku*,
then the two stone crosses, the first buildings, and finally stop in
front of a yellow villa. Stefan likes the brewery, and Helena likes
the great big house.

BARBARA

There is no future in Windyki. Basia has already outlived her
brother, father, and mother. The only one left is her sister, who has
her own little gang of children. Baśka would be yet another mouth
to feed—perhaps one too many. Posters go up in the village telling
people to go west, where there's work to be found and places to
live, where you can start anew. But Barbara Wójcik doesn't trust
a word the government says, even printed in black and white. It's
1946. She gets on a train and goes to see for herself. She goes all
the way to Wałbrzych. She sees factories, mines, and crowds of
people. She asks about work. Then she hurries back to Windyki.
There are others like her there, waiting for good news.

And then westward. Two of them set off together—she and
Zenka Jankowska. They use their ticket money to buy food, then

climb onboard the train through a window. They ride part of the way on the roof. They make it to Kowary, well beyond Wałbrzych, before a conductor catches them. They're thrown off the train for riding without a ticket, so they climb in through a window again, but this time it isn't such a good idea. The conductor is furious and calls the police. Once the police arrive, there's no way of getting out of it, their pretty smiles and giggles do no good. They're taken to jail in Strzelin, twenty miles south of Wrocław.

The judge is compassionate, but he says:

"If I don't put you in prison you'll spend your whole lives fare-dodging."

It's common sense. They get a month in a women's prison. Baśka will come away from it with three memories—the dirty prison panties she had to wash, the endless hunger, and the feeling of isolation. Though that's a feeling she eventually becomes accustomed to.

They're released thirty days later, and Zenka's sister picks them up. She brings fresh bread, which they devour right at the gate. Then they go south to Kłodzko. People in the area say they're looking for spinners there and if a woman wants a job, that's where she should go. Twice in Kłodzko, Baśka does not die.

THE FOURTH DEATH

Fighting for her life, Barbara Wójcik braces her arms and legs against the work counter and prays someone will come, because she can't hold out like this for long. It an unequal fight—Baśka is barely sixteen years old, has had typhus, and is still poorly. She is weak, and the machine is strong. It only took a moment's carelessness for the spinning machine to snag her apron. A few days ago, Baśka saw what one of these machines could do to a person when a German woman was pulled into one—only shreds of a human being remained.

Barbara Wójcik doesn't want to be shredded—she wants to live. She braces herself with her legs and arms, the machine pulls, Baśka screams. Finally, people come running and switch the machine off. Once again, she's made it out alive.

JAN, OR JASIEK

It's the tallest mountain he's seen in his life. He has to tilt his head far back to make out the end of the road and the buildings rippling with heat off in the distance. Mama calls out, urging him on, but Jasiek's strength has left him, he can't run any faster, his bundle relentlessly weighs him down. Finally, his mother gives up, slams the door, and the car that could have driven them to the top of the hill leaves without them.

"We'll walk."

Jasiek would follow his mother to the ends of the earth. He lost his father at the front. They spent the whole of the war living in Maków Mazowiecki, fifty miles north of Warsaw. When the war was over, Mama left him at his grandmother's and headed westward, planning to get the lay of the land and then send for him. She found a job in a mine; she wrote it was hard work, but the money was good. He missed her terribly. When she came to Maków, he'd hang around her neck; when she left, he didn't want to let her go. That spring, she packed Jasiek's things into a little suitcase and took him with her.

Everything was new—the road to the station, the train, the conductor, the tickets, the view out the window. From Wrocław onwards, he rode with his face glued to the windowpane, because Mama said they were getting close (he was constantly asking).

He asked about Germans, too.

"There are a few left where we're going," she said. He was a little scared of Germans. He still is.

When they arrived at the train station, he couldn't believe the mountains. Mountains everywhere! All the way up to the sky.

"Mama, I won't make it up there," he said when he saw where they were going. But he'd have followed her to the ends of the Earth. He didn't even mind that the car had left.

"Come on, Jasiek, we're going," says Mama, holding out her hand.

It's springtime, the sun is shining, and he doesn't have school tomorrow. Together, they'll make their way to their new home: it's the first time they've had a trip like this for a long time.

THE FIFTH DEATH

This time it's an old, pockmarked secret policeman who decides her life is meaningless. He drives her out of town, throws her from the car, and takes out a straight razor. It's a warm fall night, slightly windy—no rain, but wet.

It all started back in the summer. She had been working for a few months. She was a hero of labor and kept winning prizes:

lard, herring, once even a beautiful yellow blanket from UNRRA (she immediately took it to the tailor and had it made into a coat for chillier days). Then they started coming for her, pounding their fists on the door. She would barricade it shut with a chair, sit in the corner and cry. She knew what they wanted. She says they never got in—they went after others instead. Sometimes she heard screaming, but mostly she heard nothing. Then the women would come to work and sit silently at their looms. Some disappeared overnight—they went off to Głuszyca or Kamienna Góra. There were looms there too, and besides that there were no secret policemen using the workers' hostels and weavers' quarters as free private brothels.

She could never hold her tongue—like when she'd screamed at the Germans in Windyki. They could have killed her, after all, but they let her go. Now Barbara Wójcik is lying on the damp roadside on the way to Wałbrzych, thinking this time she's said too much, so now it's time for her to die. Because this time when they came for her, she screamed through the door that they were animals and not men, that this Communism of theirs wasn't supposed to be like this, that she spat on this sort of Communism. She doesn't know what enraged them more, all she knows is the chair could no longer hold them off. They burst in, dragged her out by her hair, and drove her out of town.

Which brings her to the damp roadside, the man with the razor, and the night. All that's required to bring her short life to a miserable end. But suddenly, lights appear in the distance, an engine roars, and a car screeches to a halt just beside them.

Two brawny men jump out and approach the man with the razor—they say something, a scuffle begins, someone screams, someone falls. Baśka clambers to her feet and hears only these words:

"Make a run for the train station and never come back."

THE MINERS

1948. Stanisław Gruszka, twenty-one years old, sets off from Huta Przedborska, fifteen miles outside of Rzeszów. He's carrying everything he owns: a shirt, bread, butter, and a razor. He borrows some money so he can go west.

"Once I've earned enough I'll pay you back," he promises.

He's almost sure he'll earn enough—his brother is already in the west. He writes that they're opening mines there, they pay well, you just have to get on a train and come, everything will be fine. There's no problem finding a place to live. After a two-day journey, he arrives at Janowice station and asks where the mine is. They direct him to the town on the mountaintop.

Stanisław Kopczyński is on the move too, from Szczucin, near Kraków. Before 1947, he spent his time there beating the crap out of the village Communists. Then he realized eradicating the Red plague had become more than he and his friends from the Home Army division could handle. So he's heading west, because now that same Red plague has started beating the crap out of them, and he'd rather disappear for a while than disappear forever. Besides, his fiancée has already left for Trzcińsko near Jelenia Góra—her father got a job down the pit and is urging Staszek to come.

"We'll have the wedding when you arrive."

Karolina Kolis is also on her way. She's twenty-two and wants to make some money. She spent the war in Niwiski, outside Rzeszów— it was fourteen miles to the small city of Mielec, and seven and a half to the county seat of Kolbuszowa. There was poverty everywhere she turned. They had fields, but they were always flooded. If they wanted to pick potatoes, they had to wade through water up to their calves. Whatever they picked immediately started rotting. They dug drainage ditches, but that didn't help for long. Through the last two years of the war, they never got a full night's sleep—just behind the house was a military airfield, where planes were constantly taking off and landing. Sometimes they went days without sleeping a wink.

When the war was over, Karolina read on a poster how people had to go west to build the new Poland. She didn't want to build— she wanted to make money. She got on a train and went.

In Janowice, she finds the only jobs for women are farm work. Apparently a certain Wróbel in Stare Janowice is looking for someone. At the township, they tell her maybe if a mine opens she'll be able to get a job there. She should go to Wróbel's for the time being.

Then there's Bolesław Grzyb from Skaryszew, near Radom. He's coming because his brothers are here already. He's accompanied by his wife and daughter, nine-year-old Elżbieta. They settle in Stare Janowice, which is closer to Miedzianka on the hilltop than to the station. There, little Elżbieta meets her double. A German family lives in the attic of their house, and they have a girl her age—named Elizabeth. The girls make fast friends.

Elżbieta's aunt and uncle take over some old German fields and start farming. One of them—Uncle Janek—will often embarrass Elżbieta in front of her German friend. Janek can't resist prodding the Germans about who won the war, and who owns all this now. On occasion he'll walk into their apartment without knocking and take whatever he needs right then and there. Once, he needed a cow, and they had the only one in the area.

"You're getting the earth and the water," the German woman cries in desperation. She has two children to feed at home and can't buy milk anywhere. "But you won't touch that cow!"

Once, when Uncle Janek goes into town, the German woman comes to ask if she can take some supplies from the pantry. Elżbieta doesn't understand—it's the Germans' pantry, after all.

A few months later, the Germans depart, leaving nearly everything behind. Her aunt and uncle take over the farm and her dad goes to work down the mine. Almost all their neighbors work there already. They leave their houses at dawn and cut through the meadows to the town on the mountaintop. They can already make out the mine's headframes and the church steeples.

Barbara Wójcik is on her way there too. It's fall, but she's only wearing a light dress. She truly has the look of a ghost—disheveled, pale, and shifty-eyed. She speaks to no one, spending the entire journey curled into a ball in the corner. She goes to the village hall in Janowice for the sole reason that she can see it from the train station. She asks for somewhere to live and a job. They send her to a farmer in Stare Janowice. She works there for a few months until she learns they're opening a mine in Miedzianka and need workers, including women. They'll pay well. Baśka decides to take a job there, and finds a room in a hotel beside the railroad crossing. The Germans call it Kluger's hotel, though it's been long since there were any Klugers in the area. It's a twenty-minute walk uphill from there to Miedzianka.

To get a job in the mine, however, it's obligatory to make a full confession: where you used to work, what you did during the war, whether you have family abroad, why you came west.

Stanisław Gruszka says he came for bread and he found his long-lost lover in the town. They hope to marry soon.

Stanisław Kopczyński admits he joined the partisans, but he has nothing to show for it, he only pilfered coal from German trains. And he would certainly never beat the crap out of a Communist.

Karolina Kolis says she only wants to earn money and that's all she cares about.

Bolesław Grzyb assures them he spent the war working in Germany, and by the time he returned to Skaryszew, the Russians had already arrived.

Barbara Wójcik doesn't say she escaped from Kłodzko with nothing but a dress because a pockmarked secret policeman wanted to slit her throat with a razor on the damp roadside on the way to Wałbrzych. But everyone in Janowice who was meant to know that already did.

THE SIXTH DEATH

One evening Barbara Wójcik, nineteen years old, goes to bed shaking in fear. She knows now that they know. They summoned her to the police station, shone lights in her eyes, and grilled her about everything, including Kłodzko. She wept. One of them said:

"What's with the tears, Basia? Have we even touched you?" And then he ordered the light put out.

When Barbara Wójcik hears an engine rumbling outside, her whole body stiffens. Then comes the slam of a car door and silence. Then footsteps, floorboards creaking on the porch, the squeak of a door handle—did she lock the door? There's no checking it now, she pulls her quilt all the way up over her head and waits. She already knows what they'll do.

"I'll be lying here with a hole in my head," she thinks.

They're already in the hall, they're walking through the kitchen. Through a gap in the bedsheets, Barbara Wójcik can make out a dark figure and the glow of a cigarette. Then she hears the click of a pistol being cocked, and the words:

"I'm going to shoot you now, you whore."

And then it flashes before Barbara Wójcik's eyes: the utter desperation, the utter tragedy, and the utter senselessness of this situation and the story that's swallowed her up in her short nineteen years. And having seen all this, she pulls the quilt down from her face and hisses straight at that smoldering cigarette flame the words that until now have filled her with terror.

"I don't care anymore," she says, and waits for the gunshot. But she hears only silence again. When a moment later she opens her eyes, she sees nothing but darkness.

"This is where I'll stay now," she thinks, and after a while, she drifts off to sleep.

UEBERSCHAER'S TOMB

THE DISAPPEARANCE BEGINS with Ueberschaer's house. As
early as 1945, the first brave souls break down the door and go
inside. They're probably disappointed—there's nothing of value
here, only books. They go try their luck somewhere else. Three
years later, in the spring of 1948, three children appear nearby.
One is little Marysia Kaczmarska. She's six years old and she's only
just arrived in town—her father has started working down the
pit, and she herself will go to school in a few months. But for now
she's on a wild vacation, roaming the area with the other children.
When they reach the old hunting lodge, they all agree the place
is probably haunted. Marysia is afraid of ghosts, so she keeps her
distance while the boys break down the cellar door and go inside.
They run back out screaming, one wielding a saber, the other a
large knife, and the third an impressive set of antlers. They race
back toward town, past Marysia, who is hiding in the bushes.
They'll later claim they heard a rustling in the cellar, as though
someone were still there.

The next brave souls arrive a year later. They are seven children from nearby Mniszków. It's spring, either late March or early April, one of the first warm days of the year. Today, instead of getting into the buses the mine provides to take the children to school in Janowice Wielkie every day, they play hooky. The old German hunting lodge is nearby—they want to find out what's inside. Helena Rudzińska is thirteen and doesn't think this is a good idea at all. Still, she goes along with it—she's not going to school on her own.

They climb up the mountain—it's steeper from Mniszków, there are rocks scattered around and the boys have chosen a path that runs right through the middle of them. They laugh hardest when someone slips and they slide all the way down on the wet leaves. Finally, they all reach the top. In the distance, they see the wooden lodge with the broken door and shattered windows. They don't even look inside, knowing they won't find anything of value there. Someone says they have to hunt for treasure, and someone else says if there's treasure, it's definitely in the tomb. The boys get to work; the girls sit and watch, helping a little.

The tomb is massive and dug into the stone mountainside. They can see inscriptions on the partially moss-covered slab. But it is the small window located in one of the walls of the crypt that fires everyone's imaginations. It is on the side with the most beautiful panorama of the mountains. They decide to break the window and get inside that way. Over a few hours, the boys manage to dig a small hollow out of the wall of the crypt and loosen a few bricks around the opening, yet it's still too narrow for anyone to get inside. A cadaverous stench wafts out of the tomb, but it doesn't bother the boys, who keep at it. The closer they are to achieving their goal, the further the tightly packed group of girls stands from the tomb. They all know they're doing something wrong, but no one has the courage to call a halt to it.

Finally, they pick the smallest one of them, grab him by the legs, and push him up to the hole. He doesn't fit all the way in, but he manages to get a grip on the coffin. If there's treasure in the tomb, it's got to be in there. The little boy grabs the coffin and pulls it toward him. The ones outside pull him by the legs, and he manages to lift the lid slightly; it then falls off with a crash. He only catches a glimpse of the corpse laid out inside before his friends haul him out and they all run screaming toward Mniszków. The smallest boy, the one who was inside, will later say the body in the tomb was missing its legs.

Even though Helena kept her distance, she is still wracked by pangs of conscience. To make matters worse, her father found out about them playing hooky, and when she told him where exactly they'd been and what they'd done, he gave her a terrible spanking and, on top of that, ordered her to confess everything to Father Matwiejczyk. Nevertheless, they all return to the scene two days later. They steer clear of the tomb and don't say a word about it—they want to see what's in the house. They go inside. The interior is shrouded in a pleasant semidarkness, because most of the shutters have been left intact and locked, while only a few windows are missing their panes. The house is relatively tidy—enormous wardrobes painted with wildflowers stand along one wall, completely empty. Helena could have fit in any one of them without the slightest difficulty. They go upstairs, where they discover masses of books. Giant, thick volumes fill the shelves, cover a small desk, and are piled up on the floor as well. Some have been torn to pieces, as though someone were digging around for something inside them. Those lie open. The children attempt to look through them, but most are written in old-fashioned letters and are in German besides. There are almost no books with pictures at all, so the young visitors rather quickly lose interest. Only Helena finds two anatomy books. Each drawing shows a person and what can be found inside them. All the pictures are in color and highly detailed. Helena is most struck by the illustration of the human heart. Both books go into her schoolbag. The children hang around the house a little longer, then finally decide to return to Mniszków. They never go looking in there again. Helena carries her trophy proudly; over the weeks to come, she will pore over the books so many times she'll nearly have them memorized. Then her interest will wane, and her sister will take the volumes to the used bookstore in Jelenia Góra. With the money from selling them, she returns to Mniszków with a new, warm sheepskin jacket.

*　　*　　*

The next brave soul is Zdzisiek Jankowski, age twelve. It's 1969 or 1970—now no trace remains of the lodge on the hill, but there are no ruins haunting the site, so it must have been dismantled by local farmers. That means Zdzisiek knows nothing of the painted wardrobes, the ornamented shutters, and the stacks of books that once filled the attic. He has his eye on something else. He and his friends love to climb into any hole, drift, or tunnel left behind from the mines and still accessible. All these activities are kept strictly secret from his father, who worked in the pit and knows how dangerous it is down below: he himself lost his legs down there.

But it will take more than the threat of severe punishment to deter them, for the boys have found a new cave not far from the tomb of the "old German knight" on the road to Mniszków. For a few days they dig earth out of a rock cleft and finally manage to slip inside. At first they think they've merely discovered a large cavern, but now they're making their way farther and farther, lighting the way with a carbide lamp, unable to see the end of the rock tunnel. When they finally spot a pale glow in the distance, heralding an exit, to get there they will have to swim through ice-cold water. They emerge onto the surface soaking wet and freezing. They are proud to discover they've passed underneath the entire town—they're standing on the opposite side, and can see the road to Ciechanowice as well as Mayor Nowocin's property.

They can't stop thinking about the tomb, and a few days later, they return. They dig out one of the walls, working with a pickaxe, to try and get inside. Finally, they succeed. Shortly thereafter, all three of them parade through town. One wears a Prussian helmet with a large spike on top, the second a tin breastplate with German writing on it. Zdzisiek leads the way, waving an entirely authentic saber. People come out of their houses, there is much laughter, and a few even give them a salute. Then the police arrive on the scene and the game is over. At home, Zdzisiek gets a whipping for digging in the graves. He never goes back to the crypt again. Anyway, it won't be long before they move to Janowice and Miedzianka disappears.

In the late nineties, a mysterious car arrives in Miedzianka with four men inside. No one would have taken any notice if not for the fact that in order to reach their destination, this peculiar group chooses the old road to Mniszków, which, as everyone around here knows, leads only to the old tomb—any further and the road is so overgrown that only an off road vehicle can make it through, and this car is not one of those.

The car stops past the village, and the men take backpacks out of the trunk then disappear up the hill. After a few hours, a powerful explosion wracks the area, and stones go flying through the air. Smoke rises between the trees in the direction of the old tomb. A little later, the men load up their bags and hurriedly drive off.

Paweł Nowak, a resident of Janowice Wielkie and a history aficionado who's been fascinated by Ueberschaer's tomb for some time, hears about the car's arrival and the explosion. He rushes to the site, his heart heavy with the worst possible feeling of dread. Lately, more and more enthusiastic treasure-hunters have been arriving; after reading in the papers about the town that disappeared, they decide to try their luck there. Some search with metal detectors, others with explosives. Paweł knows enough about the town to be sure none of them will find anything. And so it goes this time as well. The whole area is littered with scattered fragments of stone, and a few hastily dug holes can be seen around the tomb and in the place where the wooden lodge once stood. Yet the tomb itself has remained intact, and all there is to see is a powerful crater the explosion left beside it. No one has gotten inside, there's no doubt of that.

A few years later, an elderly man with a cane slowly makes his way toward the solitary tomb. He knows the way: his name is Karl Heinz Friebe. No one pays particular attention to him, and in any case there's hardly anyone here anymore. He passes the overgrown cemetery and the last buildings of the Pławiak farm. The road cut from the side of the hill finally reaches the site, and he carefully makes his way down the sloping ground to reach the reinforced concrete slab. A beautiful view of the Falcon Mountains stretches out from here. Despite what he promised himself all along the way, here, at old Ueberschaer's tomb, Karl Heinz Friebe's eyes once again fill with tears.

THE SECOND CEMETERY

"THEY'D LEAD YOU TO THE END of an inactive drift and tie you to the shoring. Then they'd go back and blow up the entire corridor. They buried dozens of people there like that. Only no one talks about it, because even now people are frightened."

"We didn't talk about the mine at home, because it was a secret and no one trusted anyone else. My mother always came home from work bundled up in her miner's jacket and with a few layers of foot wrapping. But she never told us what she was doing there. Because if we let slip in school or out playing with the other kids that she was mining uranium, they'd have killed her down in that mine and we'd have lost our mother."

"We knew what they were mining, but no one said it out loud. Anyway, what difference did it make if we knew, since no one told us how harmful it was? They didn't tell us the uranium was killing us, we only found that out in the nineties, but by then it was too late because half of us were already six feet under."

"People said there were two cemeteries in Miedzianka. A German one, up the mountain, which by that time was already overgrown with bushes, and a Polish one, underground. Dozens of people were buried alive in that mine—they'd disappear overnight, along with their entire families. You'd just come to work and someone would be missing. And then after work it would turn out their house was empty or somebody new had moved in. But no one asked any questions, because there were informants everywhere in the pit. If there were four miners standing together on break, the secret police were already watching them. And if there were five standing together, you knew one of them was an informant, so everyone would talk about the weather.

"Then the informants had a hard time because people down there knew who was snitching, so they'd stay on their guard when those people were around. But that meant the informants had nothing to write in their reports, so they'd raise political subjects themselves. And then the other informants would squeal on them and it would turn into a big mess. I'm sure at times one agent accidentally snitched on another.

"In 1950 I'd already been a foreman on the night crew for six months. We were only taking uranium at that time, and my teeth would hurt every day. In April 1951, a machine operator, a Russian, came up to me and I confided to him that if I worked at the uranium all day, my teeth hurt. Then he explained to me it was because of the uranium and that in Russia, people who worked with uranium would also complain of toothache at first, then afterward they would die. He just asked me not to tell anyone, because they'd throw him in prison for saying that. I kept working until the fall of 1951, then they sent me to a sanatorium. After I got back, I asked to quit, without revealing anything to anybody."[*]

"They always had soldiers standing at the gate, carefully checking with Geiger counters to see if the miners were taking out any spoil. So everyone would dust themselves off very thoroughly before going out the gate, especially their shirt and pant cuffs, because even a tiny pebble could cause you a whole lot of trouble. There were times when one miner didn't like another, and right after dusting off but before reaching the gate, he'd put a little radioactive dust in the other man's pocket and the man would get in trouble or just disappear."

"You could only get into the mine by showing a special pass. The only problem was not all the soldiers checking them knew how to read. So if someone wanted to and had a bit of luck, they could get in on someone else's pass. But maybe nobody was that brave. Afterward, when command HQ caught on that some of the guards were illiterate, they always posted at least one man at the gate who could read.

"The senior registrar ordered rabbit hutches set up in the yard by the mine clinic. We had someone there looking after the rabbits part-time. They had everything they needed: oats, milk, carrots. But there was something else—each cage held a container

---

[*] Letter of 1/22/1971, in *Akta osobowe górników Zakładów R-1 nr 184447* [Personnel Files from Miners at R-1 Mines no. 184447], State Atomic Physics Agency, Department in Jelenia Góra.

of uranium. People didn't say it out loud, but they knew anyway: after two months, every one of those rabbits had bitten the dust. We were like those rabbits. Only for the most part we lived a little longer."*

"There was this one smart-ass working in our laundry room. One day on break I guess he got drunk and started reciting a little poem: 'Stalin gets to eat / our bacon fat and meat. / But stupid me I go / to the kolkhoz even so.' We never saw him again."

"The Russian overseers and machine operators working down the pit were greatly superior to the Poles. Once, one of them told me in confidence not to sit on the canisters of spoil or anywhere the Geiger counter would creak. They also advised me to go up top when I was on break and not have breakfast until then. And never to drink the water in the mine.

"Uranium had a particular smell and the Russians and the foremen knew how to use that to find a vein. They'd walk into a drift with their lamp out and sniff. The uranium reeked like something decomposing in water, it stank like a corpse when we found a vein.

"Sometimes when we couldn't find a vein, a machine operator would come and search. On more than one occasion, after investigating like that the operator would back off quickly, but he'd tell us: 'Get digging, boys.'

"There was so much radiation in the pit that the miners' watches stopped. But no one complained. One man said when

---

* Piotr Dziewit, *Uranowi ludzie* [Uranium People], *Panorama* 14, 1991.

he was drunk he knew why his face stung after work—then they beat him to death and threw his body into a ditch.

"It was all well thought-out, the Russians were betting no one would survive the conditions in the mine and that would be the end of their Miedzianka problem. But they miscalculated. If they'd known that then, they certainly wouldn't have left us here. We would have been left underground long ago."

"This little runt would come with letters from the secret police. And as soon as he showed up at the pit, everyone was seized with blind fear. Because whoever got a letter from him usually didn't return to the mine. This messenger came a couple times a week, always holding a bunch of those letters. People didn't want to take them from him, so sometimes he'd put them on the floor at a miner's feet and then walk away."

"First they'd beat you unconscious with truncheons. Then they'd wake you up and do it again. They'd do it a few times. And if after all that you didn't confess, they'd bring you into the mine, shoot you in the back of the head, and fill in the shaft. And once some-one had disappeared without a trace, no one would really speak up for them anyway."

"They hit him in the teeth and on the head with a pistol butt, no mercy. They beat him and took him off to the filled-in shafts."*

---

* Michał Mońko, "Gułag Miedzianka" [Gulag Miedzianka], in *Odra* 4, 1995.

"The radiation in Miedzianka wasn't so bad. But in Kletno, the miners couldn't last underground and they'd faint. So they took them out of there, but I'm sure some stayed underground forever."

"The ones who talked too much got taken to see the secret police in Janowice. Back then, they had a little pond next to the station. When the secret police moved out of there, they filled in the pond with sand, and reeds and bushes started growing. When at the end of the seventies, the township wanted to dig out the pond and fill it with water again, some big shot showed up and told them they weren't allowed to. Apparently there were a lot of miners' bodies lying at the bottom of that pond."

"If anyone doesn't even want to talk about the mine today, it's probably because they have something to hide. Because every one of us there had something to hide, and no one paid for any of it. So it's not fear keeping people from talking about the pit, it's the shame of knowing they were such bastards back then."

"Once an NKVD officer came up to me and told me not to miss a single lump of uranium, or I'd get to see what polar bears looked like. A few weeks after that, I quit and went to work in a paper mill.

"We used to load the spoil into trucks, and where they took it afterward I have no idea. People said it went to Legnica, and then on to Russia, but who knows. A Soviet soldier rode in every truck, carrying an automatic pistol. Somewhere along the route they also switched out the Polish drivers for their own, so even the Poles don't know where they went."

"There were no Geiger counter inspections at the gate, people have made that up to make these stories sound even more hair-raising. No one ever checked me. What was there to take? Some rocks? Usually a soldier stood at the gate of the mine and checked passes, though because some of them couldn't read you could often get in on a pass that was two months old.

"Everyone knew what they were mining and everyone talked about it. The whole town knew what was going on down the pit, because some of the shafts were right next to private homes and weren't blocked off with anything. You just had to be careful your kids didn't hang around there."

"They gave the miners half an hour before the end of their shift so they could dust off their clothes before the inspection at the gate. We also had washrooms and a laundry room at the mine, but not all the miners used them. Some of them went straight home from the pit wearing clothes covered with that radioactive dust."

"I didn't ask about anything, I didn't know anything about them killing people there—what you're telling me here is the first I've heard of it. I wanted to work, make some money, and have peace and quiet. Anyway, I managed to survive the mine without knowing anything, because what good would knowing have done me?"

LONG LIVE MIKOŁAJCZYK!

YOU CAN TELL WHO WORKS in the mine from their constant spitting. A man is walking down the street, he hocks, and saliva comes spurting out of his mouth. Or he works his tongue around the inside of his mouth, coughs, and steps outside for a moment. He comes back and wipes his mouth. Some try to rinse it out, usually with vodka, or if the bar is closed, with moonshine. The rinsing only helps for a bit.

"You can't cough this shit out," they say, and order another double vodka. They throw their money around, which is another telltale sign. On payday the bar is packed to the rafters and the air is gray with smoke. Up here everyone talks about the weather. You can talk about work down below. Doing it the other way around will get you sent to hell—even though officially hell does not exist.

HEAVEN

Ludwik Kaczmarski is about to find out whether hell is real. It's Sunday, a little after 11:00, and his wife and daughters are just getting ready for church when he appears at the door. He's pale as a ghost and has come crawling on all fours; now he's lying in bed, asking them to massage his body to soothe the terrible pain. His wife Anna Kaczmarska gently unbuttons his shirt; their three daughters—Marysia, Bronka, and Natalka—stand beside her in their Sunday best. They gaze silently at their father's gray skin and their mother weeping. A fourth daughter is on the way—Anna Kaczmarska is heavily pregnant.

"What did they do to you?" she asks, sobbing, but Ludwik no longer responds. Yesterday he went to Janowice to celebrate the name day of Mikołajczyk, a miner from Trzcińsko. No one knows, or is likely to ever know, what this Mikołajczyk's first name was, whether he really existed, and whether he really was as dreadful a figure for the miners as it will later turn out.

Supposedly, this is what happened: the boys had a few drinks, got their courage up, and started making toasts. There was a toast to Grzyb, to Kaczmarski, and also to Mikołajczyk. Mikołajczyk got more toasts than anyone, and finally he bought a round for them all. Someone was passing by the bar, someone overheard. And maybe the secret policemen even heard it at their station—it wasn't far, just a few buildings away. Mikołajczyk had been a bad name to hear ever since Deputy Prime Minister Stanisław Mikołajczyk had defected to the West. So Mikołajczyk was the worst name possible—a name not to be uttered at all except in a whisper and with absolute revulsion. To chant that name was a sin, and for a sin like that, you'd find out if hell was real.

They burst into the bar and grabbed hold of whomever they could. Whoever'd drunk the least and was still steady on their feet made it out the window and into the woods. Whoever's reflexes failed them was left behind. Kaczmarski was one of the latter. They took him to the station and held him all night. They probably weren't trying to kill him, because if they'd wanted to do that, they'd have beaten him anywhere they felt like, but he only had bruises below the neck, mostly on his back and stomach. They did a real number on him, and early the next morning, they threw him out. Struggling, he dragged himself back to Miedzianka. He crawled up the old road, which might be why no one found him earlier—these days everyone takes the paved highway. It was fall, a cool early morning, and fog hung over Janowice. By the time he reached home, he was barely alive. Twenty minutes later, he is dead.

HELL

Stanisław Gruszka, age twenty-three, can't get his throat clear. He's doing piecework, like all the other mine workers. At first he worked with the carts, but he quickly advanced to the pit face. Drilling in granite is tough, though—the rock is hard and it breaks off in large pieces, and he has to be careful he isn't crushed. Sometimes two workers will throw their weight behind a drill and the rock still won't give way. Other times, one blow of a pickaxe is enough for a big chunk to fall off on its own. The rock in the pit is unpredictable and all the miners fear it.

When mining, first of all you have to drill holes in the rock. The drilling is done dry, so there's always so much dust in the air of the galleries that two miners wearing lamps and walking single file can't see one other. At one stage they're given masks, which after a few minutes get clogged up and people start suffocating in them. It's easier without the masks. When the pit management introduces wet drill bits and dust reduction, the miners keep drilling without water anyway. It's faster that way, they get higher output, and therefore more pay. Nobody's down here for pleasure, after all.

Blasting takes place once the boreholes are ready. The explosion has hardly died away before the men are sent into the gallery. No one waits a few hours, as they do in other mines, for the dust to settle and for whatever is hanging from the ceiling after the blast to fall down as well. There's no time for anything like that.

If you want a lot of output, you've got to make friends with the Russkies. They're the ones with the machines and who know how to analyze the rock. They can tell where veins are up to twenty feet deep into the face. So if you're not buddies with one of them, you can work like a dog and not get anywhere—the Russky will point you to a useless vein, so all your effort will be wasted. If a vein is good, you don't even have to try that hard to do well for yourself. Russo-Polish friendship must therefore flourish underground.

Staszek Gruszka prefers Russian supervisors to Polish ones. You can always get along with a Russian. Say you've got a big wedding to throw—you go to the engineer and ask him to put you down for a little more spoil. Then you get a higher fee and a first-class wedding. It's also a Russian machine operator who at one point tells Staszek something that sticks in his memory:

"Eat your breakfast up top. And don't drink the water from down here, because it's harmful."

HEAVEN

It all began in 1948. First the Russian experts arrived and trekked through the German shafts, taking measurements. They found over 150 such sites all over Lower Silesia. The first shafts open in Kowary, Kletno, and Miedzianka itself. One day, two army companies are quartered in the manor house and everyone can tell something is up.

The mine is administered by Ore Production Facilities (known by its Polish acronym ZPR-1, or R-1 for short). The mines' headquarters are in Kowary, near Karpacz, where forty-four Soviet engineers and their families also live. They supervise the work in every branch of ZPR-1.

There's no shortage of job applicants in Miedzianka. The ground here is infertile—tilling rocky soil like this from dawn to dusk is backbreaking work. But word is they pay well at the pit, and so they do—when the miners collect their pay after the first month, they can't believe their eyes. Each one has received four thousand złotys or more. A liter of vodka costs eighty złotys. The tavern is immediately jam-packed. Word quickly gets around the area that the miners up in Miedzianka are as rich as Croesus. Those who have to carry their pay home to neighboring villages ask for armed soldiers to guard them, since there are men already lying in wait for them in the forest, keen to earn a little extra on the side.

You've just got to keep your mouth shut and not make a fuss about what you're doing. Karolina Kolis keeps her head down. Her job is simple, though demanding. She collects carts of spoil from the hoist and pushes them down the rails to the spoil tip.

The hardest part is when she has to turn the cart over and dump out the spoil. Then she clears the cart out with a pickaxe and rolls it back. Eight hours a day, rain or shine. It's worst in winter, when they're given wooden clogs that get caked in snow. Every few steps you have to knock them off so you don't fall flat on your face. Karolina knows what's in the carts—it's uranium. But that knowledge does her no good. She doesn't know what uranium is for. And she doesn't want to know, because people in the mine say the less you know, the better. So Karolina sits tight and doesn't talk much. Only once does she speak up. At a cart workers' meeting the director asks:

"Now, ladies, tell me, how would you like to be paid: a day rate or do you prefer a percentage?"

Only Karolina raises her hand:

"Mr. Director, I'd like to be on percentage."

He replies:

"Comrade Kolis, you're the smallest one and you want to be on percentage? Are you planning on working like a dog?"

"Well, if I'm supposed to break my back on these carts, I want to get something out of it."

Once they'd collected their pay, all the women thanked Karolina afterward. And she explained to them that since all the miners down there were on percentage, that meant they would go all out to make more money. And if they went all out, there would be more spoil. Someone up top was going to have to take the spoil to the tip so work didn't get held up.

Baśka Wójcik works the mine carts too. They call her Little Basia, which is sort of a joke, since Basia isn't little at all anymore.

She pushes the carts like nobody else, and quickly becomes one of the leaders, training new women for the job as well. The mine carts are tricky, and if you don't know how to handle the damned things you can end up in serious trouble. You have to roll them down full, and it helps a lot if you use a stick for a brake. But you have to know just where to put the stick so you don't knock your teeth out. If you don't slow the carts down, at best they'll run off the rails at the bottom, and at worst they can fall on one of the women. You push them up the hill empty, so they're a little lighter. But still heavy.

HELL

Staszek Kopczyński came to work as a miner; later they made him an electrician and a welder, still down the pit. They hired him right away, but now he's a little scared the people up top will find out what he was really doing in the Home Army and fire him. He needs the money badly. His father-in-law kept his promise—they held the wedding as soon as Staszek arrived in Janowice. He's having a kid soon.

Yet what Kopczyński fears most is that human stupidity will cost him his life. It's dangerous in the pit, so before you do anything, you have to think three times. If you don't think, there's plenty that can go wrong.

On three occasions, Staszek didn't think. The first time, he got the idea that instead of taking the ladder he'd go up on the spoil hoist. He grabbed onto the cable and on the way up it spun him around so fast he saw stars. He almost lost his grip—if he had, the only thing left of him would be a wet splotch on the ground. From then on, Staszek uses the ladder, like you're supposed to.

The second time, they ordered him to weld something underground. He went down, walked into the gallery, and started welding. It was the end of the day, his thoughts were already up on the surface, so he forgot the ventilation down there was switched off. He was breathing in zinc particles—he has no idea how he made it back to the surface. He lay down in a ditch and lost consciousness. They didn't find him until that evening—he was barely alive.

The third time he was working the pumps. They were activated using a special switch, and only an electrician could do it wearing insulated gloves. Staszek forgot the gloves and turned them on with his bare hands. An electric current burst out of the switch, and from then on Staszek knew not even to walk up to the pumps without gloves on.

Underground accidents like this are increasingly common. The mine hospital in Kowary sees a thousand patients a year. That means one out of ten mine workers in that town have accidents. Most often the cause is human carelessness and stupidity. On September 24, 1949, two miners died because one of them was carrying explosive fuses and primers around his neck and his carbide lamp set them on fire. In August 1951, another mine worker extracted himself from a broken elevator cage and decided to climb down the shaft wall. As he was doing so, the elevator came down right on top of him. He fell to the bottom and died from severe injuries. Yet another miner fell from a forty-five-foot scaffold, another was using an extractor even though he hadn't been trained to. It struck his coworker in the head and the man died underground. Ten miners die in the R-1 mines in 1950 alone, and the total number of accidents comes to 1,039. The next year there are 757.

The most serious accident Staszek witnessed in the pit was when Józek Sarul was crushed working the rock face. He will never forget the sight—sometimes he just wonders whether Józek was being that stupid or if the rock was that unpredictable. After that, Józek spent the rest of his days barely alive.

HEAVEN

There are a few rules the miners have to follow on their way to the surface. They stop working a half hour before the end of their shift and head up top. They have that whole half hour to dust off their clothes. Few of them leave their work clothes at the mine. They don't tend to use the washroom either. Most of them live right nearby and prefer to go home. They unroll their cuffs and turn out their pockets, they take their boots off and knock the dust off them. There can't be even the tiniest speck of spoil in the folds of their shirts, even a single pebble or grain of dust.

Soldiers stand at the gate and check them with Geiger counters. When a counter creaks, they unroll the man's cuffs and check his pockets. If they find anything, the man disappears. Whispered stories are already going around about men who weren't careful enough dusting off their clothes. No one has seen them again—they are probably dead. In reality it varies. Officials from the mine's secret police station will take the culprit from the gate and interrogate him. If the man is lucky, he gets off with a warning and a note on his file. He won't be able to count on working a good vein anymore. If he's unlucky, they order him to pack his things and leave town that very night. He disappears, and the miners start swapping far-fetched stories. In 1949 alone, as many as fifty-five people are purged from the mine in this way.

So everyone is frightened and takes care when dusting themselves off. The dusting is a real test of camaraderie—people check one another over, help one another out, and look under one other's collars. They dust off in silence, focused, sneaking glances in the soldiers' direction. Once they're clean, they line up for the gate. Sometimes it also happens that one man doesn't like another, or has heard around town that a guy has been visiting his wife. Ordinary human matters. Then it's enough to slip a stone into the other man's pocket after they dust off but before the inspection. Then there's no need to worry about your wife's fidelity. This sometimes happens down the pit as well.

There's also a rule on the surface not to talk about what you were mining, how many mine carts were sent to the hoist, or how work went. Best not to say anything at all, answer questions about work by smiling, changing the subject, and looking up into the sky. It's best not to talk at home either. Jasiek Majka, the one who first hiked up to Miedzianka with his mother, only asks once what she does in the mine. Barbara Majka, née Kmiecik, has a mind-numbing job operating the spoil hoist, but she knows enough about the facility that her son's loose lips could cost her her job—at least.

"Sweetie, you're better off not knowing. What's the point of talking about it at school? It would cause problems for all of us."

HELL

They can't let their guard down underground either. The miners are constantly moved from one work crew to another, changing up their tasks, work locations, and crewmates. They're never in one place for more than two or three months. This is so people don't get to know one another too well. The secret police have got agents here, tasked with working just like the others and listening to what people say on break. The miners have a fairly clear sense of who's on their side and who's ratting them out. But as a precaution, they trust no one, especially new arrivals. They say if you see five men standing in a group, one of them is definitely informing. In reality, the secret police have got barely two agents at their disposal for every hundred workers in the mine. Those two can't be everywhere, they won't hear everything, they won't find out every subversive word or thought that crops up in the labyrinth of galleries beneath Miedzianka. But the atmosphere of fear ensures no one broaches sensitive subjects.

Of course the secret police attempt to recruit new informants, and have their methods of doing so. The first ones to go are anyone caught with something at the gate, along with any others who've somehow fallen short. They're accused of treason or revealing the facility's secrets—they're threatened with being deported east, or with prison. Some give in and sign. They end up in their old crews, but now everyone there knows what the secret police asked them to do. So suspicion grows, and people talk about the weather. Those who are forced to rat out their crewmates soon lose their enthusiasm—they wiggle their way out of informing and stop being of any use. The ones paid for their information are much more helpful. Money is not the only way they are compensated—that must be picked up somehow, documents must be signed, it has to be withdrawn from somewhere, and something done with it. All that puts people off. As far as the miners and the surveyors are concerned, the best reward is a good rock face. For that reason, people down below are of a mind that if a man always finds a vein, it's not that he's lucky—it's that he's hiding something and you should keep your distance.

HEAVEN

They buried Ludwik Kaczmarski on November 1 in Janowice, in the graveyard next to the church. Before that, in one of the ex-German tombs, some big shots from Jelenia Góra performed a quick autopsy. They told Anna Kaczmarska his death was due to injuries to his internal organs—his kidneys, liver, and lungs. They didn't say who gave him these injuries. Anna takes a picture of him before they close the coffin. In it, he lies on his back in a white shirt, his hands on his chest. Someone has placed a hat beside his head. They bury him with no shoes on. She asks them to write on the gravestone that he died tragically and "May his soul rest in peace." The big shots say no.

A few weeks later, another grave is dug in that same graveyard. There, they bury a little stillborn girl. They give her the name Ludwika. She will lie a short distance from her father.

Kaczmarska and her daughters are now living from hand to mouth. The oldest sister, Natalka, goes to work in the mine. She deliberately falsifies her papers to do so—otherwise they wouldn't have accepted her. Little Basia trains her. Natalka will later say that if not for Basia, she would never have gotten the hang of the mine carts. Basia Wójcik's response to that compliment is that someone had to look after a weakling like Natalka, and she just happened to be nearby.

Jan Miroś, a baker from Miedzianka, also helps out Anna Kaczmarska and her daughters. He tells the girls to come every morning for fresh rolls and bread. Whenever Anna appears in the door of the bakery with the intention to pay, Miroś only waves the money away, then leans over the counter and whispers conspiratorially:

"For you, everything here is free."

He keeps his promise for over a decade. Even when he relocates the bakery to Janowice, the girls go to his store to get bread, and he never accepts money from them. Besides, all of Miedzianka goes to Miroś's for bread, because no one makes it better than he does.

There's no discussion of Kaczmarski in Janowice, and especially not in Miedzianka. It's a taboo subject. Especially the people celebrating his memorial name day hold their tongues. Though several months have passed, they're afraid that before he died, he let slip a few names.

In the mine, Janek Czyżyk, an orphan, hands out summonses to the secret police station. He showed up in town a couple months ago looking for work. He was too young for the mine and nowhere else wanted him. He was starving, so the secret police took him in and told him to carry letters between the mine and Janowice. Every afternoon, Janek takes a sack of letters and heads for the shaft. There, he waits for the miners to finish their shift. He hands them envelopes as they come out onto the surface. Some don't want to take them—then he lays the letter on the ground, right in front of them, and walks away.

One day Staszek Kopczyński gets an envelope of his own. The summons says he is to leave his house on a certain day at a certain time and look around. In the distance, he will see a man who will lead him via a roundabout route to a location where officers will ask him a few questions. Staszek is afraid, he knows he told a lot of lies in his CV and now they're probably going to ask about what he actually did in the Home Army in Szczucin. But there's no way he'll tell them he was beating the crap out of Reds, and all he cared about was making sure he left every part of their face swollen up.

At the appointed hour, Kopczyński steps out of his house, hoping not to see anyone. But he spots a secret policeman in the distance who, upon catching sight of him, turns around and slowly goes on his way. Staszek follows him, as he was ordered. Though he's afraid, it feels a little like he's in a spy movie. Or a comedy, really, because none of this cloak-and-dagger stuff makes any sense. Janowice is not a very large village—everyone knows one another here. They all know if a gloomy secret policeman walks past followed by a terrified Staszek, that means the former is leading the latter to old Piela's apartment, where the security services have a secret interrogation room.

They walk in circles around town like a pair of idiots, until finally they actually arrive at Piela's apartment. Inside are a desk, a lamp, and a large portrait of Stalin hanging on the wall. They give Staszek a piece of paper and a pen and order him to write his CV. When he finishes one, he is to write another, and then another, and then another. He produces a dozen or so of these CVs, and they take each one out of the room before returning a moment later and ordering him to write one more. Finally, they ask him straight out about Szczucin and the Home Army. Staszek sticks to his story and talks about the coal. But they don't care about that, now they ask about young Krochmal.

They knew each other back in partisan days and became friends. When Krochmal settled in Janowice, Staszek found himself a home next door, so they live side-by-side. Now the secret police want to know if Staszek could become even closer friends with him and check him out a little. Then maybe he could end up with a better face down the pit, maybe even a promotion—they need a foreman somewhere and they could make it so that foreman was Staszek.

"Your offer is exceptionally attractive, Comrade, however I can't be as friendly with Krochmal as you'd like. The problem is our wives have had a falling-out and I'm not allowed over to the Krochmals' and they're not allowed over to our house. So I would very much like to help, but I can't."

The comrades go a little purple in the face, and they take out paper and a pencil.

"Then, Kopczyński, you're going to sit here and write CVs until the end of your goddamned miserable life!"

HELL

So on the surface there are secret policemen, while down below there's radon. This is a product of decayed radium, which, in turn, comes from uranium. Radon is a silent killer, a radioactive gas that enters the lungs along with rock dust. So black lung, an occupational mining disease, takes a tremendously arduous toll in uranium mines, since for the entire period the radon is decaying, it is radioactive black lung. It causes tumors and cellular degeneration. More and more of Stanisław Gruszka's friends are complaining of bad health. After two years working in the pit, he himself decides to quit. He's overheard too much from the Russians about what it actually is they're mining. The rock dust scratching the back of Staszek's throat keeps getting worse. He's also noticed he washes his hands obsessively, trying to rid himself of the gray residue that coats them in the mine. He even rubs his hands when they are clean and washed. Another factor in his decision to leave is a recent accident underground. His crew went down into the gallery as usual and activated the drills, but before they could even get to the face, one of them fainted, followed immediately by another few. Staszek doesn't remember when he lost consciousness himself. He woke up back on the surface alongside the others. There hadn't been enough air down below. The mine director arrived, wringing his hands—he forbade them to go to the doctor, and each of them was only granted ten additional days of leave. Then everyone went back to work.

All they can do is follow the rules the Russians have passed on in secret. By now everyone in the mine has probably gotten a warning from a friendly "comrade." They don't drink the water, they don't eat underground, they don't sit on the ore canisters. But it's not only the miners working with uranium, for there are also the women transporting the mine carts of spoil. One of these is

Karolina Burzawa, née Kolis. She married recently, and now she's pushing carts without yet knowing that she's pregnant. When she finds out, she hands in her notice. Karolina is lucky, and a few months later she gives birth to a healthy girl.

Julia Jaroszewska is not so lucky. She's also been working with the uranium, and is also pregnant. She doesn't quit, but does go on maternity leave. Her child is born sick, and fairly rapidly contracts a tumor. When Jaroszewska explains to the doctors in Jelenia Góra where she's been working, they can't believe their ears.

There never have been and never will be any notices about radiation in the pit. Officially, there are no additional risks associated with mining uranium. But even if the miners had known about the lurking threat, there wasn't anyone in particular to whom they could raise a concern. The Mining Inspectorate operates in the facility, but it reports directly to management, so in spite of its remit it performs no checks. Before 1956, not a single one of the R-1 mines investigated potential occupational hazards. The first measurements, carried out long after the mine in Miedzianka was closed, showed the concentration of radon in some of the mines exceeded acceptable norms by six hundred times. But the uranium extraction is shrouded in absolute secrecy, and no problem can be taken beyond the grounds of the facility. When an occupational inspector arrives from the Main Board of the Union of Nonferrous Ore Mines, the soldiers in the guardroom immediately call "Number 15," meaning the secret police station in the mine. Before long, the inspector finds himself in a window-less room, where he will spend the next few days receiving only bread and water. Upon returning to headquarters, he files a report ending with the words: "They ordered me to pass on the message that we are to send no more inspectors there."

HEAVEN

The four years the uranium mine is open are years of plenty. As before the war, the town has a pharmacy, a few stores, a bakery, a meat processing plant, and workshops. A community center has now been set up in the former German tavern. It holds dances every Sunday, which mine workers and people from Miedzianka— as well as nearby Ciechanowice, Mniszków, and Janowice—attend. The community center also organizes screenings once a month by a traveling movie theater. It's brought by the Russian soldiers guarding the mine, and each time they show a different film praising the gallantry and valor of Soviet soldiers on the fronts of the Great Patriotic War. Entry costs a few złotys, but the local children have their own method of seeing the movies for free. On the day of the screening, they sneak into the community center and dart under the makeshift stage where the image will appear. When the lights go out and the projector rattles, that's the signal they can abandon their hiding place without being seen, and watch the movie in peace.

The miners are rich. You can tell at first glance who works in the mine and who doesn't. Some buy motorcycles, others renovate their houses. In February 1949, Baśka Wójcik collects a paycheck of 28,000 złotys—some fifty times the average monthly salary in Poland. And Stanisław Kopczyński occasionally brings home twice that. Once again, the wealth concealed in the ground is causing the town to blossom. These days it's here, not in Janowice, that life is vibrant. More people are constantly arriving, eager to work in the mine. The authorities estimate the local population peaks at nearly 3,000 people. The town has never had so many inhabitants.

However, the origin of this success must remain unspoken. In official documentation, the uranium mine in Miedzianka is registered as a "Paper Factory in Janowice Wielkie." Even in internal communication, the word "uranium" is avoided like the plague—substitute terms are used instead, such as "diatomaceous ore," "R-2," or "P9."*

After the extracted ore is pure and cleared of additional rock, it is manually packed into heavy metal canisters. These are produced on-site in a special workshop. This is so no information makes it into the wider world about the number of canisters coming out in a given day. If the mine had to order them from somewhere, someone would have to make them, someone else count them, and someone else finally transport them to Miedzianka. Every one of those people would have to be checked, followed, asked questions about their contacts, their past, their family in the West. There would be a huge amount of work involved with ordering the canisters.

Once the ore is packed up, trucks with Polish drivers come to the mine. Each truck is loaded with a few dozen canisters and a Russian soldier with a machine pistol. Then the convoy drives north. On the way, they stop at a predetermined location, where

---

* Robert Klementowski, "Uranowe mity. Kopalnictwo uranu w Polsce w społecznej świadomości" [Uranium Myths: Uranium Mining in Poland in Social Consciousness]. Manuscript provided by the author.

empty trucks are already waiting, along with Soviet drivers. They switch trucks. The Russians drive their trucks off toward Legnica, and the Poles return to the mine with the empty ones.

The ore mined in Miedzianka contains around 0.2 percent pure uranium. That's why tens of tons of rock waste are necessary to obtain a few tons of ore, from which barely a few kilograms of uranium will be produced. The quotas are increasing; mining runs in three shifts and nearly 1,500 people are working in the mine. The majority of them live in the town, but some come in on mine trucks from neighboring villages, and some make their own way across the mountains.

Mineshafts now dot the entire area, and spoil tips pile up around each of them. No one knows in exactly how many places uranium is being mined in this mountain. Over four years, twenty-five miles of tunnels have been dug. Some speak of a few, some of over a dozen, some of dozens of mining posts. Suffice it to say that all the mining drifts of ZPR-1 put together run a hundred miles long, and if all the mineshafts were combined into one, they would reach a depth of nearly twenty miles.

Some of the uranium mining tunnels in Miedzianka were dug by the Germans. These have been appropriately secured, and the mining authorities have access to all the documentation. It's a different story with the new drifts. In the pit, the rule is you follow the vein, and the machines direct you where to dig. Hardly anyone thinks about what's above them. The miners tell stories about digging a drift right up under the surface of the ground. That's not so bad if it's a field above you—then one day the farmer will find a large crater, and a few dump trucks full of sand will need to be brought in and that's that. It's worse if the miners follow the vein under the town, which happens as well. Then the sinking ground causes yards and cellars to collapse, and puts cracks in the walls of buildings. The mining authorities try to fix the situation, supporting the houses with wooden props and filling in sinkholes at their own cost. Their efforts are increasingly for naught.

HELL

Aside from the ordinary mine workers, soldiers work in the pit as well. They arrive in trucks from Ciechanowice, where their barracks are located. There's almost no contact with the soldiers— they work in their own crews, and even eat separately. Word in the mine is they're only nominally soldiers, and actually they're political prisoners. There's much truth in that.

By the fall of 1949, a "special mining recruitment initiative" is introduced in some units of the Polish Armed Forces. The economy, which is gathering steam, needs hands to work, and where it isn't possible to find willing civilians, the decision is made to look among the soldiers. Not many volunteer, however, and the majority of those who do are sent to the coal mines in Upper Silesia.

In February 1951, the Minister of Defense, Marshal Konstantin Rokossovsky, signs an order permitting commanding officers to assign soldiers to labor battalions. From then on, a mine posting is yet another tool of political repression. You can end up there for singing Home Army songs, for not joining the Party, or for refusing officer training. All the enemies of the people are sent underground as well—aristocrats and their sons, clerical families, landowners and private businessmen, the sons of prewar policemen and kulaks. And groups who merely seem unreliable are turned into miners—Silesians, Mazovians, Kashubians, Slovaks from Spiš, returnees from Yugoslavia. Finally, members of independent scouting organizations, veterans of the Warsaw Uprising, Home Army soldiers, the former Peasants' Battalions, and members of the anti-Communist underground all get pickaxes instead of rifles. They're told straight out: "You learned how to shoot in the forest."

In the whole of the R-1 facilities, there are two battalions of miner-soldiers working, assigned the numbers 10 and 11. They both make up the Tenth Labor Brigade, which at its peak numbers 2,755 soldiers. The Second company is quartered in Ciechanowice, three miles from Miedzianka. The soldiers are restricted to a few buildings, their shifts usually last from eight to eighteen hours. They dig in the most difficult sectors, where the height of the drift does not exceed three feet. The other miners keep away from such places, because there's no escape in the event of an accident—all you can do is call for help, and maybe someone will hear. They work almost every day, Sundays as well. Soldiers are entitled to barely a few days off a year: May 1, July 22, October 13 (Polish Armed Forces Day), and Miner's Day—December 4.* As a rule,

---

* Specific information regarding soldier-miners' working conditions comes from Robert Klementowski's article, "Skazani na uran. Kopalnie rudy uranu we wspomnieniach Żołnierzy Batalionów Pracy" [Sentenced to Uranium: Uranium Ore Mines in the Memories of Labor Battalion Soldiers], in *Studia nad faszyzmem i zbrodniami hitlerowskimi*, no. 21, 2009.

they also go hungry. In the barracks, they're given bread, thin soup, and black coffee with no sugar for breakfast and dinner. Lunch only differs in that they eat it in the mine, and sometimes the soup has a couple potatoes floating in it. It's a good bit better on days when inspectors come to see the unit. Then the soldiers get buckwheat or goulash with noodles, and for breakfast they also get cottage cheese and hard-boiled eggs. They only truly escape their hunger on Polish Armed Forces Day—when they receive a two-course lunch and a liter of vodka for each brigade.

The harsh conditions and backbreaking work mean the productivity of the soldiers' battalions drops dramatically. Aside from that, they cause constant problems—since they don't care about earnings, they dodge work if they can. Sometimes they even come into conflict with the Internal Security Corps soldiers guarding the mine. In November 1951, the soldiers disappear from Ciechanowice, and no longer appear in the mines either.

HEAVEN

The town is constantly wracked with rumors of spies being arrested trying to steal the mine's carefully guarded secrets. There's no hiding the fact that Western intelligence is interested in the facilities. There's an arms race underway, in which the construction of atom bombs is an absolutely key factor. The West wants to know all about the uranium Stalin might use in the future. That's why Western consular and embassy employees come to the area on vacation so often. But Kowary, where the facilities' headquarters are located, is a closed town. Only soldiers and civilians with the proper authorization have access, while gates and armed soldiers block the entrances to the town. Any lost travelers who disembark at the train station here are immediately packed onto the first departing train.

Similar, though less severe, restrictions apply in all the R-1 mines, and in Miedzianka as well. But it's all theoretical, because in practice it's another story. In their reports, the secret police are constantly appealing for literate guards to be sent, and for the fencing off of some of the mineshafts, since the mining is taking place in direct proximity to people's homes.

Things that remain obvious for locals must absolutely be hidden from visitors, especially representatives of Western governments. Meanwhile, the area is teeming with people who have decided to return to Poland after years spent abroad in France or Benelux. Many even work in the mines—in fact, they're the perfect experts. They've acquired specialist knowledge in the West, which they can now make the most of for the glory of Communist Poland. Not all of them speak perfect Polish, so they have their own work crews to make it easier for them to communicate in a language no one here knows.

The secret police monitor them closely, the more so because they contact the French embassy in Warsaw and the consulate in Wrocław ever more frequently. That's because a few years living in Poland have left them disillusioned with conditions here, and they've decided to return to the West.

At the end of the forties, a young returnee from Belgium, Stefan Burzyński, is hired in one of the R-1 mines. He is one of many, so no one pays particular attention to his poor acquaintance with the Polish language. Burzyński has no difficulty finding a job in a pit, but mine work is only a cover. His real name is Louis Quievreux: he's a native Belgian and an agent of one of the Western intelligence services. His task is to convey information about specific mines, the scale of mining, and the types of ore being extracted here. For a few months, Quievreux—alias Burzyński—performs his duties flawlessly. He even manages to sneak out a specimen of the ore, which he passes on to his handlers. He then rapidly receives orders to withdraw immediately through a prearranged smuggling channel. But the young Belgian has unfortunately fallen in love with a certain beautiful woman from Jelenia Góra. He drags his feet for more than a week, not wanting to leave without her, and this is his downfall. He's captured and given three death sentences. He's jailed in Warsaw's Mokotów Prison. He quickly becomes a curiosity and a mascot for his fellow prisoners. He's not serving his sentence with just anybody. He eats lunch in the prison cafeteria with the elite of the Wilno Home Army: Maciej Jeleń, Roman Woźniacki, and Jan Pętkowski. Quievreux impresses them with his extraordinary fortitude, despite their dire situation. When on one occasion a warden goads him, he replies proudly that he had the right to defend his homeland as he did, since he considers international Communism a threat to its independence.[*]

Despite this impertinence, his punishment is quickly commuted to fifteen years in prison, and he is transferred to an institution

---

[*] Mieczysław Chojnacki, "Mokotowskie więzienie. Rozprawa – wyrok – pobyt w ogólnej celi śmierci" [The Mokotów Prison—Trial—Sentence—Stay in a Shared Execution Cell], *Zeszyty WiN-u* R-1, 1992.

in Strzelce Opolskie, seventy miles southeast of Wrocław. There, the trail runs cold. He is probably sent to the West in an exchange of captured spies.

HELL

But spies are lurking everywhere, even among the Poles. If you lie to the authorities, the authorities will squeeze the truth out of you. All night long they squeeze it out of the young miner Czesław Dull. When they hired him, he was ordered to write six CVs. They had a seventh in their archives, and they knew he was hiding his family in the West from them. He spent all day at the station with no food, then that night the commandant came and said:

"Have at him!"

First they beat him around the head, then they tied him to a bench and battered him with rubber truncheons. He lost consciousness, so they revived him. They took him home and ordered him to tear up the doorframes and floorboards with his bare hands. They were looking for weapons. They didn't find any.

They arrest Teresa Stegnarska at the train station in Jelenia Góra. She works sorting uranium, and suddenly she receives an order to go to Kielce on official business. As soon as she's on the train, two plainclothes officers appear at her side out of the blue. They say someone has informed them she took uranium out of the mine. She is accused under Article 7: espionage. During the interrogation they say they have her brother-in-law's confession, thanks to which they even know which pocket she hid the samples in. Stegnarska demands to confront him.

The answer comes: "You're not in charge of us, bitch."

She spends the next fourteen months imprisoned in Wrocław. Then she's sent to Mokotów. She's held there for another year, without sentence and without formal charge. Once she's released, she's unable to find work for many months.

Some stories are terrifyingly similar. On July 27, 1950, the tavern in Janowice hosts another party. The place is full of mine workers, including Bolesław Grzyb, a younger miner who came to the pit all the way from distant Skaryszew. Andrzej Pacholski, a steel fixer in the mine, is also there. He's young and fairly handsome. He, his wife, and their three daughters live in a building on First of May Street at number 24. They're barely a stone's throw from the tavern. Pacholski is passionate about soccer, and he spends every spare moment on the field, kicking the ball around with his friends. But this time he's come to the tavern to drink the health of his colleague from the mine—Mikołajczyk.

They drink all night long, there's singing, and toasts, as well: to Grzyb, to Pacholski, to Mikołajczyk. Before long, the secret police burst into the tavern. Pacholski and Grzyb are the slowest to escape. They're taken to a station in the park. They hold them all night, interrogate them, and take turns beating them up. They let Grzyb go after a few hours, he has a hard time making it home, and will spend another few weeks recuperating. They drive Pacholski to Jelenia Góra, where they start all over again. They beat him unconscious, then drive him off to Janowice and throw him out right next to the health center. Baśka Wójcik is passing by that night and gets a fright from the wheezing drunk lying in the ditch. She runs away. His neighbors find him the next morning and carry him home. An ambulance arrives in time to drive him to the hospital in Miłków, twelve miles away. He dies there. They bury him in Janowice, in the graveyard by the church.

HEAVEN

By 1951, the easily reachable uranium deposits under Miedzianka have already been exhausted, and the Russian specialists know this perfectly well. The miners begin to sense it too, since their earnings, though still high, are much lower than when the mining began. The staff in the Miedzianka pit is therefore cut. Some of the workers quit on their own—including Karolina Kolis and Staszek Gruszka. Now she looks after her children, and he's found work in the paper mill in Janowice. He earns a fraction of what he did before, but at least he doesn't have to worry about the dust that used to tickle the back of his throat.

Baśka Wójcik is transferred thirty miles away to Radoniów, and Staszek Kopczyński eighty miles to Kletno. Natalka Kaczmarska marries Staszek Kołoda, the chief of the mine's fire department. She won't have to push carts anymore. She and her husband often visit her father's grave. When news arrives that the mine will be closed, some miners move to the area around Lubin and Legnica. Copper mining has just gotten underway there, and they need a few thousand specialists in the pits. Everyone who comes will get a new house.

The mine is closed in 1952, the drainage pumps are shut off, and the drifts and shafts slowly fill with water. As the water rises, so does the locals' conviction that the mine closure is masking some secret. There are more and more rumors about people left underground, German treasure, mysterious trucks, secrets, and spies. The more water there is, the more of these stories go around Miedzianka.

The miners who didn't make arrangements beforehand find themselves unemployed. They spend all day long sitting outside their houses, coughing and reminiscing about when they could afford everything. Now they hardly have enough for anything at all. Besides, even if they wanted to, there would be nowhere to spend their money. As time goes on, Miedzianka shrinks, houses empty out, and the stores and workshops disappear. The town is quickly turning into a ghost, one which will haunt the area for twenty years to come.

POSTSCRIPT

"*NYET*, MR. DIRECTOR, the hunting dog's not up to it. No meat today!" shouts Bronek Hac with a laugh to Director Pavlovich, who has a stern look on his face. Jack, their coarse-haired pointer, really is sick today—he's lying in front of the office door and doesn't even lift his head. That means the geologists from Miedzianka won't get chicken soup, but they will have a quiet evening. What usually happens is Jack brings them a chicken clenched in his jaws and they eat lunch—which the indispensable Lena cooks for them—then a farmer arrives and raises hell, saying something's wrong in his henhouse again.

The students swear no one has trained Jack. So you could say he's a natural-born chicken thief. The director looks kindly on the pranks the dog and the students play. Only once did he lose his temper, when a large placard was hung in his room, reading:

IT'S NO USE GETTING OUT OF BED.
WHY NOT HAVE A DRINK INSTEAD?

Colonel Richard Pavlovich is a nice guy, for a Russky. He thinks everything Soviet is best. He works as a specialist in the Union of Non-Ferrous Ore Mines in Złoty Stok—before that, he was director of the Konrad mine in Iwiny, and now they've moved him to Miedzianka. He speaks Polish, but doesn't write it so well, so he employs Lena for that. She's the only one who has to get up early—still in her pajamas, she walks to the office and sits at the typewriter, while the director paces the room, dictating official correspondence.

Meanwhile, the rest of the guys, mainly geology students from Wrocław, are slowly getting ready for work. This is where their summer practicums take place, but Pavlovich pays them to spend a few months here and not return to school until November. Every day their task is the same. For weeks, they've been mapping closed drifts and shafts in the uranium mine. The pits have been closed for a year, and now the students have to find out what's really in them. The Russians took all the plans with them as they left, and flooded some of the mines. The students are not allowed into anywhere with even the slightest layer of water, because some of the drifts and shafts are completely unmarked above ground, so if you go into them, the earth could easily give way under your feet and you'd never be able to swim to the surface.

They enter through a drainage shaft, the only one that wasn't destroyed when the mine was shut down. A local miner guides them through the labyrinth of tunnels. They call him Mr. Kot, and over the course of their few months in Miedzianka it never occurs to anyone to ask his first name. Kot knows the layout of the mine perfectly. He also knows where to look for copper.

Wandering through the inactive galleries, Bronek is constantly coming across geological specimens of copper ore untouched by the miners' hands. He knows they were only interested in uranium. But now he will mark each such discovery on his maps, as the authorities are investigating renewed copper extraction in the mine. The surface analyses performed here by engineers from Wrocław have given promising results. Now, before getting to work in the underground tunnels, they have to check if what's on the surface is also confirmed underground. This is the job of Bronek and his friends.

But they don't have to go into the interior of the mountain to find copper. Impressive quantities of it lie in the spoil tips. Realizing this, Director Pavlovich decides to commence exploitation of the mine.

Upon receiving the proper permit from headquarters, he hires the few miners remaining in town and orders them first to clear out the rubble and then to commence blasting operations. The miners obediently clean out a tunnel, and soon the first explosions wrack the area. However, only five people are working on blasting operations—there's no way they could segregate and process the spoil. But there is absolutely no need to. The miners are clearly enjoying their job—all they have to do is make sure a boom rumbles through Miedzianka every now and again.

Pavlovich hires over a dozen other people, this time with no mine training, to work on the spoil tips. This is where they'll get the copper, which is later sent to Gliwice. The ore is picked out by hand. Headquarters pays by the ton, taking into account not only the amount of ore obtained, but also the tonnage of all the spoil. So Pavlovich always orders a little debris to be dumped into the trucks already laden with pure ore. This ensures the proper ratio of recovered material, and means his employees receive an additional bonus for their work.

This procedure lasts a few months, and after mapping all the tunnels, young Bronek Hac and the other students join in as well. Once, Bronek even asks the director why they're performing these fake blasting operations.

"The paperwork must be in order. Copper is extracted underground, not from slag heaps. Order is important above all," answers Pavlovich.

But once all the slag heaps are cleared of ore, Pavlovich orders an end to the pointless detonations, and now they know no one will ever go underground again. The documentation the students have compiled is clear: the surface surveys made incorrect predictions of copper deposits in the area around Miedzianka.

But their underground escapades do more than just convince Bronek Hac there is no longer any point starting up the mine, for Mr. Kot leads him to places where you can see how the area was overexploited while hunting for uranium. Bronek and his friends manage to get into a few cellars in Miedzianka from underneath, and Kot keeps stopping to tell them which building they are currently under. Once, he even shows them the way to the basement of the mansion standing near the church. These tunnels under the town are only held up with makeshift shoring. The posts won't stand the test of time, and the town will eventually collapse. Bronek knows that is a fate Miedzianka can no longer avoid.

And then everyone departs, Pavlovich to Wałbrzych, the boys to Wrocław to finish school, and the miners once again sit outside their houses, hands resting on their bellies. The mine disappears before their eyes. The last shafts are already filled in, the drifts are covered up, the scrap is shipped away, and the barracks are demolished. In a few years only the spoil tips, sprouting with weeds, will be the only sign that anyone went below ground in this place.

THE LAST ONES

THE LAST ONES LIVE ON THE OUTSKIRTS of town, occupying only a few houses, not making themselves obvious. No one knows if they still hold out hope, or if they've stayed simply because they no longer have the strength for change.

The Blümke sisters occupy one floor of number 98. They're elderly, wear black dresses, and usually cover their tightly wound hair with black headscarves. Some people in town call them "the wraiths." The younger one helps out at the Spiżes', looking after their children. Baśka and Stefan call her "Grandma Blimka." They're a little frightened of her, because Grandma doesn't speak Polish (she speaks to their parents in German), and she treats the children strictly. Only once did Baśka Spiż catch Grandma Blimka brushing her hair in front of the mirror. Baśka had to make a run for it right away, because the old lady was furious and went chasing after her, spitting out German curses.

In twelve years of living in Polish Miedzianka, the elder Blümke sister has left the house barely more than a few times.

It could be she goes out at night, but regardless, few in town know what she looks like. If you knock on the Blümkes' door, most often it will stay shut. The sisters aren't expecting anyone. Sometimes the door will crack open slightly, and the visitor will hear a few incomprehensible German sentences. Then the door will shut.

There's also a gravedigger living at number 98—Alfred Neumann. He's the one who digs properly proportioned graves for the remaining ones who've reached the end of their lives here. He buries them facing away from the town. There's not very much work, though. Poles are buried in the cemetery in Janowice.

The Gliszczyńskis are here too. That's what people in the town now call Maximilian von Glyschinsky and his family—his wife Lotte and their three children. Maximilian runs a sparkling lemonade bottling plant out of his house at number 21. It's right near the square, a stone's throw from the brewery. Maybe that's why the Glyschinskys make friends with the Spiżes. Stefan speaks perfect German, so they have no trouble communicating. The men enjoy themselves over cold beers, while their children—Basia, Stefan, and Hania, and then Peter, Kristine, and Margaret—play hide-and-seek together behind the brewery.

The Polish children respect Maximilian. He's missing one leg, so he clunks around on a wooden prosthesis. From time to time, he hires the bravest of the little boys to work in his factory—he gives them the task of cleaning the glass lemonade bottles. They receive a few złotys for an hour's work. They can only collect it in cash, though many would prefer to be paid in the lemonade Maximilian produces. But the old German sticks firmly to the established rules—he pays the children money and once it's in their hands, they must decide how to spend it.

The last year the Germans can leave Poland under the postwar repatriation is 1957. To do so, it's necessary to submit the appropriate paperwork in Warsaw. All the Germans living in the town at that time choose to do so. Stefan Spiż comes home one day and says that soon no Germans will be left here, and they must help them arrange their departures so they have the best possible memories of Miedzianka.

The first to leave are Grandma Blimka and her sister. Spiż assures them at great length that they can stay in Miedzianka as long as they like, and he promises to take care of them until the end of their days. Yet the decision has already been made. Grandma cleans the apartment carefully, then places a padlock on the door, wrapping it in a rag soaked with machine grease so it doesn't freeze. She says goodbye to the children, gets into the truck, and drives off. Young Baśka and Hania Spiż cry.

Soon afterward, the Glyschinskys disappear. Maximilian hands the little factory over to Staszek Pławiak. Over a few days, they transport their furniture and all their possessions to the station in Janowice—there's a train car already waiting there to take everything west. Finally, Lotte and the children get on a passenger train and head off for the border. Maximilian will ride in the freight car with all their possessions. He stays another few days tying up loose ends. On July 9, 1957, he says a heartfelt farewell to Stefan, locks up his house, and heads down the road toward Janowice. He's the last German to leave the town.

On November 7, 1957, Maximilian von Glyschinsky writes a letter to his old friend, Count Christian Friedrich zu Stolberg-Wernigerode:

> The manor house in Johannesdorf is now a nursing home. The gardens are being maintained, and the farm buildings are in good condition. The tax collector's cottage, where the Stief family lived, has fallen down, as has the tenant's house. The manor house in Rohrlach now belongs to the government.
>
> Kupferberg looks the worst. From 1948 onward, it was the largest uranium mine in the East. The main mineshaft was located in Gräbel's field. The farms were simply demolished and in their place, mineshafts were dug a thousand feet deep. Debris was piled up on agricultural land downhill. Your Lordship's estate was liquidated entirely, the stables were converted into workshops, and the courtyard into a storage area. Two companies of Russian infantry were quartered in the manor house, as guards for the mine. After the pit was shut down, the house served as a summer camp for children. Altogether, thirty-four mineshafts were dug around Kupferberg and the same number of waste heaps were piled up. Bergmühle was closed down. The turbine was scrapped, but the rest of the machinery remains. That Pole that Mayor Fürle brought in still lives there. The wooden bridge over the Bober River was destroyed, as was Mr. Teige's house. Near

Bergmühle, there is a water-pumping station for Kupferberg. Large amounts of water were needed to cool the powerful compressors providing air to the uranium mines. To that end, a large reservoir was also built, situated uphill from the cattle market.

This general state of savagery is giving way, however, to dread.

DON'T TOUCH THE GRAVES

"THE LAST ONE BURIED THERE was some German or other, and by then it was a Polish priest who did it. The German must have been really short, because I was struck by how small the coffin was.

"There was a wrought-iron gate leading to the cemetery, and stone angels standing where the footpaths crossed—one at each intersection. Each was about six-and-a-half feet high. Of course, we were kids back then, so maybe we only thought they were that big. We also thought the wall wrapping all around seemed impossible to climb, but we got over it somehow.

"The rich Germans' tombs were at the back of the cemetery, as big as the ones in Jelenia Góra by the garrison church. There was room for a few coffins in each. Once, we snuck out of the house and carried a sleeping pallet into one of the tombs. We spent the whole night like that; it was warm and it never occurred to anyone to look for us there. There were no coffins left in the tombs at that time. I don't know what happened to them."

"They came on tractors, no one knew who they were. They hooked chains onto the gravestones and pulled entire slabs into the road. Then they loaded them onto their trailers and drove off. All that was left were these uncovered graves, and after a while human bones started turning up all over town. One day, the kids played soccer with a human skull."

"We burned the wood in our stoves. You'd go into a tomb and pull the coffins apart. There were no bones inside, because the Germans only put empty coffins in the tombs. That's why it was all right for us to burn the coffins."

"The guys who ended up coming for the stones were from Bielsko-Biała. They drove from village to village all over Lower Silesia, collecting German tombstones. Then they scraped the old inscriptions off them and reused them when a Polish person died. For a couple pennies, I helped load the stones into their cars. Our graveyard only had bushes growing everywhere, no one was making any use of it."

"We were all little kids. We walked there one day and the boys went into one of the larger tombs. We stayed outside because we were scared, and besides, someone had to watch and make sure no one was coming. The boys opened both coffins. The first one only had one person inside, but the second one had a woman, I guess, because between her legs there was a little skull. As though she and her child had died while she was giving birth, or just after. The boys stuck the little skull on the end of a stick and ran through the whole village with it, then threw it into the bushes.

"Afterward, that night, I had a dream about that little skull. I woke up screaming and told my mother everything. Then I got a nasty whipping. My parents ordered us to find that skull and put it back where it came from. Then Mama also told me I wasn't allowed to touch anything in the tombs."

"I witnessed the soccer game with the skull myself. It happened because, when the children asked whom the tomb belonged to (it was a small stone chapel with one wall smashed in), a local told them it belonged to a German pharmacist who poisoned many Poles. So they treated the skull that way to take revenge."

"The cemetery was where our social lives could blossom: we went there to drink beer, play cards, or if we wanted to hide from a girl. But no one did anything bad in the cemetery, nothing like that happened there."

"When the Germans started showing up in town again, they went straight there. They would go to the cemetery first thing. And they'd walk around, although you never saw any of them angry. They didn't even ask why this had happened. They'd just walk up there and back again. And I'll tell you—the fact they didn't ask us about anything, that was the worst part."

"I don't remember the cemetery, but we moved to the town fairly late. People told me there had been graves there, but by then there was no trace of them. I used to go there before the Corpus Christi celebrations to collect branches for my mom and grandma to weave into wreaths."

"My mother often told us, 'don't touch the graves,' but everyone went there, you know? We even held contests to see who could pull more of those little silver angels off the coffins. For a while, those little angels were even something like a currency at school. It was easy to get a hold of new ones, because the cemetery was right across the street, so at recess we would run there and the boys would pull those angels out of the tombs for us."

"They pulled out the last skeleton in summer. It was just before I went to tech school, at the end of grade school. They were bored, they pulled it out of the tomb and left it at the base of the wall. It looked like it had walked out of the tomb by itself.

"They took the wall apart too, because it was made of good stone. All that was left there afterward was a meadow where a few farmers grazed their cows. And I could see those cows out the window of our apartment, and I kept track of who they belonged to. And then I would run to my mom and tell her not to buy milk from those farmers because their cows were grazing on the graveyard. Back then I thought it was disgusting to drink milk like that."

"What happened to the cemetery afterward?"
  "After what?"
  "Well, after it was looted."

"But nobody looted anything there! Nothing happened to it afterward."

"But it's gone now."

"Yes, it is. There's only the memorial plaque. That German left it there. I don't know what happened to the cemetery afterward, whether it fell apart on its own. I have no idea."

THERE WAS THIS FEAR

"MY MOM OFTEN LEFT US AT HOME, and when she did I had to take care of my younger sister. We lived in this gray house all the way up the hill, by the bend in the road. Apparently there had been a German tavern there, but there was no trace of any tavern when we lived there.

"One day we had the whole house to ourselves. It was almost noon when I had to go outside for something. And when I walked up to the door, I heard this racket from the stairs, as though a crowd of children were running down them. I went straight out, but there was no one there, and the door upstairs was shut. I spent all day sitting in my room, scared to budge."

"During parties my father always sent Wacek to Janowice for vodka. The stores were closed at night, but if you wanted vodka, everyone knew who to go to and whose window to knock on. Wacek usually took the old road down to save time. Once, he set off, but not fifteen minutes later he was back with a wild look in his eyes.

He said this dark figure had blocked his way in the forest. And he tried to get past it, but when he went left, it did too, and when he went right, this figure followed him. And it was just about to give Wacek a smack in the face when it dissolved. And it seemed like he would be able go on to Janowice to get the moonshine, except he had lost all desire for a drink and came running back."

"One of the people who looted the cemetery got visited in the middle of the night by a skull and crossbones, which said to him: 'You are to return to me what you have taken.' He was so terrified, the next day he ran to put the skull he'd taken back in the tomb. And then everyone got a lesson afterward that we shouldn't touch the graves. There was this fear everyone had that the Germans had left their ghosts behind out of revenge, and they were going to give us trouble."

"On the old road to Mniszków there was the tomb of some noble-man or knight. And on November 1, there would always be a candle burning there and no one would know who'd lit it, because to get there you had to walk past the Pławiaks' house, and the Pławiaks made sure no one traipsed through their fields and never saw anyone going out there with a candle on All Saints' night.

"Once, when we were walking past that tomb in the evening, we saw this bright glow coming through the trees, as though someone had lit a thousand light bulbs. And we never went there again."

"The town was full of ghosts, but only in people's minds. Grandma used to scare us, saying that in the pigsty, where we never kept any pigs, at night you could hear the squealing of slaughtered piglets. So we always kept our distance from the sty. But grandma was just trying to keep us from going in there, because it was falling apart and something could have fallen on our heads.

"Grandma also used to scare us by saying we had to behave, because if we didn't we'd be visited by the ghosts of children the Germans had apparently buried alive under the floors of our house. It was those buried children that frightened us the most."

"One of the shafts was haunted. When I was coming back from the afternoon shift at the factory in Marciszów, I used to walk past it. It was usually after ten o'clock and you could always hear this rumbling and screaming, it made your skin crawl. Then I would walk a different way just so I didn't have to hear all that."

"The forest, which you had to walk through on your way from town to Janowice, was haunted by the spirit of a chimney sweep, who'd killed himself there for love. And we always did our best to run through the forest so we wouldn't see or hear anything, because we were absolutely terrified of that chimney sweep.

"At the edge of the forest there was this enormous tree with a partially burned trunk. Boys would often hide inside it wrapped in sheets and frighten us when we were walking back from school. But those were the only ghosts haunting Miedzianka."

THE GERMANS ARE COMING

IN AUGUST 1961, a reporter for the local newspaper *Nowiny Jeleniogórskie* writes:

> It is said there are places against which all the evil roaming the earth conspires. In these stunted towns and villages, it always hails while neighboring places are spared, and lightning strikes most often, setting fires blazing. At least that is what superstitious people say.
>
> Others, who focus on earthly matters, claim that if a bus route is canceled somewhere, it's always in in these stunted places.
>
> Doom and defeat have staked their claim here, and adding insult to injury, heartless people are working hard to worsen the misfortune of one such stunted place. Miedzianka is dying, a town half-alive, unlikely ever again to return to its former glory. Miedzianka is dying day by day. Out of forty abandoned buildings, ten have already collapsed into ruin. All over the

marketplace, damaged roofs threaten to fall in. Each day ever more windows and doors, casings, thresholds, and floors rot away. Then the rain leaks in and the buildings tumble down like a man whose legs have been cut off.

1

Bogdan Spiż's first memory from Miedzianka: the wind pushes over a colorful box, sending glass bottles clinking down the road toward Janowice. Bogdan looks on helplessly. He is six, maybe seven. It's the mid-1950s and the pharmacy on the square has just closed down. For a little kid like him, everything left behind in there is a priceless treasure. He grabbed as much as he could and was heading home just as the wind whipped up. He doesn't know what to do—save what's fallen out, or keep going and bring whatever he can home.

Bogdan Spiż's last memory from Miedzianka: his father is crying.

They live in the yellow villa in the lower part of town. The brewery isn't far away, and Stefan Spiż is the brewmaster—he has nearly twelve workers under him, so he spends all day there. He constantly repeats the old brewers' maxim:

"There are three rules of making beer: the first is order, the second is order, the third is order. There are no other rules."

There's a hop kiln in the cellar of the brewery, and tanks upstairs where the brewing takes place. Elsewhere stand huge blocks of ice to cool the area. The brewers look after the Spiż children as though they were their own. Basia, Hania, and Bogdan are allowed to skate on the nearby pond. Of course, whenever they show up there, all the other kids from the area come running too, and soon it's so crowded there isn't room to skate.

The company roofer also builds a sled for the little Spiżes, while Bogdan amuses himself constructing a pigeon loft in the attic of the villa. He never gets anywhere with it, because a goshawk stalks the area and each time the flock of pigeons takes wing it ends in tragedy. The company driver, Stanisław Czapla, also allows Bogdan to sit in the passenger seat of their large Soviet-made truck, and whenever he can, he brings the boy along on his route around the restaurants and stores that order their beer from Miedzianka. These trips take them to Szklarska Poręba, Karpacz, Świerzawa, and even Złotoryja and Gryfów Śląski. Small, specially produced barrels of Złoto z Miedzianki—the new, Polish name of Kupferberger Gold—are also sent to the Szwajcarka hostel. The best part of these journeys is not only that he gets to ride around in a giant truck, but he also gets to drink sparkling lemonade, for alongside nearly every brewery is a second bottling plant dedicated to making this delicious treat. It's the same in Miedzianka—after all, until recently old Glyschinsky had his bottling plant right next to the brewery. Bogdan went there many times, and Maximilian was friends with his father. The boy even promised himself that when he grew up he would make sparkling lemonade too, and then he'd have as much as he liked.

2

It's 1959 when *Nowiny Jeleniogórskie* reports: "A worker at the brewery in Miedzianka, Mr. Pisarczyk, has for some time been regularly removing significant quantities of barley from the brewery, unpunished until now. He has been so bold that one night he stole nearly a thousand pounds of barley. But this time his luck ran out. The night guard spotted him carrying barley sacks and alerted the brewmaster, who in turn informed the police station in Janowice. They immediately ordered a search of Mr. Pisarczyk's apartment, revealing 2,800 lbs of barley rightfully belonging to the brewery. Mr. Pisarczyk was arrested and jailed."

A few issues later, the newspaper announces the Jelenia Góra city council has decided to build a new housing project on a fifty-acre plot on Legnicka Street. The complex will feature not only comfortable apartment buildings, but also a retail chain, a movie theater, a restaurant, and all the essential services. The first twenty-five acres are to be finished by 1965. In total, the new project will feature around 1,500 residential units. By March of the next year, the newspaper's editors, along with the presidium of the city council, are organizing a contest to name the housing project. Locals send in several dozen entries. Among those the jury considers are: Bolkogród, Peace and Friendship, Unity, Progress, Żwirko and Wigura (after the famous aviators), and Fawn. The winning proposal is to call the project Piastowskie—after the Piasts, Poland's first ruling dynasty—but it quickly emerges another Piastowskie has just been built thirty miles away in Bolesławiec. The employees of the city health department come to the rescue. In their opinion, the housing project should be named Zabobrze, meaning literally "beyond the Bóbr," since the project will lie across the river from downtown Jelenia Góra. "The following arguments support this proposal: it is formed from the existing, very old Slavic name of the River Bóbr; it is constructed in accordance with Polish naming conventions; and it lends itself to everyday speech," explains the newspaper.

3

Miedzianka has been losing people ever since the closure of the mine. Its population is now around three hundred. Most of them work in the paper mill in Janowice and in linen factories in Marciszów. Some go as far as Jelenia Góra for work. A bus stops in town four times a day. There are more and more abandoned homes here, some fit for demolition, others in need of renovation but which are probably still habitable. Only one store and old Zygmunt Pikus's slaughterhouse are still open. For bread, the people of Miedzianka go to the Miroś family bakery in Janowice Wielkie. They still have the community center, and every week the Farmers' Wives' Association holds dances, which Hanna Spiż helps with.

The township realizes that losing its population will quickly become a problem, and therefore resolves to salvage the situation. In the late fifties, someone in the Industrial Coal Union in Wałbrzych gets the bright idea to renovate a few houses in Miedzianka and settle retired miners there. The climate in the town is healthy, it's peaceful and quiet; if it could only return to self-sufficiency, it would be paradise for retirees.

The first renovations are soon underway. The houses that were in best shape are quickly prettied up. But the retirees never appear, for during construction they discover the majority of the houses stand on unsafe ground. Workers discover collapsed basements and cracked walls, while landslides and sinkholes appear overnight. The plan with the Wałbrzych miners only makes sense if they're able to settle a significant number of seniors here. Moving in only a few would condemn them to barely scraping by under hardly acceptable conditions.

Still, they quickly find takers for the renovated homes—people who have no idea about the mining damage. A final group of settlers arrives in town. They come from central and eastern Poland, and also include repatriates from Ukraine and Belarus.

The Gębuś family lives at number 34. They've come from Częstochowa, 150 miles east. They were unable to find an apartment there because they ran a stall selling devotional items outside the Jasna Góra shrine and one of their sons is a priest. That was all it took for the authorities to make their lives difficult. They rent the building where the pharmacy used to be—from which little Bogdan Spiż took those treasures of his not that long ago. During the war, the building belonged to the pharmacist Kurt Haenisch—one can still make out the faded letters on the front of the building—while before Haenisch, the hunter Rotter lived here. He left a large number of hunting trophies in the attic, including an impressively large twelve-pointer shot years ago. Now, little Hanna Gębuś takes this treasured set of antlers, and her friends make them into brooches and pendants for her.

At more or less the same time, the Kluba family arrives in Miedzianka. They disembark at the station in Janowice weighted down with bundles. Baśka Kluba is five, she's never seen a mountain so steep, so she has a hard time keeping up with her parents. Janek, barely three years old, finds it even harder. Everything seems enormous: the trees growing along the roads and the mountains surrounding the town. When they reach the first buildings in Miedzianka, the local children rush to meet them, and housewives peek out their windows in curiosity. The Kluba family makes for a peculiar sight—two children in shabby clothes with their parents, and each one loaded down with countless bags. The locals stare at them in silence. Then, behind her back, Baśka distinctly hears some words she will never forget:

"The Germans are coming!"

For years to come, that is how she and her family will be known.

Irena Barwicka is one of those who arrive in the town in the late fifties. In 1958, she's still living with her husband in Andreyevichy in Belarus, working on the railroad and living in a pretty apartment inside the station building, where she is raising a one-year-old daughter, Alina. One day her father-in-law comes and says:

"Listen, we're going to Poland. We can't keep living here."

He is a Pole, and ever since he refused to sign up for the kolkhoz, he's found it more and more difficult to farm here. Poland is still accepting repatriates, but the family can't postpone it any longer. Irena sits down at the table with Władek and they think it through. They're doing all right, but without his parents they won't manage. They decide to apply. A few days later they receive a refusal, and Władysław Barwicki is summoned to the NKVD station.

"Well now, Barwicki. Aren't you fond of the *Sovietsky Soyuz*?"

Władek knows if he gives the wrong answer he'll never see Irena again. He explains he was born in Poland and now his parents are going there, and he wants to go so he won't miss them. And that's the only reason. He is refused permission, but they tell him to try in Hrodna. There, he barely opens his mouth before they say: "You have ten days, Comrade, or you'll be stuck here for good." They quickly sell their chickens and their piglet, pack their bags, and get on a train. Meanwhile, a letter arrives from Władek's parents. They say they're living in Miedzianka in Lower Silesia, they have a two-story house and a large field. The letter concludes: "There's no railroad work to be had, but we're doing all right farming."

The journey to Poland takes a few hours—at the border all their Soviet-issued documents are confiscated and they're allowed to continue. The repatriation station is in Biała Podlaska, thirty miles across the border from Brest. The Polish officials ask if the Barwickis know where they want to go and suggest some towns near the German border: Zielona Góra or Gorzów Wielkopolskie.

"We already have family in Miedzianka," they respond. "That's where we're going." Irena receives a ticket and heads west on the local train with Alina. Władek will come later, on a freight train with all their possessions.

Irena Barwicka and little Alina arrive at Janowice station before dinnertime on April 25, 1959. She asks people on their way back from church the way to Miedzianka. They say you have to go up the hill, and once you've passed the brewery, you'll be there. They walk, Alina gathers flowers, Irena looks around the area. They pass the two stone crosses, and then the brewery. Then Irena stops dead in her tracks. The town looks like the Eastern Front just passed through it. Houses with no windows and the doors torn off, debris strewn everywhere. One of the churches is in utter ruin, the second is locked up tight. She asks for the Barwickis and someone shows her the way. When she lays eyes on the house where she is meant to live, she bursts into tears. Her sister-in-law comes running out to her, then Władek's parents. Irena doesn't hold back:

"Where have you dragged us to?! They were sending us to Zielona Góra or Gorzów, to new apartment buildings. Anywhere would be better than here! Even Andreyevichy."

They go inside, but it's no better there. Irena can't get a get a grip on herself, and she's also afraid what Władek will do when he sees the three crumbling, unheated rooms the eight of them will now be packed into. Sure enough, as soon as Władysław Barwicki gets out of the truck loaded with their possessions, he only says to his father through clenched teeth:

"Is this the worst shithole you could find?"

For the next few weeks, Władek doesn't speak a word to him.

4

The first television in Miedzianka stands in the little community center set up in the villa by the brewery. In theory, this space is reserved for the brewers, but in practice everyone in town makes use of it. Bogdan is in charge of operating the TV set. Only he knows how to turn it on and off—he also knows what to do when the reception goes bad, and that it's no use banging your fist on it. The trouble is they only need the boy when they have to fiddle around with something on the TV. The moment a picture lights up the glass screen, the grown-ups kick the boy out. But Bogdan knows how to stand up for himself. When the picture suddenly cuts out in the middle of a murder mystery, everyone shouts for him to come. He decides he's going to preemptively act offended, and stubbornly refuse to do anything for a good fifteen minutes. Finally, after they've promised he can stay, he once again twiddles this knob or that. From that day forth no one pushes their luck, and the boy has a guaranteed front-row seat.

Baśka Spiż also knows how to capitalize on the potential the town's only TV offers. She decides to collect ten złotys for entry from each of the children who come to watch the evening kids' shows. She's exposed that very night, when the little ones come home crying and their outraged mothers descend on the Spiżes' house. Baśka has to go around all the houses in town and return the money, and she gets a whipping from her father on top of it. That's a rare occurrence, for Stefan Spiż is a calm and level-headed man. In fact, he's a quiet and extremely mild stoic. No one in town remembers ever seeing the brewmaster angry, and few can even recall Spiż raising his voice. Every time he has to give Baśka or Bogdan a spanking, he'll come to them that evening and explain:

"If I spanked you it's only because you did something bad. But I love you and I don't want you to do bad things. Do you understand?"

Mama is a completely different story. The employees even joke that Stefan is the brewmaster, but Helena is the one to be afraid of. She's an energetic woman, confident and decisive. She's capable of whacking you upside the head or wiping the floor with you. They occasionally get the feeling she's got Stefan wrapped around her little finger. But it's all appearances, and Stefan is no innocent himself—he's quite the drinker, and at the brewery there's even a motto with the employees use to start their day. As soon as the brewmaster arrives they shout, "Pour the beer, the boss is here!" Then almost the whole team sits down together, and if it's cold in the yard, they warm up the fresh beer in special canisters immersed in hot water. Along with the beer, Stefan likes to eat two or even three raw eggs. Only after thus fortifying himself may work begin. He drops into the brewhouse a couple times over the course of the day. Friends of his, township officials, and policemen are constantly showing up at the brewery. He has to have a drink with each of them. Here, beer is just a drink like any other. They have a drink before their midmorning snack, then a chilled one to quench their thirst in the heat. On days when too many acquaintances pass through, even Stefan gets a little tipsy. When he does, Helena gets mad at him. The children never forget their parents' arguments. As a rule, they hear their mother's shouting and their father's soothing tone.

Their parents' arguments are probably also caused by the rumors that periodically make their way around town. People gossip that if Stefan Spiż is going to hire a girl in the brewery, the girl has to be pretty, or else she's got no chance of getting a job.

Baśka Sobieś is pretty, but it isn't her beauty that gets her a job in the brewery. It's a referral from the employment office, where she signed on right after graduating from school. They checked her registered place of residence—Miedzianka—and therefore sent her to the only industrial facility in town. Her job is to ferment the beer, and as soon as she arrives at the brewery, people start to whisper. This is perhaps because Stefan Spiż is particularly effusive in his praise of her. When inspectors from Wałbrzych come visit the facility one day, Spiż introduces the girl fermenting, saying:

"And this is Baśka, my prettiest employee!"

Anyone who doesn't know the brewmaster very well might think there's something more behind these compliments. Such gossip falls on fertile ground—occasionally so fertile that it causes a scandal. There's beautiful Adela, who's been working in the brewery for some time—she was transferred from a brewery in Lwówek Śląski to work in Miedzianka. She works in the office, and therefore often spends time with Stefan. People talk about them constantly, and point their fingers at Adela in town. Finally, she can't take any more of it—she quits her job in tears, and leaves Miedzianka.

Then there's Werka Butyńska. People gossip about her too. Werka came from the East, she lives in Janowice and has a little child, but she doesn't have a man, because as soon as he learned he was going to be a father, her man fled Poland. She was left on her own, unemployed and with a child to support. On Christmas Day of 1965, it even made her want to kill herself. She was changing her child's diaper when her uncle came home. Werka asked him to close the door, since a blizzard was raging outside, and the little one might catch cold from the draft.

"You've had one kid already, you slut," came the reply. "So if that one bites the dust, you'll just pop out another." She snatched up the child and ran to her attic bedroom. She laid the child on the bed and pulled some pills out of a drawer. She intended to swallow them all, but couldn't work up the courage. She looked at the little baby lying beside her and resolved that whatever her life might look like, it would not end that day.

None other than Stefan Spiż lends Werka a helping hand, offering her a job in the brewery and not minding if the young mother brings her baby to work. They lay out some sheepskin bedding in the hop kiln—it's warm and dry there, and there are always people around, so the workers keep a constant eye on the little kid. When Sławek gets bigger, they make him their mascot and he's the darling of all the staff.

Werka is beloved in the brewery. She throws herself into her work and impresses the men by being able to lift a 110-pound sack of barley on her back and carry it to the third floor all on her own. Then when it's time to drive to Janowice and unload supplies from the cargo train, Werka gets in the truck and goes along with the others, just like a man. But what sticks in most of their minds is when Werka shovels the brewers' grain drying in the basement wearing nothing but her underwear. It's so hot down there, especially in summer, that the only way to work is half-naked. So when it's time for Werka to go down to the basement, Stefan Spiż orders all the men out of there. The most curious ones try to peek through the basement windows, so sometimes Stefan will quietly sneak up on them and tan their hides with a stick he keeps on hand for such occasions. Maybe that encourages the village gossip about a fiery romance between Werka and the brewmaster.

All this chatter reaches Helena Spiż, meaning that when Stefan gets home from work he has to put up with her swearing at him. One of these fights even ends in a temporary separation—for a few days, Stefan is banned from the house, while Helena is not allowed onto the grounds of the brewery. Yet the workers suffer most, especially when it comes to keeping her out—caught between a rock and a hard place, they dread getting in the brewmaster's bad books, but lack the courage to go up against headstrong Helena. But in time everyone's anger subsides and all is as it was.

5

In 1962, Bogdan and Baśka Spiż finish grade school and Bogdan decides to remain true to his boyhood resolution: to have a lemonade bottling plant. While there are no technical high schools teaching lemonade-making, there is a brewing school in Tychy, outside Katowice. Baśka has a harder time because she keeps changing her mind. One moment she wants to be a teacher, the next, a nurse. She has a hard time coming to grips with it. Finally, she chooses neither, deciding instead—at her brother's encouragement—to go off to Tychy as well. The brewery in Lwówek Śląski, which their father's facility in Miedzianka is a branch of, covers their tuition and accommodation. The agreement is simple—the brewery is investing in their education, so once they've graduated they will work in Lwówek Śląski or Miedzianka.

They leave that August. From now on, they'll see Miedzianka rarely—twice a year, for the holidays and on summer vacation, but only when they haven't got work placements to do in other breweries. The whole Spiż family leaves town for a few months in the fall anyway. Stefan is tasked with taking over production in Lwówek Śląski, and while he is away, Jerzy Słowiński takes over as brewmaster. He subscribes to the same principles as Stefan Spiż:

the secret of good beer is order, order, and order once again. The next-most important thing is high-quality water—and that is starting to run out in Miedzianka. Each year, the brewery produces over a quarter-million gallons of beer, meeting one-fifth of the demand from the thirsty inhabitants of the region: each citizen of Jeleniogórskie County drinks as much as twelve gallons of the amber-colored brew a year. Setting aside children and the very elderly, it works out that the average county resident in the prime of their life drinks fifty-three gallons of beer per year. So brewing definitely has a future—the question is whether that future lies in Miedzianka. The brewery's water intake is unable to meet the demands of the facility, and more and more, Słowiński has to resort to the municipal aqueduct. Maybe that's why he talks from time to time about the possibility the brewery might close, though no one who's tasted the beer from Miedzianka takes that rumor seriously. After all, this is the only brewery in the region. Miedzianka's beer has always taken pride of place at provincial beer-tasting contests, where Stefan Spiż is often asked the secret of its exquisite flavor. With an impish grin, he answers that success lies in maintaining the right temperature and in the quality of the water used to produce beer in Miedzianka. He prefers not to mention his three principles of beer production to journalists or his competitors.

6

In 1963, the cherry tree in the Czaplas' garden disappears. It's July, but rain is pouring down like it's October. Vacationers are wandering aimlessly around Janowice or packing their bags and making a run for it. Rivulets flow down from the peak of the mountain. Some reach as far as the river, which turns brown and muddy; others get lost somewhere on the way. People already know what this means, and don't take their eyes off the ground beneath their feet—a long rain bodes ill here more than anywhere else. The ground becomes saturated and heavy.

Early one morning, old Czapla comes to see Jerzy Słowiński, who looks depressed. Right now Czapla is meant to be driving a shipment of beer twenty-five miles to Złotoryja, and the truck is already loaded up.

"I'm not going, Mr. Słowiński, I'm not coming into work at all today. I'm not coming because the cherry tree in my garden has disappeared on me."

They go look. The cherry tree used to be there and now it's gone. There's just a hole in the ground with water pouring in. And if you shine a flashlight into the hole, you can make out the top of a little tree with a few cherries no kids had managed yet to pick. Some kids stand at the edge of the hole too, gazing down in silence. Mrs. Czapla just keeps holding her head in her hands and thanking God all this didn't happen at night, because the whole family had to walk past that cherry tree to get to the outhouse.

"Just think, if anyone had gone out there at night, they'd have been buried alive," she says.

They wait a few more days for the tree at the bottom of the hole to stop sinking completely, then old Czapla takes a van from the brewery and gets some rubble to bury the tree. For a month, he keeps on dumping in rubble until there's no trace of the hole.

All that happens after that is is Mrs. Czapla goes around asking people for a little fruit to make preserves, telling everyone that, after all, their cherry tree is a long way underground.

7

Kazimierz Milcuszek is in charge of educating Miedzianka's children. He first comes to town back in the early sixties. He enjoys hiking, often driving into the Giant Mountains and periodically to the Rudawy Janowickie range as well. He's a loner, traversing most of the trails on his own. When he arrives in Miedzianka, the town doesn't make a positive impression. Milcuszek later says it had the stench of something coming to an end.

When he finishes his teacher's training in Wrocław, he decides to look for work in Jelenia Góra. At the time there are no positions open there, but the little school in Miedzianka is urgently seeking a teacher. Perhaps more reluctantly than not, Kazimierz Milcuszek becomes its schoolmaster. The school has four grades with as many as sixty children. The number goes down year after year. There are, however, some Roma coming in. Kazimierz Milcuszek has a bit of a tough time with them, because the Romani children aren't especially inclined to learn or stay in class when they're supposed to. Yet rather than punishing them, he decides to implement a carrot and stick approach. So he buys all sorts of musical instruments—from cymbals and drums to triangles and hi-hats. He shows them to the Romani children, who can hardly wait to play them. But he strikes a deal with them: they can't play the noisy instruments until their third and fourth breaks, and on the condition that they sit attentively in every class beforehand. This scheme eliminates the truancy problem among the Roma, though of course that doesn't mean it's gone from the school in Miedzianka entirely. Periodically gales so buffet the hill that entire classes are unable to make it to school.

Mustering their innate talent, the Roma attain such a level of musical artistry that they soon grace every one of the school—and even the township—assemblies with their playing and dancing, earning admiration and acclaim from their audiences. But it never occurs to them the people of Miedzianka will come to remember them for a different reason.

While the children go to school in Miedzianka, and the older children and teenagers go to schools in Janowice and Jelenia Góra, preschool care is a problem for those who need it, since neither Miedzianka nor any village in the area has one. Mothers are therefore forced to cope with their tiny tots on their own. It isn't a problem for those who don't have jobs, but most women in Miedzianka go to work in the linen factories in Marciszów. So their children stay home alone or are looked after by a neighbor or relative.

One such child is Urszulka Wyka. Her mother Helena Wyka works three shifts in Marciszów, so the neighbors and her mother's sister look after the little girl. But on October 12, 1965, there's no one home. Two-year-old Urszulka gets into a small kitchen cabinet and pulls out a bottle of gasoline. The bottle is only partly closed, and in a few moments the child has covered herself in its stinking contents. Tragedy strikes when she reaches for the matches. Urszulka's clothes don't burst into flame, but they smolder for around half an hour. The locals don't realize what's happening until smoke starts pouring out of the apartment. The women next door raise the alarm, break down the door, and rush in. Urszulka is lying on the floor, badly burned. Only her turtleneck sweater didn't catch, and the flames haven't damaged her face. The doctors called to the scene don't know how to handle the child without making the pain worse. Urszulka survives for another few hours. Nearly all the townspeople come to the funeral, many bringing small bouquets of white flowers—the kind the little girl most loved gathering around their house.

8

It says in *Nowiny* that they're going to film the hit World War II-themed TV show *Four Tank-Men and a Dog* in Miedzianka. It's 1968, and Irena Siuta, the wife of a respected local doctor, has just become the new head of the township in Janowice. Before moving to Janowice, she was a teacher in Jelenia Góra. People say she's Russian. Irena Siuta knows nothing about a possible visit from the jolly tank crew—she's new here, she doesn't know anyone, and anyway, decisions like that are made at the county, or even provincial, level. It wouldn't have been hard for anyone up there to argue in favor of bringing the film crews to town. There is probably nowhere in the region with so many ruins, nor any Lower Silesian town that looks so much as though the air raids had just ended. This in a place where, in actual fact, not a single bomb fell.

The ruins keep causing more trouble. At night, some buildings let out hair-raising noises, they crack, creak, and groan. People are now saying the houses have started to sing. So at night they lie in bed, close their eyes, and listen closely. Those who can't stand their houses' nighttime groans any longer pay a visit to the township. They demand action—no one wants to live in a ruin. Finally, a commission on mining damage comes to town all the way from Katowice. They roam from building to building, entering basements and peering into attics. They find something almost everywhere—cracked walls at the Barwickis', bent windows at the Majeks', and at the Żureks', a roof that only by some miracle hasn't fallen on someone's head, because it's hard to work out what's holding it up. In a few backyards, the inspectors pause in amazement, gazing terrified into the black caverns that open up here after each heavy rain.

The commission finds the ground under the town can be fortified and the old mine drifts secured. In practical terms, this means pumping an almost unimaginable quantity of cement into the ground. No one here has the time for that, much less the money. Besides, no one knows exactly how many of these drifts there are. It would be an enormous job—practically speaking, an impossible one. In one article on the subject in *Nowiny*, the paper admits plainly: "Cost, excessive—purpose, none."

There's an easier solution—to resettle, as quickly as possible, the people whose houses could collapse at any moment. Resettle them where? That's not the mining damage commission's problem. But it is still a problem, and not a small one at that.

First, people start migrating within the town. Over a dozen families receive orders to vacate their buildings immediately. These are the ones whose houses have been singing the loudest.

They move where there is less mining damage or none at all. The western part of town—where the school, a few small houses, the Spiżes' yellow villa, and the brewery are located—is holding up best. But available spaces in Miedzianka soon begin running out, and people don't want to be packed into poky little apartments. The first townspeople start looking for places to live in Janowice. They want to stay in the area.

The abandoned buildings fall into even greater ruin. People from neighboring villages come to Miedzianka for free bricks and wood, which are at hand here in abundance. All you have to do is go into one of the abandoned houses and take what you need. No one watches over the ruins—there are two policemen in the entire township, and they prefer not to venture into Miedzianka. People start thinking of the town as the Wild West, giving shelter to smugglers, vagrants, and wandering Roma. *Nowiny* even reports on the peculiar entertainments of the local youth:

"WHAT A WORTHLESS STORE: To the Editors: There is a grocery store in Miedzianka that sells wine to the fifth graders from the elementary school. The store clerks encourage the boys to buy alcohol, which they then consume in the nearby ruins and drunkenly accost passersby, throwing stones at them."

"WINE ONLY ON RATION CARDS: To the Editors: In response to the letter criticizing the store in Miedzianka for selling alcohol to minors, I wish to explain I sold wine to a boy who had brought his mother's ration card with instructions to purchase wine."

"FROM THE EDITORS: Madam, it would be better for you to sell the child bread or butter on his mother's card, not wine."

It sadly begins to occur to the town's two hundred permanent residents that their days in Miedzianka are numbered. Rumors also start up that the whole town will be resettled in the new housing project in Jelenia Góra: Zabobrze. Apparently there's a plan to squeeze them all into two, maybe three apartment buildings.

9

There are different kinds of mud—there's watery, fluid, overflowing mud with the consistency of oil paint that covers everything dipped into it in a thin, shimmering layer. There's also spring mud, heavy and clay-like, which sticks to a person's boots so that after only a few steps they must stop and somehow free their feet before they can continue. Then there's frozen mud, hard as rock, the kind that can twist an ankle or break the heel of an inattentive pedestrian, because, accustomed to soft mud, they resign themselves to plunging their foot in. Then at last there's ultimate mud, where a person halts at its edge and gazes at it, knowing that they will have to find another way to get to the other side, to "the far bank." In the worst cases, there is no way around it. Ultimate mud is what they have most in Zabobrze.

From the very beginning, the residents of the housing project have fought heroically to survive. The first ones moved in as long ago as 1965. The next few buildings were occupied over the next three years. In the project, a surrealism prevails that is entirely in keeping with the era of its construction. For instance, when the weather begins turning cold in 1967, it quickly becomes apparent that the construction teams forgot to connect a few buildings to the boiler house. Now they have people living in them, but hooking them up will take a few weeks.

Besides that, everyone in the new project has problems with their heating. They freeze in October and January, while in May they complain the boilers are running full blast and it's unbearable in the apartments. There's also trouble with the water. The rule is: the higher up you live, the later you bathe. Tenants on the first few floors can start thinking about a bath by around eight o'clock in the evening, while those on the top floors don't do their dishes or wash until after midnight, when the pressure in the pipes has built up and the water has made it to their floors. Of course that's assuming this time a muddy, reeking fluid doesn't dribble out of the taps—which happens fairly frequently here.

The editors of *Nowiny* keep dedicating more space to the project. Letters from upset residents of Zabobrze arrive almost daily:

"A year ago I moved into the building at 12 Szymanowski Street. I found the drain in the kitchen clogged with plaster. I called the plumbers and they brought an old-fashioned snake, and while they were trying to push it through, it broke. Five feet of it was stuck in the pipe, but the plumber said it wouldn't do any harm because the coil would rot away. The sink still did not work, however, and water started flowing into my neighbor's kitchen. I complained once again and received an appointment on March 20 at 8:10. It's now July, and no one has come yet."

"The basement of the recently finished building on Szymanowski Street is already flooded with water. It turns out the drains are clogged and the gutters don't work. I asked for them to be checked out. The super told me I had to wait for it to rain. Before it could rain, a pile of building materials was laid on top of the drain. There was no question of having it checked out."

"There's a drying room on Szymanowski Street, but it has no heater, which is why laundry rarely gets done in the building, especially considering there's no water."

"Even though building 5 has only been standing for six months, our laundry room is out of order. When we raised the matter with the administration, they told us there was a shortage of burners for the gas rings. As he was leaving, the repairman advised us to stop complaining about the laundry room, since we could wash our clothes in the river."

"Gaps are appearing in the walls of fairly recently built rooms, running in a zigzag from floor to ceiling, wide enough to hand each other soap and other items through them."

"A window in our apartment between the kitchen and the living room simply fell out. Meanwhile the parquet floor has dried out so much that gaps of an inch or more have formed in it, the radiators have been leaking for two years, and every three or four days the bathroom floods with filth. There's absolutely no way we can go on in this freezing, stinking apartment."

*

Theoretically Zabobrze is part of Jelenia Góra, but residents have to trek as far as two miles along the shoulder of a busy highway to get downtown. There's no bridge over the river connecting it to the new neighborhood. Meanwhile, the lightest drizzle drowns them all in mud, because despite the first buildings being finished, the project is still a giant construction site. In fact, there's nothing here besides the apartment buildings—no phone booth, preschool, or post office. The project was assigned to a postal zone far on the other side of town. The residents and the mailmen curse whoever thought up that idea, since they have to walk almost four miles to collect a registered delivery. They could take a taxi, but Zabobrze has no taxi stand. When one finally is built, the taxi drivers don't want to wait there, because too often driving to the project results in broken suspension or some other damage. No wonder the residents jokingly call their project *Zabłocie*: "beyond the mud."

There are also problems procuring basic groceries. Despite several hundred families living there, and the target being several thousand, there still isn't even the tiniest vegetable stand, to say nothing of the promised shopping pavilion. The residents haul all their purchases from town. When the first grocery stand opens in Zabobrze, soon followed by additional shops and retail units, a new wave of letters makes its way to the editors of *Nowiny*.

"Observing the two clerks at the grocery stand in Zabobrze, customers standing in the long line feel like they are watching a slow-motion movie about labor heroes whose greatest joy in life is work."

"We're glad to finally have a stall with vegetables in Zabobrze, but it saddens us that the seller is unscrupulous. He not only hands you your vegetables with his hands dirty and mud under his fingernails, he also reaches them into the sauerkraut and pickle barrels. We suggest the health inspector address this."

"The man running the fruit and vegetable stand in Zabobrze is a real shark. He systematically refuses to weigh potatoes in the nylon bags the customers bring, saying they 'have their own weight.' But then he loads expensive items into a filthy bowl, which we think very much 'has its own weight' itself."

"On April 13 I waited six hours for a haircut in the ladies' section of the hairdresser. Mrs. Litwin the hairstylist took care of a whole string of customers who apparently had appointments, ignoring me. It's a shame she didn't tell me right away there was no point in waiting."

"On August 22 I wanted to buy two pounds of lemons. The saleswoman told me I would only get them if I bought a grapefruit at the same time."

In spite of all these annoyances, officially Zabobrze is paradise and the salvation of Jelenia Góra. The town's population has skyrocketed ever since industry started up here, and the ex-German apartment buildings downtown have long since been bursting at the seams. Jelenia Góra also attracts people from the nearby towns—work is easier to find here, there are more schools, there are cinemas and a theater. But Jelenia Góra is more than that for people from Miedzianka. It's the dream of leaving a ghost town where the houses groan and where after every heavy rainfall, you have to check before leaving the house whether there's still a scrap of land outside to set your feet on (while going out at night is highly inadvisable). They already know their town will disappear soon. They also know the township has managed to buy two whole buildings in Zabobrze, numbers 9 and 11. Soon more will be added: 37, 39, and 45. The money to purchase them comes from compensation for the mining damage, paid to the township by the the Mining Industry Union, which oversees the abandoned mines in Miedzianka. Theoretically, this money should be spent saving the town, but the township prohibits renovating the crumbling buildings. Few people believe anything is salvageable here.

10

There are very few people who want to stay. Staszek Pławiak says he won't budge even if he's left alone among Miedzianka's ruins. He doesn't know that that is almost exactly what will happen. For now, he has plenty of fields and a barn full of cows, and he finds leaving all this for an apartment in a cramped building simply unimaginable. So for the time being, the Pławiaks constantly change houses, living successively at numbers 88, 46, 75, and 44. But every house where they try to live is fit for demolition, so an eviction notice arrives and they occupy yet another house abandoned by people who've left for Zabobrze.

Old Mrs. Płaksa, who lives in the school building, doesn't want to move out either. The last schoolmaster, Kazimierz Milcuszek, was one of the first to depart. He settled in building 9.

The Spiżes don't leave either. Helena and Stefan are now arguing routinely and the whole town knows about it, but on this matter they remain remarkably of one mind. They absolutely will not move away from Miedzianka. Their situation is easier than others'—there is almost no mining damage under the part of town where the brewery and villa stand, nothing is crumbling down here, the houses don't sing, so they can stay without fear. But they know that when the town disappears, the brewery will go too. There will be no one to work in it, and after all, transporting workers to the middle of nowhere won't be profitable for anyone. Whether Stefan likes it or not, the brewery's days are numbered. The employees, most of them living in the town, know it too. They'll only work in the brewery as long as they live here. No one plans to commute to Miedzianka from Jelenia Góra, especially because the bus service linking the two towns now only runs twice a day. Baśka, his "prettiest employee," realizes all this. She's just married Janek Majka, and as a wedding present from Stefan they received a keg of the finest beer. Now the Majkas are expecting a child.

The anxious atmosphere infects everyone, even the hitherto self-possessed Stefan. Despite Baśka's advanced pregnancy, the brewmaster orders her to carry heavy sacks of barley. The employees watch with disbelief, yet no one protests. Baśka does her best to argue, but it's no use, they both quickly go from talking to shouting. No one has ever seen the brewmaster like this before. Baśka runs out of the brewery in tears, and Stefan slams the door furiously.

After a while, Józef Sobieś—Baśka's father and a good friend of Stefan's—shows up at the brewery. He takes Stefan outside and screams in his face at the top of his lungs.

"And if you ever order her to carry sacks again, you son of a bitch, I'll fix you so good you'll never work another day in your life," he says on his way out, and Stefan searches for his hat in the deep snow. Sobieś is in the Party, he knows people who could help him follow through on his threat. For his part, Stefan knows he's gone too far. Both men realize the incident has relieved the tension. Soon they'll meet again over a beer, feeling no resentment toward each other.

In 1969, the Barwickis leave. All it took was letting the damage commission into their house and receiving an eviction notice. It was the same with old Mrs. Majka, Janek's mother—she left the same year, and now lives in Zabobrze in building 11. The next year, departures include the Klubas, who were taken for Germans twelve years before, and the Żureks, who not long ago were glad to get a new loft apartment on the town square. The loft soon started singing. For the past two years, Janina Żurek has had trouble sleeping, because instead of dozing off she would stare at the ceiling, thinking it could collapse on her at any moment. For the Żureks, the Barwickis, and a dozen or so other families, moving to Zabobrze is true salvation and relief.

11

After finishing technical school and completing his work placements, Bogdan Spiż joins the army. He was drafted right after graduation, and he traded a keg of beer to arrange for his service to be in Jelenia Góra. Bogdan's nickname there is "Miedzianka." Sometimes Private Miedzianka is given a rather peculiar mission—to zip up to his father's brewery on a motorcycle and sneak out a small keg, then bring it back to his unit at breakneck speed. He's not even aware stealing beer is a long-standing tradition here, set in motion by the young Georg Franzky. Thanks to top-quality beer facilitating good relations within the unit, Bogdan's military service passes pleasantly. But as his discharge approaches, Bogdan thinks more and more of streamlining the brewery his father runs.

When he returns to Miedzianka for good, he finally has time to examine the place closely. He knew it was emptying out, and kept seeing more familiar faces on the streets of Jelenia Góra. Yet not until walking its devastated lanes does he come to grips with the scale of what his father has been so pained to tell him. Only a dozen or so houses bear no signs of damage. The remainder are missing windows, doors, beams; some even lack entire walls. The township has ordered warning signs placed on some of the ruins, saying entry can result in death. In some, you must cross through a ruined first floor to reach the second floor, where there are people living. Flowerpots on the windowsills tell you not to take any load-bearing beams from inside. In 1971, barely over a hundred people live in Miedzianka, the clear majority of whom are Romani. They were resettled from Płoszczyna, ten miles away, as per regulations ordering the settlement of the Roma population and prohibiting their nomadic lifestyle. The Roma have occupied uninhabited buildings, but they assure people they won't stay here long and will soon move on.

In the first wave of departures in 1968 and 1969, scores of people move away. Their houses remain unoccupied. The community center, where not so long ago Helena Spiż threw raucous Saturday parties, is closed. There are no stores in town—the last one shut down due to unprofitability. Nearly every conversation touches on the subject of decline. No one kids themselves that the town can be saved, and people speak with a certain respect for those who've decided to stay in the face of adversity.

Bogdan is one of those. Baśka Spiż got herself a boyfriend and a job in Wałbrzych; she didn't want to go back to Miedzianka anymore. Bogdan, on the contrary, sees all his dreams fulfilled in the brewery his father runs. He has the proper education and manages to introduce a few innovations at the facility. His father allows him to do so, only supervising the most important matters and giving advice when necessary. Collaborating like this is a golden opportunity for Bogdan, while Stefan gets to hand off some tiresome tasks.

However, the young brewer's ambitions are out of step with what headquarters in Lwówek Śląski intends; they inform the Spiżes straight out that the brewery will not survive the town's liquidation. No surprise, then, that headquarters is furious when at the start of the 1970s, Bogdan sends special, unmarked bottles of his beer to the brewing fairs in Munich. Złoto Miedzianki wins a high second place in the tastings. When it emerges the beer was sent from behind the Iron Curtain, a small international scandal breaks out. The phones in Lwówek Śląski and Miedzianka ring off the hook and the people in charge at headquarters go ballistic, because the victory of the Spiżes' beer undermines their argument for shutting down the brewery. Bogdan receives immediate orders to dispose of all the bottles specially produced for the occasion, along with the beer inside. So he calls up his friends, the three of them sit down, and over more than twelve hours they dispose of the beer nonstop. One of them, Bogdan Markowski, will later say that never again in his entire life did he have a hangover like the one from disposing of beer in the brewery on the mountaintop.

"Disposing of all that left us pretty indisposed," he adds with a roguish grin.

1 2

On May 13, 1972, the final decree is signed. The provincial assembly in Wrocław resolves to liquidate the town of Miedzianka. The document includes a schedule of demolition activities. The brewery is to be closed that same year, and the final inhabitants are to depart by the end of 1973. Thereafter, the town will be demolished in three stages—first the buildings will be dismantled, then the debris will be shipped out along with larger pieces of the foundations, and finally a forest will be planted here.

The last families leave Miedzianka on schedule, in 1973. One of them is the "prettiest employee in the brewery"—Baśka Majka, with her husband and her young son. They learn they've been allocated an apartment on March 19, during her father's name-day party. Right then they're sitting in a bar in Janowice, when someone from the township bursts in bearing flowers.

"Józef, as a name-day present today, you're getting three apartments in Zabobrze, for you and both your daughters."

Józef Sobieś cries, although perhaps not for joy. Nothing in the world would make him want to move to the city—he would be fine in Miedzianka if not for the fear that something might collapse on him at any moment. Baśka and Janek think differently. For them, Miedzianka is a real source of concern. They've been waiting eagerly for an allocation, and are actually living out of their suitcases. Before May is over, they rent a dilapidated Volkswagen Beetle and move into the apartment building at 45 Karlowicz Street. They get an apartment on the fifth floor. For a few years to come they'll set their alarm for one in the morning, so they can get up and, half-asleep, take a bath. In spite of this, they never regret making the exchange.

That year anther few families move out of Miedzianka—the Chutyrkos, the Mądreckis, the Wędzels. Even the Roma disappear: some go to neighboring villages—Trzcińsko, Janowice, Radomierz; others head off to Kowary; and yet others scatter off elsewhere in Poland.

Now the only ones in the town are those who've decided to stay despite the authorities' urging. That amounts to around a dozen people: the Spiżes, the Pławiaks, the Płaksas, the Łuczaks, and also the Dudeks beside the road to Ciechanowice. Their houses aren't threatened by the mine damage, and the authorities can only make the case that after the liquidation of the town they will remain here alone, in the absolute wilderness, with no means of survival. However, those arguments do not convince them.

To make things worse, one of the stone crosses placed here centuries ago disappears from the side of the road leading to Janowice. Who knows why the thieves were tempted by the one without the faint inscription. Maybe they took the cross at night and didn't notice the difference. Or maybe they wanted to take both, but someone chased them away. One way or the other, now only one cross has been left by the roadside, with *Memento* carved on the crosspiece. Soon after, one of the local farmers will move it to a completely different place, on a balk on the opposite side of the road.

At the end of 1972, a deafening noise draws the last inhabitants of the town out of their houses. An enormous excavator is climbing up the road from Janowice toward Miedzianka, and behind it comes a truck full of workers. They stop in the square and go off in all directions, examining, knocking on walls, and gesticulating vigorously.

Bogdan Spiż watches them. No, he no longer has any illusions; this is the end now. He just doesn't know how he's going to tell his father.

WHOSE FAULT

"EVERYBODY WHO'S SUPPOSED TO KNOW already does, and people remember. Everything went to ruin. But that's not all that happened, is it? Mrs. Siuta, the doctor's wife, the big fancy lady, she smelled business and that was it for our town. She did so well for herself on Miedzianka's misfortune all you can do is envy her. And that's why people hate her so much.

"Siuta was a Russky, from the East, she showed up out of the blue to cover up all the remains of what the Russians had left behind. She made herself out to be this fancy lady, just like her mother was, who was actually never Polish to begin with.

"There were two kinds of people who believed in the Communists: the ones who believed because they were poor, and the ones who believed because it was more comfortable that way. She didn't know what poverty was, and the government never did her any harm. So take a guess why she was such a Red.

"For a while she had a cover working in a school, teaching Russian, but before long they made her head of the township.

After that she ran Karpacz and was a governor. People were scared of her, they said she had friends on the Central Committee itself, even in Moscow, since that's where she came from, after all. And now she had instructions from them on how to wipe away every trace of the town. Nothing left but bushes—and sure enough, that's all our doctor's wife left us with.

"Mrs. Siuta demolished Miedzianka and if not for her, the town would still be there today. There were even plans to fix up the empty houses and settle retirees from Wałbrzych here, and since they'd made plans, that means nothing was caving in. The damage was just a pretext for her to send in the demolition squads.

"By '69, it had started. They tore down house after house. They used bricks from Miedzianka not only to build houses for teachers in Janowice, but to build the Palace of Culture in Warsaw, too. The train carrying the bricks was waiting at the siding next to Stare Janowice and they unloaded the trucks there."

"We called her 'our Mrs. Siuta,' although she wasn't one of us, and she certainly wasn't a lady. Except that she was pretty, her face made up, her hair done, and she drove around in a car.

"She had an insatiable appetite for antiques—as soon as she got her eye on something, she was liable to come into a stranger's house and take it. But back then you didn't say no to people in authority, so folks just handed things over. She collected a whole house's worth of those antiques and then sold them all over the place. She made a pretty penny selling Miedzianka too. She couldn't have built a house on the river with her township salary."

"I've got nothing against her, because she didn't do me any harm, personally. But everyone will remember her for trying to sell the bells in Radomierz for scrap. She drove there herself to take them down, she only brought this beanpole of a guy with her, but that was more than people would take and they weren't having it. That day the whole village turned out. They made a giant scene. Mrs. Siuta got up on a ladder, so people pulled her down. You can't take down Catholic bells, especially antique ones, but she was a Communist and she didn't get that. It wasn't until they chased her away with pitchforks that she gave up, got in her car, and went. We never forgave her for those bells."

"The Gypsies took Miedzianka apart, and Mrs. Siuta, the president of the township, brought them here specifically to do that. The way it happened was the Gypsies would get moved into an empty house and they'd live there until they'd burned everything up. They tore up the floors, steps, parquet blocks, and window frames, and burned it all on the first floor. If there were no stoves left in the house, then they would light their campfires right on the kitchen floor. When there was nothing left of the house anymore, the Gypsies would tear off the roof as well, then move on to the next one. House after house like that.

"The buildings the Gypsies finished off would get torn down by demolition squads. This great big excavator would come, we called it Big Bertha, it would hook its bucket on a window and tear the walls down, one by one. Then the workers would go in and pick out the good bricks. And then Big Bertha would raze it all to the ground."

"Miedzianka really was caving in, but no building caved in from below, it was all from above. The mine had nothing to do with it. For a few years the town was a source of free construction materials for the whole region. Whoever needed bricks came to Miedzianka and took them for themselves, as many as they needed. I built myself a coal hole behind my house with them, it's there to this day, because that was good brick the Germans left behind. Quite a few houses in Janowice were built from that brick.

"And it's not true the Gypsies finished the town off. There were dozens of buildings there, so how many Gypsies would there have to have been to take care of it all by themselves? They only wrecked the town as much as the other residents did. Someone would be living on the first floor and be so cold that they'd go upstairs, tear up a piece of the floor or saw off one of the roof beams, and burn it in the stove. And when water started pouring in on their heads or the walls started cracking they'd go to the township and ask to be allocated somewhere new to live. Miedzianka was the Wild West, and a ruin."

"The Gypsies finished off the whole town. Mrs. Siuta brought them in. And they were top dogs here for a good few years."

"They were the ones who finished off all the buildings?"

"Sure were, building after building, they'd move into the empty ones and wreck them."

"How many Gypsies were there?"

"Two families came, first they lived in the manor house, but they multiplied fast and after a year, Gypsies made up half the people in Miedzianka, until the Poles started fighting back, because they were running the whole town into the ground."

"Were they causing problems?"

"In the church, the one that's gone now, they butchered horses on the sacred altar! Old Mirga would lead a horse inside, whack it on the head with this great big club, slit its throat, and the horse would bleed to death. Then they'd cut the horse into big pieces and kids would run home with the meat still steaming. They cooked the meat in laundry cauldrons, and the whole of Miedzianka stank of burning horsemeat."

"Did you see this?"

"No, but everyone in town said the Mirgas were slaughtering horses in the Catholic church. The blood would flow down the steps into the street."

"People were tricked out of their houses. Mrs. Siuta would come and say the building was getting renovated, so the residents would be moved into another one. As soon as the people were out, the bulldozers would show up and knock it all down.

"Then, when they were running out of empty buildings to move people into, they resettled a dozen or so families in apartment buildings in Zabobrze. They said it was only for a year, while the renovations were going on. People believed them and only took essentials from Miedzianka. And when they came back a year later, there was no trace of the town or their houses, just tall grass."

"People didn't want to leave the town, because it was beautiful there and there were no cave-ins. But the government had made up its mind and there was nothing to be done, we just had to pack up and go. Some they relocated to Janowice, but when there was a shortage of apartments there, they bought two buildings in Zabobrze and squeezed us all in there. And right after that they leveled Miedzianka to the ground, so there wouldn't be any trace of the mine."

"She was more of an icicle than a woman. If someone had something to sort out with the township, they'd rather go to Słowińska than Mrs. Siuta. People were scared of her; besides which, she wasn't from here and who knows who was pulling her strings. But her husband had a warm heart, he was a doctor, and for a few years he rode his bike in the Peace Race. Everyone was amazed at what a grip she must have had for him to stick with her. Dr. Siuta was always there for you, he'd even come in the middle of the night and not ask for any money. Maybe she wasn't so bad either, maybe she just had to do what they ordered in the county or the province. But what does it matter to us if she had nasty bosses?"

"How did it happen that Miedzianka is gone?"
    "How did it happen? It was Siuta, God damn her to hell."
    "What do you mean it was Siuta?"
    "She came and pushed us out."
    "She pushed you out herself?"
    "Well, she had her minions, thieves, people like her."
    "Wasn't the town caving in?"
    "Sure, but not everywhere. And she drove all of us out and ordered it all plowed under. There were other ways to do it, you know, without pushing everyone out."

"What other ways?"

"How should I know? Are there any cave-ins in Miedzianka now? No, nothing, so there wouldn't have been any cave-ins back then either."

THAT EVIL WOMAN

THE NICEST THING THEY SAY ABOUT HER is that she has a wonderful husband. Other than that, they only speak ill.

"It has nothing to do with revenge," they emphasize, "but she shouldn't think we don't know. It's just a shame she got away with it. She made a fortune, she built a beautiful house, who knows, maybe a few more. Our doctor's wife."

That Evil Woman says:

"Please give me a few days, I have to remember everything. I'm eighty years old, I know what my name is, I have no intention of dying yet, and I'm not ashamed of anything."

*　　*　　*

She is just returning from summer vacation with her parents when the planes appear in the sky. The family is rushing to Volhynia in the Polish part of Ukraine, to the towns of Zahajce and Tytylkowce, where her father has estates—they want to hide out there. Before long, those estates will be nothing but memories.

Like a mantra (in old age he will become a Buddhist), Father repeats to Irena that Hitler could declare war on Britain and France at any moment and everything could turn out all right. After the Russians invade, he stops talking that way. Red Army soldiers enter the village, and the NKVD immediately turns up on the Kamieńskis' estate. They take her father away and hold him for two days. Irena is terrified. Rumors are going around the area that the bourgeoisie will be deported to Siberia or executed on the spot. Papa is bourgeois.

The peasants defend Kamieński. They form a committee and go to the NKVD officers, begging them to let him go. They say he's their noble lord, not some oppressor. Their intercession works, and Kamieński goes free. Before the night is over, these same peasants come to the estate and escort the whole family out of the village. They have been informed that the next day could be too late to save them.

And so they head west, to the Germans across the river. The river is the Bug. But the Bug is a long way away, so they have to walk, pay for guides, sleep in barns, hide from peasants, Ukrainians, Russians. Hide from everyone. They don't know who's a friend and who's a foe. They're Polacks, exploiters, and since they're hiding they must have something on their conscience. They don't like Polacks here—at least that's what people say. So they have to flee as far away as possible, at night, taking side roads, or cross-country through forests and fields. And if they can't go on, they'll lie low somewhere and wait, hidden, until they can set off again. As long as it's toward the river, westward. West is better than east.

They trek this way for two months, covering their tracks, awaiting the right opportunity, and then in December they reach the river. They rent a boat and hire yet another guide. Irena gets in with her mother; her father and the guide wade through the water, pulling them across to the other side. They're in Nazi-occupied Poland, although they are certainly not safe yet.

But their father has contacts here—he's friends with Count Maurycy Stanisław Potocki, lord of Jabłonna outside Nowy Dwór Mazowiecki, nearly a hundred miles away. They reach the estate right at the end of the year. Potocki hires Adam Kamieński as a meter reader, and they're able to feel safe here for a while.

Jabłonna is much larger and lovelier than the Kamieński estate they left back in Volhynia. Yet the splendor of the manor house and the gardens surrounding it contrast strongly with the hard reality all the residents have found themselves experiencing. They are poor and hungry in the house, and soon after coming to Jabłonna, Irena must go to work. She finds a job in a sparkling lemonade factory, where she washes bottles every day.

Jabłonna has its positive aspects—it is still a large landed estate, with everything that goes along with that. This includes horses. Back in Volhynia, little Irena fell in love with horses, and missing them was perhaps what upset her most during her family's autumn travels. Yet that love of horses will eventually cause problems. One day, a German officer arrives at the Potocki estate. He comes on a horse, having ridden from the nearby Modlin fortress. Irena senses no danger, and paying no heed to the rider, she approaches the horse, strokes its muzzle, and kisses its nose.

Perhaps the girl doesn't know to connect the figure of the German officer with the signs she saw once on the benches in the park: *Eintritt für Hunde, Juden und Polen verboten.* Or maybe she simply wagers their shared adoration of horses will momentarily break down the barrier between her and the soldier. Whatever she might have imagined, she's made a fundamental mistake. The German soldier erupts in fury and orders little Irena to report the next day to the fortress. There, she will be his servant and ensure that breakfast and fresh coffee are laid out on the German officer's table first thing every morning. It will also be her job to polish his boots and keep his house tidy. The work itself is neither too arduous nor too difficult: all it takes is working meticulously and keeping her head down. The route to work is a different story entirely. It's what Irena fears most. To reach the fortress, she must not only pass through several villages and settlements, but also traverse the bridge that is the Germans' favorite place to stage roundups. On several occasions, the name of her "employer" saves her life.

In August 1944, the Uprising breaks out in Warsaw, and nearby Legionowo is the only place outside the capital where fighting is also taking place. The insurgents' task is to defend the capital from the north. The Germans crush the resistance fairly quickly, but the Russians attack from the east. It's only a matter of time before they break through. Adam Kamieński knows this, and now yet again must locate shelter for himself and his family. He finds it in the nick of time in nearby Baboszewo.

The Russians reach Jabłonna before the end of September, and the Germans burn the Potocki estate as they retreat. Before long, Red Army soldiers are in Baboszewo. That's when Adam Kamieński makes a mistake that only by a miracle doesn't cost him his life. Not recognizing the Soviet uniforms, he races toward the soldiers—and greets them in German.

The war ends, but the Kamieńskis have no hope of returning East. The displacement machine has just been activated, tearing hundreds of thousands of people away from their homes and hurling them westward. The Kamieńskis are wondering what to do. Volhynia is no longer in Poland, nor is there any sense in remaining around Warsaw, for the capital itself now resembles nothing so much as a heap of rubble. But once the war is over, father's longtime contacts come back on the scene. His old friend and comrade, Czesław Centkiewicz, returns from a concentration camp in Neuengamme. Irena still remembers hearing stories before the war of his polar expedition and other extraordinary journeys. Now, too, she listens with bated breath to tales of his battles in the Uprising. Soon Centkiewicz is offered a job in the Energy Union. He is to be technical director of the Lower Silesia District. There are obviously opportunities that come with a job like that, and Centkiewicz wants to make the most of them to help his friends. Therefore, he proposes that the Kamieńskis come west with him. There's really nothing to think about. They go.

From the ruins of Warsaw, they reach the ruins of Wrocław. From there, they head southwest. They're in Jelenia Góra by May 1946. For the first few days, Irena wanders the city, unable to believe her eyes. The buildings here have roofs and windows, there are no ruins anywhere, German *Hausfrauen* sweep the sidewalks every morning and hose them down every evening. Polish government offices are operating and trolleys are running. It's as though there was never a war here.

The Kamieńskis and the Centkiewiczes occupy a villa on Aleksander Fredro Street. The building isn't very comfortable, but it has one enormous advantage: as property of the Energy Union, it's defended by the Industrial Guards. That's important, because around the area and in the city itself, they keep hearing more about looters and gangs of ordinary thugs, taking advantage of the confusion following the war to clear out apartments abandoned by the Germans. There's even a street market in Jelenia Góra, so-called Swag Square, where you can buy literally anything.

Father gets a job in energy production and Irena goes to school. Just like many people in Jelenia Góra, they do their best to forget about the war, exploring the city and starting to get to know the region. During one Sunday expedition, Irena Kamieńska discovers Miedzianka, a charming town soaring high above the area. She walks along its steep lanes and stops on the triangular market square, gazing upward. The peace and quiet here delight her. She adores all of it, and promises herself she'll return here another time.

People will curse her for that.

*   *   *

That Evil Woman lives with That Good Man in an apartment in Cieplice, right beside the highway from Jelenia Góra to Szklarska Poręba. When everything changed in Poland, this is where they decided to disappear to. They handed over the house in Janowice to their son. It wasn't that they wanted to hide, they were just tired. In Cieplice, they rest.

It's sort of the back of beyond. You have to drive through the entire spa town and head north. In a couple miles you come upon a multifamily, ex-German apartment house—a sorry sight from the outside. No extravagances, just a prosaic suburb transitioning fluidly into the countryside. The interior is a little better—paintings by her father hang on the walls.

"That's Zahajce, that's Tytylkowce. I only went back there once. I didn't recognize anything but one large oak tree. Everything had disappeared, not a stone remained standing of anything we'd left behind."

It was already time for them to go when a woman ran out of a nearby house and asked timidly, "Miss Irena?"

"I don't know who she was. We both wept."

On her business card with a panorama of the Giant Mountains, Irena Kamieńska-Siuta has a Latin motto: *Nummis praestat carere quam amicis*—Better to go without money than without friends.

Irena Kamieńska-Siuta's greatest friend for years has been her husband, Stanisław Siuta. He's the one people say has a "heart of gold," and she has it all wrapped up for herself.

* * *

It's the mid-fifties, Irena has just returned from college in Warsaw—she majored in Russian and is now hunting around for work. She wants to be a teacher. She doesn't have the greatest family background, so it's best not to speak up about her heritage.

"A landowner's daughter from the East"—in times like these, there's no way that could sound good.

She'd joined the Party even before leaving for Warsaw. She was seventeen—she worked in the Youth Organization of the University Workers' Association. Now, after returning home, she has a little free time, so she establishes a Jelenia Góra branch of the Polish Youth Union and becomes its first president. Yes, Irena Kamieńska believes in Communism. Aside from that, she has a surfeit of energy, but a shortage of athletic skill. She could definitely enjoy herself on the field or the court, but when she hits a ball it never goes where she wants it to. Czesław Centkiewicz even took her cross-country skiing one winter. They were meant to go as far as Bierutowice. Irena fell down 113 times on the way, and after that she stopped counting. But each time, she picked herself up and pressed on. No, there's no need to read too much into this: simply put, if she hadn't gotten up, she would probably have been abandoned in the mountains—Centkiewicz wasn't in the habit of looking behind him.

The only thing Irena likes to do is swim. "I can swim through water as well as I can swim through life," she will say years later, with an ounce of pride.

At last, she gets a job at Jelenia Góra high school. There she meets Staszek, a handsome PE teacher, soon to become a medical student. She is a beautiful black-haired woman, vivacious, a bit of a go-getter who makes everything her business. Like quicksilver. Meanwhile, he is quiet, calm, and composed. They go well together, even though they're like oil and water. The combination suits them. They begin seeing one another and stay together forever. When he goes off to school, she launches herself like a whirlwind into work. She not only teaches, but also works for the Youth Union. She becomes president of the Education Commission of the city council in Jelenia Góra, and also runs for county council. She organizes, educates, and monitors. She is ambitious, she wants to aim high. She is persuasive in an interview given to a local newspaper in 1965:

"We've made plenty of useful initiatives, but we could have accomplished even more if the local government and the community had worked together more closely. Above all, the Commission did not hold enough meetings with educators, parents, or even the students themselves. I hope the new Education Commission will address its predecessor's shortcomings."

After Staszek Siuta returns to Jelenia Góra from medical school, they quickly marry. They must hurry because he's just about to go into the military to fulfill the service requirement for doctors. This second separation does not last long, however, and he's hardly had time to take off his uniform before he's offered the directorship of the health center in Janowice Wielkie. They don't really know where that is, and look for it on a map. When they find it, they only take a moment to consider—Staszek finishes his service, they pack their bags and go. He becomes the director, and she a teacher in the local school. People eye them suspiciously. They come around to him faster—he's a doctor, he keeps in touch, he treats their children. She remains a riddle.

An elementary school in the countryside is not the same as a high school in Jelenia Góra. There are different problems, different students, and entirely different conditions. For many children, getting to school in winter is nearly impossible—for instance from Mniszków, which has no school of its own, it's nearly a four-mile walk. If the road is buried in snow, there's no way you can arrive on time. Aside from that, it's much harder for country schoolteachers to ask for educational assistance or additional funds from the central office. When Irena lived in Jelenia Góra, she could corner whomever she needed and make concrete arrangements. From Janowice that's nearly impossible.

So increasingly she comes home disheartened and fuming. It takes a lot of energy to fight a losing battle, and there's no point hiding the fact that she prefers working with older children. Her students sense this and start walking all over her. Her dream job is turning into nothing but trouble.

"You can quit anytime you like," Staszek says one day. After all, money is not a concern. He is well paid as director of a health center, and they could live a life of ease in Janowice on just his salary. But it's not money keeping Irena at work: rather, it's her energy, which requires some outlet.

"But if not the school, then what?" she asks.

*   *   *

"I didn't know they hated me," she says, surprised. "We did everything in our power to save those people." She slowly and distinctly enunciates the word "save." She actually repeats it several times after that. "I never particularly felt disliked by anyone because of what happened."

On the table are cake and curious-looking cups full of tea, and the sound of children frolicking in the garden comes through the window. Yet in the room, all is quiet. A clock ticks, a fly buzzes, her upstairs neighbor's floorboards creak. That Evil Woman says nothing, her eyes fixed on a saucer, turning it over in her fingers and tapping it delicately with a polished fingernail. Her face reveals no light half-smile—her mind is clearly somewhere else entirely. She doesn't look surprised, but rather resigned. That Good Man sits beside her, peering at her as though expecting her to say something.

"They can choose not to believe me, but I really have no other nationality. My mother was Russian, but I'm Polish. This is an exceptionally strange nation. We have a spectacular history, spectacular literature, and are often spectacularly crude. In one of Melchior Wańkowicz's books, someone he was interviewing asked him if vodka-drinking was the Poles' most troublesome characteristic. Wańkowicz responded that drinking is not the problem. The problem is gratuitous envy."

"What were they most envious of?"

"We had more than they did, and I was a Communist. Isn't that enough?"

*   *   *

It's the spring of 1969. A powerful storm has just passed over Komarno, one of the villages in Janowice Wielkie Township. In the space of about fifteen minutes, winds tore off roofs and water washed away the village's only access road. Animals have broken out of smashed-open enclosures, and the electricity has gone out in the town. People are running helter-skelter, not knowing what to grab onto or what to rescue first.

Township leader Irena Kamieńska-Siuta drives to the village. She organizes a meeting in the least damaged of the barns. Kamieńska is short, so she stands atop a hay bale placed on the ground. She assures them the township will help, and asks what they need most urgently. One farmer asks what to do with their studs on the loose. Siuta turns bright red, she can tell it's a provocation, but she takes a deep breath and embarks on a schoolmarmish lecture about raising young people and how to deal with young hooligans violating village girls. The farmers stand there listening, and some scratch their heads. When Kamieńska reaches the point of suggesting the township could organize classes for the young men in order to occupy them with something constructive (after all, there is so much that needs to be done these days), someone finally good-naturedly interrupts her.

"He means our bulls; they've gotten into the forest, and none of us has a damn clue how to catch them now."

Because Irena Kamieńska-Siuta, though she's been leader of the township for a year now, is not from around here. She was working on the council when it was proposed she run the entire township. That was a year ago, after she'd quit her job at the school and was looking for work. She always found organizing and taking action appealing. The problem is, and has been all along, that the township is rural, and she simply doesn't know how things work in the countryside. Of course she spent her childhood on her father's estate, but everyone called her "mistress" and she really learned nothing about the countryside while she was there. Then came Jelenia Góra and college in Warsaw. Here, people see her as city folk, and rightly so—she is from the city. She has people in her office who are familiar with rural issues. Usually, if someone has something to sort out with the township, they go to Irena Słowińska, the township secretary, not to the leader.

People complain to Słowińska that "Mrs. Siuta doesn't get what we're talking about."

So relations with the new township leader waver between suspicion and forbearance. But she doesn't mind.

Her mother once jokes, "Hang a sign in the office saying you only accept poultry that's been slaughtered and plucked." But truthfully Irena Siuta rarely receives such tokens of gratitude.

Of course, part of the problem is Siuta is a "Comrade." That plus her Russian roots makes people suspicious of her true motives, and of what connections might be supporting her. Gossip goes around the countryside that the people upstairs sent her here specifically to eliminate all traces of the Soviet uranium mine in Miedzianka. Such rumors naturally do nothing to widen her circle of sympathizers. Either out of malice or carelessness, during a May Day parade the platform on which she is to deliver her speech collapses underneath her. The workers placed it on round barrels, so when Siuta stands at the microphone, the whole platform slowly starts to tilt. People roar with laughter, and officials rush to their boss's aid. Luckily they manage to wave the whole incident off as a joke.

It's probably not until Radomierz that she finds out what people really think of her. In the early seventies, a priest from Szklary, next to Nowa Sól and about eighty miles north of Jelenia Góra, arrives at the office. He's building a church in his town, and now he's driving all over Lower Silesia gathering up accoutrements for the church from items priests aren't using in their own parishes.

The county conservation officer granted him permission to take the unused bells from the old church tower in Radomierz. It's all meant to take place at his parish's cost, the township leader need only issue the necessary approval to remove antique objects from the district. Irena Kamieńska-Siuta sees no problem—the steeple in Radomierz is at risk of collapse, no one there is using the bell, and right next door is a newer church that celebrates Masses. As a result, she considers the priest's initiative a positive solution to the problem of a ruin that will soon become a danger to the townspeople. She signs the necessary documents and soon forgets the matter.

A few weeks later, she and Irena Słowińska are on their way back to Janowice from Jelenia Góra. In Radomierz, they spot a crowd gathered around the old bell tower. They stop the car and decide to see what's going on. Even from a distance they can hear raised voices. In the center of the crowd stands the frightened priest from the parish in Szklary. He's not wearing his clerical collar, just work clothes, and there is terror in his eyes. Meanwhile, the townspeople surrounding him shake their fists and call him an impostor and usurper.

The township leader does her best to ease the situation, explaining the bell is to be taken to another church, because here it is decaying and could be dangerous for the locals. It takes her a moment to realize the bell is already missing from the bell tower.

"They've hidden it and aren't willing to give it up. They don't believe I am who I say I am," the priest says apprehensively.

"We won't surrender Catholic bells for scrap!" shouts a voice from the crowd.

Someone else brandishes a pitchfork at them. Others form a human wall in front of the empty steeple. People are building their courage up, and hurl vulgar epithets at Irena Siuta. Finally, a burly constable from Janowice appears on the scene and negotiations go on for another quarter of an hour or so. Yet no amount of explaining will help. In the end, the township leader and the priest give up, get in their cars, and leave. A few days later, the bell once again hangs in its place. For years its defenders will go around town glorying in their victory.

* * *

Today, Irena Słowińska lives in Janowice Wielkie in a small house at the top of a hill. It's her husband Jerzy Słowiński who was brewmaster in Miedzianka for nearly a year, and to this day he's retained the habit of calling the place "my little brewery." Słowińska worked in the township office almost her whole life, and retired in the late nineties. She also remembers those events in Radomierz perfectly, and has a simple way of summing them up.

"Right then I was afraid, because some of the people were being aggressive. Irena was the picture of composure."

She remembers her former boss well, though now they're in fairly infrequent contact. Their paths diverged when everything changed in Poland.

"She was demanding and strict, you had to constantly work to earn her respect. She'd hardly ever coddle anyone. But the other side of it was, if one of her employees was having problems, she'd bend over backwards to help them."

When Irena Słowińska is asked why no one in the area likes Siuta now, and some outright despise her, a silence momentarily falls over the room.

"She wasn't a likable person. She was just different: better educated than any of us, with ambition and city manners, she was pretty, fashionably dressed, always wearing eyeshadow. She drove her own car, her husband was a doctor, she collected antiques. He made good money, so she worked out of passion, not for financial gain. Well, maybe a little for the glory she loved people saying good things about her. But who doesn't? And what sort of glory is there anyway in a township or a county?"

* * *

It's in the early 1960s that people from Miedzianka first start bringing complaints to the township. In 1966, Janina Karwacka is still heading up the local government, and she miraculously manages to find replacement housing for thirty-three families whose homes in Miedzianka have recently begun to fall apart. They end up resettled in Janowice and Jelenia Góra. But the problem grows. When Irena Kamieńska-Siuta becomes township leader in 1968, a fairly impressive stack of papers concerning the town caving in lands on her desk. In theory, compensation for the mining damage goes to the township treasury and is earmarked for renovations. In the first year of the new leader's tenure, the amount totals more than 200,000 złotys, no small sum, but it's a drop in the ocean when the town is drowning in need. Instead of investing in the ruins, the township decides to call in specialists from Katowice for a site visit, to assess whether it makes sense to build or refurbish anything in Miedzianka. Before this can happen, however, the county must give its approval. They are somewhat reluctant to take on such a complex issue. They find it much easier to say it will sort itself out, or, to be precise—disappear into a hole in the ground. The lobbying and negotiations last many weeks.

Finally, experts from Katowice arrive on-site. They park their cars in the middle of the square, and the township leader is with them (afterward people will say she arrived one day in a black Volga with the guys she sold the whole town to). After a few hours of inspections and analyses, there's no doubt in the engineers' minds—sooner or later, the town will cave in, as only a small western part is unthreatened. But even there it's best not to conduct any large-scale construction. Nevertheless, the people on the square and its neighboring streets must be relocated immediately and all refurbishment must be abandoned, because it will not be successful.

There are a few ideas about how to solve the problem. The mining compensation money could be used to construct new houses on safe ground; it could also be paid directly to people and they would manage on their own. Yet the first solution is likely beyond the organizational and financial capacities of the township, and the second, for its part, is freighted with risk of not everyone making responsible use of the money granted them. There's no hiding that over the last few years Miedzianka has become a hotbed of social ills, and the Janowice police are called there with increasing frequency because of drunken brawls or people having accidents while they plunder the ruins. Of course, law-abiding citizens also live there, simply stuck in the town for various reasons or not wanting to abandon it out of sentiment. They are most likely even the majority, but the town's recent reputation is a product more of notoriety than fame. Still, there is yet a third solution—a new housing project is being built in Jelenia Góra, and the money from the mining compensation is precisely enough to buy a few dozen apartments and settle the people of Miedzianka there. To Irena Kamieńska-Siuta, this solution seems the most logical. Soon townspeople begin receiving allocations in the apartment blocks on Karłowicz Street.

*   *   *

In 1972, letters start coming into the township from the Jelenia Góra Tenants Association, with complaints about the new residents resettled from Miedzianka. Their neighbors accuse them of keeping chickens and small pets on their balconies, and responding aggressively when it was pointed out this is not the place to raise animals. Meanwhile, *Nowiny Jeleniogórskie* publishes letters from outraged readers who have no desire to see rabbit hutches and drying laundry on the lawns of the new project. So Kamieńska sets off for Zabobrze to see for herself how people are living in the new conditions. She hopes to establish whether the tenants' complaints are justified. Sometimes Irena Słowińska accompanies her on these trips. Yet over dozens of visits, they see no chickens. They speak to people who complain that there's less room in the buildings than the ex-German apartment houses and that the views out the window aren't the same as in Miedzianka. But it's close to school, there's work at hand, and they don't have to walk far to go shopping either. Even the Miroś family started transporting their bread to Zabobrze, once they figured out that's where the whole of Miedzianka lives now.

"I never got the impression from those conversations that people held anything against us or that they came out of this change worse off," recalls Irena Słowińska. "Of course they missed Miedzianka—after all, it's a beautiful place, it's difficult not to miss it. But they lived more comfortably in Zabobrze. Everyone treated us either kindly or at least with polite indifference. But not everyone had to love us, did they?"

* * *

In 1981, one Jelenia Góra newspaper publishes an article on Irena Kamieńska-Siuta, calling her the Vampire of the Giant Mountains. The carnival of Solidarity is underway—a little more than a year of rationed freedom, which will end with the declaration of martial law. In the factory halls of the Gencjana company in Jelenia Góra, meetings are being held between union activists and local government representatives. Their goal is to hold those in charge of the province responsible for their actions. These meetings culminate in a strike at Gencjana from late January to early February 1981, which ends with the signing of an eleven-point agreement. Point ten requires three people to resign from the positions they have hitherto held—including a deputy governor of Jelenia Góra Province, Irena Kamieńska-Siuta.

By 1972, Kamieńska has said farewell to the township office in Janowice and been made mayor of Karpacz. She managed to do so thanks to her assertiveness and confidence; energetic officials are needed in the province, especially in sectors as challenging as one of the region's most important tourist destinations. At a Party meeting, an official from a neighboring township jokes he'll have a cactus growing out of his hand before she manages to finish the teachers' residences she's resolved to build along Polish Armed Forces Street in Janowice. A year later, Kamieńska addresses these words to him:

"Comrade, please show us your cactus. Our residences are built, and teachers are living in them."

A few decades later, Irena Kamieńska-Siuta adds with a smile that those residences are her proudest achievement, and she doesn't understand why that street in Janowice isn't named after her.

During her tenure in Janowice, Kamieńska also twice wins her town the title of Lower Silesia Model Tourist Township. Now she is to repeat the achievement in the larger town of Karpacz.

Things go fairly well for her there; in four years she is promoted from the mayoralty into the office of deputy governor. At that time, the province is led by Stanisław Ciosek, later Minister for Industrial Relations, Employment, Wages, and Social Affairs—and after 1989, ambassador of the Republic of Poland to the USSR and Russia. Unluckily for Irena Kamieńska-Siuta, her remit includes trade and... agriculture. She is not particularly familiar with either.

When Solidarity is legalized in 1980, in Jelenia Góra it's time to settle scores. Someone recalls that during her tenure in Karpacz, Kamieńska permitted a fifth of an acre of forest to be cut down underneath a chairlift without undergoing the necessary formalities. Since the forest was located on the grounds of a national park, the Forestry Department ought to have given approval for it to be felled. The public prosecutor's office has looked into the case already and it was dismissed due to the "action's limited social harm." However, it is brought up again as part of the wave of score-settling, and the provincial authorities decide to make an example of the former mayoress, knowing full well the punishment will be disproportionate to the crime. Yet the court does not issue any verdict on the charges filed against her, instead taking advantage of a recently announced amnesty.

"I've been reprieved from a sentence that was never handed down," she tells her husband after the final hearing. But this is not the end—now the newspapers, even those loyal to the authorities, are writing at length about Kamieńska. This is when she's dubbed a vampire, and her dismissal becomes a demand of the strikers at Gencjana.

* * *

"I can stand at the mirror and look myself in the eye," says That Evil Woman. "I'm eighty years old, I know what my name is, and I'm not ashamed of anything. I can't control what they say about me. Honestly, it doesn't bother me one bit," she says confidently. But obviously it does.

To this day, there are people in Zabobrze who say she almost forcibly threw people out of their homes ("not us, but our neighbors said so"), that none of them wanted to move out of there, that their houses weren't caving in at all. They say she must have gotten something out of it. Apparently she was getting orders all the way from Moscow. She was said to be the Soviets' woman on the inside, there to wipe away all traces of the secret uranium mine. Except by the seventies the town's past was no secret. Nor, actually, was it twenty years earlier, when Bronisław Hac and the other geology students were running around in the mine galleries.

"We all knew what was there, how much they'd mined, what happened afterward," says Zbigniew Pawęska, Kamieńska's successor as township leader. "Of course nothing was said officially, because then we'd also have had to say our Soviet friends' over-exploitation caused the whole town to cave in. But it was no secret, and nowadays people are hunting around for something sensational where there isn't anything."

Yet people still wonder by what miracle Kamieńska-Siuta climbed so high. And why wasn't she ousted until Solidarity? Andrzej Piesiak founded the free unions in Jelenia Góra in the early eighties. As a Solidarity member he also took part in the score-settling after the Gdańsk Agreement, and then the negotiations at Gencjana. He spent martial law in jail in Kamienna Góra. In free Poland he served three terms in the Senate. He remembers Kamieńska-Siuta rather well.

"Those were uncomplicated times—if someone was in the government, they were evil. It was simple: you're there, you're Red, you're an enemy. I'm only now starting to think about that and see there were no shades of gray back then. We couldn't imagine there could be anyone decent among them. Many years later I realized that some of them were different, that they weren't as guilty as the rest, but you know, back then that made no difference to us. And thinking that way would have only done harm."

THE CHURCH

THE CHURCH TOOK LONGEST TO DISAPPEAR. In the only surviving color photograph, you can see it had a yellow facade, tall stained-glass windows, and that it towered strikingly above the area. Large, wooden doors led inside, while two even rows of Swedish whitebeams extended from the front of the church. They stand there to this day, though they no longer lead anywhere.

Since the end of the war, the faithful in Miedzianka—as well as the priest of the parish in Janowice, Father Matwiejczyk—have used the Catholic church standing on the lower part of the square. This is where Mass is held, and also where, according to long-standing tradition, a church fair takes place every third Saturday after Easter. The Lutheran church has not been used since the war's end. When its last caretaker, Pastor Johannes Fiedler, left, he locked the church with a padlock and a massive bar, maybe hoping that at some point the building might still serve someone. His hopes turn out to be in vain, and his security measures prove no obstacle to people wishing to get inside—and there are plenty.

First, the most valuable items disappear from the interior. Everything of any value ends up on Swag Square in Jelenia Góra or right on the scrap heap. That's also how the antique organ ends up dismantled, and locals will long tell stories about the peculiar concerts held in town back then. Each involves two musicians—the first bearing a pipe culled from the organ on their shoulder, the second following behind and blowing in one end with all their might, making all kinds of squeaking noises. These will wander through town until the final pipe disappears from the church, which doesn't take long. Over a few months, the interior of the church is stripped completely bare. All that remains are the large wooden pews where the faithful once sat, and the impressive crystal chandeliers hanging from the ceiling. The former are too heavy and cumbersome to be of any use to anyone; as for the latter, no one really knows how to reach them without accidentally breaking their neck. The chandeliers hang right in the middle of the sanctuary, far from any of the walls, and are fairly high up. For the next few years, it is these bare walls, empty benches, and untouched chandeliers that will greet anyone trying to get a look inside. Meanwhile, colored light shines in through the stained-glass windows, joining with the prevailing silence in a somewhat unreal and disheartening combination.

But this state of affairs doesn't last forever. The children work out a way to reach the crystal chandeliers. It's probably in the mid-fifties that a bizarre structure is erected inside the church. All the pews and all the fallen wood from the area go into building it. The structure sways ominously, but that doesn't deter youngsters from scrambling to the top, where their reward awaits in the form of crystal beads, which the boys tear off the chandeliers in bunches. Down below, little girls are already waiting to convert the haul into necklaces for themselves and, thus adorned, parade around town. One is Marysia Kaczmarska, the daughter of the miner killed by the secret police, and the same girl who not long ago peeked into Ueberschaer's tomb and ran away screaming. She doesn't see anything wrong with what they're doing in the church; the only thing her mother has strictly forbidden is going up the bell tower. No one at home knows what she's getting up to.

The bell tower is holding up fairly well, though, and it's the perfect spot for the older children's trysts. Baśka Spiż goes up it in 1972. She's just finished grade school and is nearly grown-up now. It's easy to get up the tower, as a spiral staircase runs the whole way and is only somewhat damaged toward the bottom. After that it's simple and easy. The top of the bell tower is where Baśka Spiż lights the first cigarette of her life. That's where many of her friends and girlfriends from school are also initiated into tobacco-smoking.

Meanwhile in town, the first serious mining damage has started to occur. The church walls crack too, yet this does not deter anyone from poking their head in, searching for free firewood. Someone spreads a rumor that the Germans hid valuables under the hardwood floor. So the floorboards immediately get torn up, but all the investigators are disappointed to discover the only things hidden under there are a few German coins, which probably slipped between the floorboards years ago and were impossible to retrieve. After the floor, next come the stairs to the balcony situated just over the entrance. After the mid-sixties, the only way of getting upstairs will be on the decoratively sculpted buttresses holding up the balcony. It's also getting harder to climb the bell tower—as the years go by, steps in the staircase keep disappearing, so before long, getting to the top will demand monkey-like agility. Some people also try to sell wood from the wreck of the church. The police do their best to combat this practice, and a few townspeople have to carefully explain the origin of the wood lying behind their houses. Still, that doesn't deter anyone—besides, they treat the abandoned houses in town the same way.

The only objects remaining in the church that appear to have any value are the figures incorporated here and there into what's left of the church fittings. They decorate banisters, the area around the altar, and once also greeted the faithful as they walked in. They've miraculously survived year after year of the building's destruction, and now they're scattered around the ruined interior. The looters probably haven't had the courage to take them away, or maybe they had no idea what to do with them. After all, officially no one in People's Poland is decorating new churches. At least that's how it would seem, but the truth turns out to be somewhat different.

It's winter in the early seventies; Christmas and a raucous New Year's have just passed. The parish priest from Janowice is visiting the homes of the faithful, as he does every year. He pays a visit to the home of Irena Wędzel. Irena, her husband, and her brother Władek live just off the square, they can see the ruined church from their window, and on occasion even worry the crumbling walls will someday lead to tragedy. Their house sings, which suggests the ground under the church is probably not too secure. One thing leads to another, and the priest asks the Wędzels a favor—there are still some beautiful wooden figures in the church, and they would be a perfect fit for the church in Janowice. Except that it's not a clergyman's place to loot a Lutheran church, so if they might be able to... An awkward silence falls. The Wędzels don't know what to say—not long ago they even chased some children away from the church who were throwing stones at the stained-glass windows. Finally, Irena Wędzel says timidly:

"Father, I think you will have to ask somebody else for help."

The visit draws to a close, the priest leaves, and soon the wooden figures vanish from the church as well, though they never appear in the church in Janowice.

Even before the final townspeople leave, Józef Kluba, a quarry worker in Janowice who lives in Miedzianka, manages to win a drunken bet by climbing out on top of the cross that crowns the bell tower. When Baśka Kluba sees how high her father has climbed, she runs to her mother and cries:

"Mama, Mama, daddy's on the cross!" But by the time people tell that story, they will be in Zabobrze.

Soon afterward, one of the walls caves in. One night the earth simply opens up, swallowing part of the church. In the morning, the few townspeople are surprised to find that now they can see into the ruined interior of the church without looking through the smashed stained-glass windows. No one is brave enough to go inside anymore. In 1974, a few dozen soldiers arrive in Miedzianka. They form a solid cordon around the area of the church, while placing explosive charges at the base of the building itself. Soon afterward, a deafening explosion rings out. Those watching the operation from a safe distance will later say the whole church hung in the air for a few moments, only to quickly transform into a pile of rubble. Stanisław Izbicki is among the onlookers. When the mine was operating in Miedzianka, he was the First Secretary of the mine's Party committee, and now he lives in Janowice. Izbicki watches the demolition of the church in grim silence. When, in the nineties, he tells a journalist from a local newspaper about the whole incident, his eyes fill with tears.

Another of the onlookers is teenaged Zdzisiek Jankowski, the same one who broke into Ueberschaer's tomb a few years ago, pulled out the saber, and paraded around town with it. He recently went into the church on his own and tore up the last of the floorboards, then brought them to his history teacher, who promised to let him move up a year in return. By now Zdzisiek and his parents live in Janowice—his father had lost his legs, but they were allocated an apartment in Zabobrze on a top floor with no elevator. So they exchanged apartments with a family from Janowice, and they live just over a mile from Miedzianka. Word gets around quickly, and when Zdzisiek hears in Janowice that an army company is heading for Miedzianka, he drops everything and runs to see.

As soon as the dust of the explosion has settled, Zdzisiek heads into the ruins and is the first to pull out the metal ball sitting at the top of the bell tower. He knows inside he'll find mementoes placed there by the church's builders. He and his friends run off into the forest with their precious find. After opening the ball, they find it holds a few coins and documents written in German gothic letters. They don't even have time to examine everything closely before two policemen appear out of nowhere. Their treasure is confiscated, while the boys end up at the police station in Janowice, where they have a lot of explaining to do. A few days later, the latest article about Zdzisiek Jankowski, the young hooligan from Miedzianka, will appear in the paper.

The day the church is demolished, Krystyna Dudek is returning home from work exhausted, as she does every day. She lives on the outskirts of Miedzianka, where there has never been any mining damage. While her neighbors are resettled, her father has no difficulty convincing the authorities he doesn't need to move out. Now the whole family lives here, even though in the span of barely a few months the area has become completely deserted and gloomy. Krystyna has missed the bus again; she takes the train and is walking from Janowice station to town on foot. On the way, she passes some soldiers fooling around—they're young, wearing grimy work clothes, smoking cigarettes and romping around on the empty highway like little boys. At the sight of Krystyna making her way up to town, one of them calls out:

"There's something missing up in Miedzianka today!"

And then they go on their way.

THE MANOR HOUSE

THE MANOR HOUSE IS NEXT TO CAVE IN. The first time the walls crack and the windows bend is in 1953. When the mine closes, the army moves out of the manor house as well. The building stands empty for a while, then the National Fire Department takes it over and runs summer camps there for its employees' children. Once summer vacation starts, the manor estate and the surrounding park once again begin pulsing with life. It's like that for a few seasons.

One year in the late fifties, a food storeroom in the right wing of the manor house collapses into the earth. No one notices in the middle of the night, and when the cooks come for provisions in the morning, they freeze at the edge of a huge hole in the ground. There will definitely be no breakfast today.

It's impossible to run a summer camp in such conditions, so the collapsed wing of the manor house is blocked off and the camp is closed down, but no one considers demolishing the building. A few families are housed in the open part—they live here for a few years, then move to Jelenia Góra. The building once again stands empty, and only children from the town and the nearby area play inside it from time to time. Like everyone here, they're looking for treasure—wherever and however they can. No one finds anything, but they leave chaos and destruction in their wake. They have no idea that a few years later someone new will end up living in the manor house.

That person is Elżbieta Jachimowska, née Grzyb, and her children. The temptation is to add "with her husband," but Henryk has once again gone on an alcoholic binge and Elżbieta doesn't even want to know where he is. It's 1974 or 1975, there is almost no one left in Miedzianka; ruined buildings haunt the square, which people from neighboring villages raid for bricks for their own building projects. So the manor house seems quite all right, especially compared to the rest of town. Elżbieta decides to move in there with her children, where maybe Henryk won't find them. Besides, until now, she's been squeezed in at her parents' place with the little ones. That wouldn't have even been so bad except that her father constantly molested her. She somehow coped with it, and since childhood she's grown used to fighting him off, but now she has to worry about her kids as well, and she doesn't want them to share her fate. Therefore, the manor house in Miedzianka is a safe haven for her and the children.

But their haven turns out to be cold and unpleasant. Drafts sweep through the empty rooms and the windows are broken, so the family covers them with whatever they can—blankets, old quilts, newspapers. Aside from Elżbieta and the children, Halina Zagrodna and a Romani family also live in the building.

The latter occupy the first floor of the manor house, where they engage in a peculiar practice: here, they have set up an equine abattoir. They slaughter horses brought by farmers from Janowice, Ciechanowice, and Mniszków. From time to time, the whinnying of a horse being slaughtered causes Elżbieta Jachimowska and her children to startle awake with their hair standing on end. Still, they somehow make it through the summer, but now the manor house is getting colder as fall approaches. Elżbieta goes to Halina Zagrodna and persuades her to come to the township with her to ask for new accommodation.

The township head is Zbigniew Pawęska and the secretary of the township's Party committee is Szymon Młodziński. They both hear the women out but can do nothing to help, because the township has no apartments available.

"How can you say none are available when half the buildings in Miedzianka are standing empty?" cries Jachimowska.

"We can't house anyone in Miedzianka, and you've been living in the manor house illegally," answers Pawęska.

They don't give up, and decide to go to the Party committee in Jelenia Góra. They don't have an appointment and no one wants to let them in. They sit down in the overstuffed armchairs in the lobby and say they won't leave until somebody speaks to them. Their stubbornness wins out. Finally, someone receives them, hears about the house with the drafts and no windows, picks up the phone, and calls the township. They return glowing with victory. A few days later, a tractor pulls up to the manor house in Miedzianka with a trailer behind it. They resettle Zagrodna first—she's moved into a beautiful cottage on Nadbrzeżna Street in Janowice. Then the tractor returns for Jachimowska's family. They ride five miles to Radomierz, where they get a fresh start.

Soon after, the Mirga family moves out of the manor house as well, and the building falls into utter ruin. Its remains are razed to the ground during the final demolition of the town in the mid-1970s. When archaeologists arrive on the site in 2009, they find only bushes, trees, and a few stones chaotically scattered around. Among these, they manage to make out fragments of a Renaissance portal from a section of the manor house Dippold von Burghaus built himself as long ago as the sixteenth century. These they transport to nearby Siedlęcin, so as not to attract amateur treasure hunters. In their report on the site, the archaeologists write:

"Approach: the highway from Janowice Wielkie to Ciechanowice and Marciszów runs through the former center of the settlement. The orientation point is the former parish church (where it's possible to park cars). 50 meters to the east of the church one can see the remains of the gates to the estate, its unkempt stand of trees, and the ruins of the manor house, overgrown with brush, forming a mound about 0.5–1.0 meters above the surface of the ground. The stairs to the cellar, partly covered with debris and inaccessible, are located on the north side of the rubble pile, but it is necessary to exercise particular caution when entering (falling earth and debris!)."

THE BREWERY

IT ALL HAPPENED QUICKLY AT THE BREWERY. In 1973, Stefan Spiż came to Zbigniew Pawęska's office. He didn't call ahead, it was almost as though he was just happening by and decided to step in for a moment. But it's a strange thing, since although both gentlemen of course know one another, they've never been particularly close. Spiż does not even remove his coat; he takes the seat offered him and is silent for a moment. Finally, he says:

"Please help me set up the brewery as a private enterprise."

Zbigniew Pawęska's eyes widen in surprise. Stefan Spiż's request not only exceeds the modest powers of the leader of a small township, but also all limits of Socialist common sense. Private beer production! Just putting those words next to one another sounds unreal in and of itself. Pawęska attempts to explain this to Spiż, but none of his arguments get through to the old brewer.

"If we don't try, we'll never find out. And this is my entire life."

Pawęska softens. He is supposed to go to the county hall tomorrow, and he promises to ask if there's any possibility. On the way there, he practices saying out loud the questions he's going to ask.

He receives a short, though comprehensive, response: "Listen, don't ask about this anywhere else, because they'll think you're out of your mind and you'll lose your job on top of it." On the way home he stops in Miedzianka. Stefan Spiż comes out to meet him.

"They laughed at me, Spiż. It's not possible."

Spiż shakes his head.

"It's not your fault, Mr. Pawęska."

They begin shutting the brewery down a few months later. Officially, it's because of the mining damage, but in this instance that's a pretense. The ground under the brewery or even the area around it has never caved in, while the brick walls have stood solidly for over a hundred years and could probably last twice as long yet. Nevertheless, production in the brewery is halted, and the leftover beer is delivered to the area's bars, restaurants, and stores. The authorities offer the employees positions in other breweries, but most of Stefan's workers have no desire to commute long distance, so they change professions and get jobs in the paper mill in Janowice or the linen mill in Marciszów. Werka Butyńska finds a job in Janowice's school.

"Werka, stay here, maybe they won't close us," Spiż says to her one day, as though completely oblivious to what's going on around him.

Bogdan Spiż becomes brewmaster of a malt house in nearby Ciechanowice, where he has the opportunity to hire his father as chief foreman. This setup is ideal—Bogdan can be in charge of running the facility, while his father will see to it that all the technical procedures flow smoothly. There is certainly no finer expert in the region than Stefan Spiż.

In 1974, a group of laborers arrives at the brewery. They remove the twenty copper tanks and roll them down the road to Janowice. It's a moment to remember: here, after 126 years, the history of brewing in Miedzianka is coming to a close. It ends with the rumbling clatter of sheet metal rolling on wet asphalt. They aren't easy to roll—the slope is steep, and it's easy to lose control over the vats, each weighing over five hundred pounds. Up top, the workers are making sure the tanks will go to the brewery in Lwówek Śląski, but at the bottom of the hill they arrive so banged up they're only fit for scrap. Stefan Spiż observes all this in silence. He does his best to keep his chin up. Or at least, as much as possible. People can see he's somewhat subdued, but he never was a volcano of energy. Those who don't know him so well might even think the sight of the vats rolling toward Janowice makes no impression on the old brewer at all. It's not until he's home that Stefan falls apart completely—years later, Baśka will recount how she's never seen her father so devastated and in such floods of tears.

The brewery is empty. For a few years, the township keeps stores of vegetables and hay there. Then most of the brewery is dismantled, and the remainder locked up tight. The pond that once supplied ice for chilling the beer dries up and becomes overgrown with weeds. Soon locals will also start dumping their trash there.

In the mid-eighties Werka Butyńska runs into Stefan Spiż in Janowice. They greet each other warmly, but the conversation is awkward. As he is leaving, Stefan flashes his slightly seductive smile, which he has not lost despite the passage of years, and jokes:

"All right, Werka, tomorrow afternoon you'll have a shift in the malt house."

"Yes sir, Mr. Spiż!" answers Werka, beaming. She can never say no to Brewmaster Spiż.

THE LETTER

"FROM 1986 TO 1993, I WAS head of mining operations in the basalt quarries in Księginki, a suburb of Lubań (where I live).

"It just so happened that at the time I was a close acquaintance of Father J. from Janowice Wielkie, who was then priest of the parish in Księginki. Father J. was building a presbytery. As you most likely remember, since there was a notorious shortage of construction materials (among other things!) during that period, projects would be supplemented by materials from demolished sites.

"In 1987 or 1988, through some networks of his own, Father J. caught wind of the ruins in Miedzianka. He even received formal approval to demolish one unused structure. This, he told me, was the remains of the local ex-German brewery. Because attempts at demolition using traditional methods did not have the expected outcome (a bulldozer trying to pull down a wall ended up being torn apart), the priest had the idea of blowing up the structure with explosives. He came to me with this matter, because my duties at the facility included overseeing blasting. I had no problem getting approval from my director to perform this task (since it was in part a question of using explosives from our quarry storage facility).

"The priest and I went to scout it out. The building was located at the center of a sizable square. The building was laid out in a U-shape, open from the narrower side. The walls were constructed of solid face brick held together with strong cement mortar. The walls had a width of around twenty inches (or, in everyday terms, 'two bricks'). The top was held together by a large, reinforced concrete roof (which is why the building was so solid). The structure seemed to be the last remnant of what had been the brewery.

"I carried out a precise survey of the building. Based on formulas designed for this type of task, I calculated the quantity, distribution, and depth of the openings to drill. I passed the data on to the priest's brother, who lived in Janowice. He was to drill the holes.

"After returning to Lubań, I set about compiling the so-called blasting specification, which was needed to obtain the necessary permissions from the area's district mining office in Wałbrzych, as well as the provincial police department in Jelenia Góra. That went smoothly.

"When we received word from Janowice that the holes had been bored, I signed out an appropriate quantity of dynamite and electric fuses from the warehouse. We loaded them into the priest's car (of course the dynamite went in the trunk, and the fuses separately in the passenger compartment), and drove with two blasters to Miedzianka. The look on the face of the policeman who pulled us over on the Jelenia Góra bypass—for speeding, of course (the priest was driving)—when we told him what we were carrying was priceless. He had a hard time believing the paperwork from the Provincial Department. But he absolutely did not want to look in the trunk. He tore up the ticket. On the way, we stopped by the police station in Janowice to schedule when two officers could come to Miedzianka to secure the area before the detonation.

"On site, it turned out the walls were so hard that the priest's brother had a very difficult time drilling the holes according to my specifications. He hadn't told us they were set too far apart, and drilled too shallowly. Seeing what he'd done, I could tell there was absolutely no point in going through with the detonation.

"However, the priest insisted we try, and so I acquiesced.

"We laid the charges, armed the detonators, and connected them. The holes had been drilled on the inside of the building, to minimize the risk of flying brick fragments. Nevertheless (and as per usual blasting methods), we covered the holes with branches we happened to find nearby, along with lengths of metal netting. The nearest few buildings were located about 200–250 feet from the epicenter. We informed the residents to keep their windows open for the next hour (this reduces the effects of the shock wave from the explosion). We also asked them to move their cars and, as for themselves, to hide in the basement when they heard the sirens. We stationed the newly arrived policemen, the mayor of the village, and a few local men around to guard the blasting zone.

"After securing the area, we connected the fuses to the blasting machine. The hand siren gave out the first warning signal. After the second, I turned the crank on the blasting machine and pressed the button. A deafening explosion followed. A cloud of dust burst through the open part of the structure. A few pieces of brick went whistling over our heads. But the building? STAYED STANDING! (For someone performing a controlled demolition, I think there is no greater dishonor! Regardless of of the botched drilling described above.)

"After sounding the siren marking the end of the operation, we went into the building. The charges had torn a wide furrow all along the wall, about four to six inches deep, depending on the depth of the holes drilled in a given location. There were no cracks in the wall! The building remained stable because of the shallowness of the holes, the size of the charges as a result, and the walls' support from the reinforced concrete ceiling.

"After the inspection, we verified no one outside had been hurt and the nearby buildings had suffered no damage. We thanked the 'guards' for their help. And what else could we do? I went back to Lubań with my tail between my legs!

"Some weeks later, Father J. informed me that they had set about demolishing the building with the help of some friends who owned a few bulldozers. Apparently our actions had somehow weakened the construction after all, because they managed to finish off the remains of the former brewery, although arduously and with great effort. But the yield of whole bricks was very modest. Solid German mortar!

"So that is how I lent my hand to your *History of a Disappearance*."

ZDZISŁAW BYKOWSKI

PHOTOGRAPHS II

HERE IS THE DRIED-UP POND full of branches and trash, and here are the remains of the brewery—a single-story ruin with broken windows. I peer inside, my vision taking a moment to adjust to the darkness, and can finally make out the first shapes: shattered aquariums, tables, chairs, oil cans, and hay scattered everywhere. A woman comes out of the yellow villa and says she knows nothing about the town, not even that it existed. Nor does she know where the mineshafts and drifts used to be.

"Is that what you're poking around for?"

I'd like to go into her house and see where Georg Franzky ate dinner and Stefan Spiż argued with Helena. But the woman stands in the doorway. The kindness vanishes from her face.

"I think you'd better go on your way, I really don't know anything."

I leave.

Mrs. Płaksa lies in bed with tears in her eyes. I ought to hear why, so I do what I can to listen. Yet I'm looking around her room, absorbing every detail that allows me to reconstruct the interior of the school from the old woman's cluttered, chilly apartment. Where the blackboard was, where the seats were, who sat where. Where they went, whether they scraped the chairs on the floor. Jadwiga Płaksa is still speaking, and I really do my best to listen; her son is pacing the room and lights yet another cigarette. I still don't know how I'll get out of here, apparently her dog has broken off its chain, the terrible beast, and is now it's running around the yard, so I'd better watch out for him.

"Do you have any pictures?" I ask.

"What would we need pictures for?"

"People keep different things."

A moment of silence.

"We don't have any."

Pictures. Snapshots barely larger than a hand, curling at the edges. Hanna Gębuś tells me to take every one that has even a bit of Miedzianka in it. She hasn't organized them—photographs from last year's name-day party are mixed in here with ones from her youth. I hopelessly sift through the box, but how am I supposed to know if what I see in the background is the town? I was never there, I never saw it, I don't know anything. I don't think I want to take them—not at all because I don't want them, I want them very much. But then she'll be left with nothing.

"I'll die and someone will throw them out. You'll get some use out of them."

Eleven photographs, ten with her in them. She was very pretty— she must have been popular. In one of the pictures she's walking on the road to Janowice with a boy. They're elegant, he has his arm around her, he presses his face to hers. They're laughing. She's looking straight at the camera. It looks like early spring, the trees have no leaves, the sun is shining, it's fairly warm, because they're wearing light coats. On the back of another photograph she's written: "Stefan, my brother, back from the army, Miedzianka—1965. Stefan." She repeated his name twice. Strange. This one looks like September or a cooler August. Her face is overexposed in the sun, we can only see she's holding her brother's hand, they're looking at one another, the road to Janowice once again. Then there's a portrait of her in the garden, as she sits at a compact table built from a single piece of wood and some kind of post. Maybe this is where that bench of hers was, maybe she had just stood on it and seen Śnieżka Mountain.

It's difficult to find Polish photographs from the mid-sixties where the buildings in Miedzianka are visible. It's rarest of all for locals to take pictures with ruins in the background. Among the photographs Hanna Gębuś gave me, only in two is part of the square visible.

Jan Majka showed me another photograph where he's with his friend Marian Sztama and the two are play-wrestling over a bayonet they'd just found in the attic of one of the buildings. Marian is holding Janek by the wrist and smiling at the camera. They're both wearing sweaters and shirts with light-colored collars. The backs of buildings are visible, a mess of country yards, low fences, sheds, and lines of drying laundry. Everything that was here before the town disappeared—everyday, ordinary life.

But what did it look like? I want to know—I won't believe it until I see it. Karl Heinz Friebe comes to my rescue. Someone visited from Germany in 1967 and took pictures of the square. In color! Karl Heinz has prints of them scrupulously organized in an album. I look at the slightly faded facades, the empty cavities of the windows, the debris spilling through doors onto the street. You can tell instantly no one from here took these photos; the townspeople would probably have been a little ashamed to do so, or maybe they just saw no point in photographing ruins. These color photographs were taken by someone who came to see whether the town still existed and how it was doing. There are only a few people in them, sitting on a bench in front of a ruined house, and a few kids. Proof someone still lives here. The ruins, the dust, and the sun at high noon, overexposing the lighter parts of the frame. And amid all this, a mailbox screwed to the wall of one of the collapsing houses. Yes, someone still lives here.

I also have pictures of the brewery, given to me by the Słowińskis. Pure inventory—most of them are of pieces of equipment whose names I don't even know. Jerzy Słowiński took the pictures when he ran the brewery for a few months. So there are indistinct photographs of the buildings and its surroundings, there are pictures of brew tanks and some other installations. A jumble of pipes, cans, and dials. A simple survey of fittings. But among the pictures is one featuring the workers. They only stepped out for a moment, there's still snow on the ground, it must have been fairly cold. I recognize Werka Butyńska right away: she's standing in front, a white scarf over her head, somewhat proud, somewhat surly. I can only guess at the others' identities, or make them up as I go.

Everyone is looking into the camera, except the brewmaster, who looks at the others with a smile. Some are laughing a little. The two-story brewery stands in the background. This is an inventory photo. The description might say: brewery building from the south side, morning shift, workers on their breakfast break, 1963—photograph not current.

ALL MIEDZIANKA'S TREASURES

"THIS IS HOW IT USUALLY HAPPENED: these Germans would come to a farm and set a bottle or two on the table. They'd give the kids some candy and crack open the booze. They could hold their drink, only they'd pretend to be lightweights. Then everyone would go to bed. And when the farmers woke up in the morning, the Germans would be gone, and so would the partition wall and the chimney. There'd just be a great big hole and a giant mess. That was how they'd get their treasure back."

"When we moved into number 27, the floorboards and wood paneling were gone, and in the attic, all the ceiling planks had been stripped down to the roof tiles, and every window was broken. And as soon as we laid eyes on all that, we knew treasure-hunters had been there before us and we wouldn't find anything valuable the Germans had left behind."

"There were people who came to the town right after the war, settled, lived here for a while, and then suddenly left. After a while people knew when someone left, it was because they'd ended up in a house with German treasure and they'd found it. And to stop people from being jealous, those families took off right away."

"During the war, the Germans kept artwork looted from all the fronts in the Karpniki Castle. It was said the greatest treasure of all was there, and no one could approach the castle because soldiers would shoot you on sight. When the Russians crossed the Oder River, that castle and all the treasure were evacuated to Germany, but the Krauts sent a few trucks to Miedzianka. And they hid it all in the mines here, because only they knew the exact layout of the tunnels.

"Then, when the Russians came and opened up the uranium mine, little by little they found the treasure in the galleries and took it home with the ore. Apparently the miners were afraid to go into the old ex-German galleries, because that's where they were digging for the treasure. Besides, the Russians did away with all the witnesses, so no miner who saw the treasure is still alive.

"There was so much treasure the Russians couldn't transport it all out of here, and when the uranium ran out they had to close the mine. So when they closed it, they shut off all the pumps and flooded every one of those galleries with water."

"In the hole under our outhouse, we found a whole tub filled to the brim with china dinnerware. Some of the pieces had broken underground, but a lot of them were in good shape and we used them for years. My sister, who lived next door, was less lucky, because she only found a silver sugar bowl. She was even a little mad at me, because we didn't want to share our china with her."

"All the cellars in Miedzianka had brick floors, so moisture wouldn't get under the houses. If you went around those cellars after the war, there wasn't a single one where the bricks hadn't been torn out and the earth dug up. Then people tried to lay the bricks down again, and the floors in those cellars lost their shape, moisture got in, and their potatoes would get moldy. I never heard of anyone finding any treasure down there. But I'm sure if someone found something they wouldn't have admitted it."

"Every now and again some items the Germans had hidden in the ground would turn up, but they had no particular value and collectors gathered them up afterward. No one here ever found gold or jewelry."

"There were a few of those families up in Miedzianka who all of a sudden would strike it rich. And at first people wondered where they got their money from, since none of them even worked in the mine, but then everyone figured out it was German treasure. Besides, their kids would sometimes brag, so if someone found something it got around town pretty quickly."

"We think some beer-label collector lived in our house before the war, because the whole attic was full of the things. They were tied up in these little bundles, held together with rubber bands. My father sometimes used them to start fires, because they'd dried out completely up there in the attic. Then Antek Szmaciarz showed up in town and bought the labels off us for the price of waste paper, so we sold them all to him and my father used old newspapers to light the stove."

"When they were demolishing the manor house, no one was allowed to go near it, and soldiers from the Internal Security Corps kept things under control. One time, a few boys and I managed to get inside. The Germans must have hidden a lot of treasure in the mansion, because when we went in, anywhere you could hide something had been cleared out. Before the workers dismantled the house, they tore up the floors and smashed in the walls to get at the valuables inside. And all we could find were the empty hiding places; we didn't discover any treasure there ourselves."

"The Czaplas found a can full of dollars and it paid for the whole family to move to Australia."

"Some Germans came and asked if they could pitch a tent under a tree and camp out for a few days. We didn't mind, so we let them. Sometimes they'd come to get water, but they mostly just sat in that tent. When they left, we went there and it turned out there was a great big hole in the ground where that tent of theirs had been."

"There was this one house in Miedzianka which the Russians had taken over immediately. They boarded up all the windows and doors and banned anyone from coming inside. Everyone in town knew the Russians were keeping treasure they'd gotten from

Germany in there. Except some people who said the Russkies had closed up the house because it was all cracked and was in danger of collapsing."

"People would laugh afterward, because when a van would show up in the area with German plates and a little digger on a trailer, we knew right away what they were coming for. They'd drive into a field somewhere or under a tree, dig for a while, then leave. No one particularly minded, it was their stuff after all, and only they knew the exact places where treasure was hidden. We spent our whole lives looking and didn't find anything but trash."

THE TOWN IS GONE

We had a house—guests came and went
The rooms are empty now, no one knows us anymore
Poison hemlock waits beyond the garden gate
And grass grows knee-high at the entrance
Although I've looked, I will find nothing
Trash and dust cover things from long ago
Shadows flit in the cracks in the wall
And crows wearily beat their wings
Above abandoned places
And no one there knows who I am

RUTH STORM*

IF KARL HEINZ FRIEBE HAD CRIED, standing in the middle of
a pasture scattered with cowpats where the market square of his
beloved town had once been, it would probably have been overly
melodramatic. But he could have been furious, disappointed, sad;
he could have seethed with hatred. All these things would have

---

* I am quoting from *Chronik über Jannowitz* by Dora Puschmann.

been possible to explain. But none of that happens—Karl Heinz stands among the nettles and calmly points with his umbrella:

"Bräuer's restaurant was there, Haenisch's pharmacy there. Where we're standing was my grandmother's living room, she would walk out from here to the entrance and then continue outside, passing under a beautiful apple tree. Once, Kupferberg was beautiful and green."

Now it is only green.

MIEDZIANKA

Back before the Iron Curtain fell and Karl Heinz Friebe was able to come to Poland with no difficulty, a certain man fell into the ground. His name was Zbigniew Antoni Sieroń and he was an electrician. It was late fall in the early eighties. No trace remained of the town on the hilltop any longer, and only a handful of the most determined residents lived in the few houses strewn throughout the area. But in a tin building on the road to Janowice, SIMET, a company from Jelenia Góra, operated its machine shops. A dozen or so people worked there, bused in specially from Jelenia Góra. One evening, Zbigniew Antoni Sieroń set out for Janowice, to repair a television belonging to Władek Trepa, an old miner and later a worker at the brewery. He returned late at night; he was hurrying a little, so he took a shortcut. But he didn't make it back to the shop.

When darkness fell, someone at the workshop noticed Sieroń was missing. They set out looking for him, in darkness and with fog enveloping the hill, just like every autumn. Finally, they found him. He lay shouting at the bottom of a sinkhole, along with a few pieces of fencing. The hole had opened up right next to the road leading to the shop. They tried to get him out, but nowhere nearby had a ladder long enough to reach. So they tied a few ropes together and descended that way. Sieroń was bruised and scared out of his mind, but in one piece. They didn't have an easy time getting him to the surface. When he got back, he excitedly told everyone the earth had tried to devour him alive. For a long time afterward, they joked that he probably deserved it.

No, the ground under Miedzianka won't let itself be forgotten. After almost every heavy rain, sinkholes and hollows open up in the fields here, which the farmers spend weeks filling with dirt. From the eighties onwards, the mining galleries collapse with increasing frequency—no one in their right mind goes into them any longer, though there are still people in the area who know where particular drifts are and how to reach them. One who knows is Bogdan Markowski, a good friend of Bogdan Spiż and, in the eighties, an employee at the dairy in Janowice. Back then, he decided to use the subterranean labyrinth under Miedzianka to store whey, which the dairy had constant problems disposing of. So Markowski and a few employees took a milk tank and drove all the way to the outskirts of Mniszków. There he located one of the entrances to the mine. They didn't even look inside, they just squeezed the whey into the mountain and left, pleased with themselves. A scandal broke out a few days later, when the water in the Bóbr turned white and started stinking.

"That's when it hit me what was really hidden under that mountain," recalls Markowski.

Leafing through local newspapers from the seventies and eighties, one will learn there was no uranium mine in Miedzianka. "In reality, from 1948 to 1952, an attempt was made to recommence mining activity and determine its profitability, but after ore was discovered in Lubin, it was found necessary to bring this to a definitive halt," writes *Wierchy*.

But the other papers were not to be outdone. *Karkonosze* adds that Miedzianka had already caved in by 1945, and *Nowiny Jeleniogórskie* says nothing had been found in the ground here since the war, so mining died a natural death. After that, Miedzianka fades into obscurity, with journalists no longer showing any interest.

When the borders open, increasing numbers of Germans begin arriving in the area, wanting to see if they can still recognize their home region. One day, an elderly gentleman with an aristocratic air stands in the office of the director of the health center in Janowice Wielkie. He introduces himself as Eberhard zu Stolberg Wernigerode, a descendant of Christian Stolberg, the last count of Kupferberg, Jannowitz, and Rohrlach. The mansion where the Janowice clinic is currently located also made up part of the Stolbergs' estate. The director is suspicious, he's already had a few Germans visit claiming to be Stolbergs, though none has been convincing enough to let inside.

So he asks, "And how am I to know, sir, that you are who you say you are?"

"Because, my dear friend," comes the reply, "if you have not changed the lock on the door to your office, I am still in possession of the key!" Stolberg then demonstrates that this is, in fact, the case.

It was Irena Kamieńska-Siuta who witnessed this scene. She had already moved on from political activities for good, and had dedicated herself to giving tours to German tourists visiting the area.

"Stolberg had been haughty, sometimes even cold, when interacting with Poles—he showed no emotion, though he stayed within the limits of courtesy and good behavior," recalls the doctor's wife. "He observed the ruins of Miedzianka, and especially the place where his mansion had stood and where now nothing remains, in sober silence. We returned to Jelenia Góra without exchanging a word. After that he began breaking off contact."

Karl Heinz Friebe returned to Miedzianka in 1989. When he saw what remained, it nearly broke his heart. He resolved never to return. But he did a year later, along with his wife. And he returns to this day. At the start he would park not far from the place where his house used to stand, and spend the night there. Then he would drive around all his old haunts, living like a homeless man among now-nonexistent homes. One day he spotted some children walking along the road to Janowice.

"I was really a small child when I left here after the war, but I felt this had been a misunderstanding, that it demanded explanation. I held onto that conviction for many years, wanting to reverse all of this. But when I saw those children, I understood the way it is now is the way it will be forever."

In 1999, Friebe decided to erect a small obelisk in memory of the town that once stood here. It was the other people from Kupferberg scattered all over Germany who convinced him. They organized a collection and chose a location. The stone was originally to stand beside the Catholic church, which is intact to this day. However, the priest of Janowice parish would not give his approval. Karl Heinz Friebe never asked him why.

"I didn't want to know the answer. He was under no obligation to tell me anyway."

So he placed the stone in the cemetery, where there wasn't much the priest could do to protest, since officially the cemetery does not exist. A modest unveiling ceremony for the monument took place on July 11, 1999. They inscribed the memorial plaque in two languages:

RUHET IN FRIEDEN
IHR SEID UNVERGESSEN

SPOCZYWAJCIE W POKOJU
JESTEŚCIE NIEZAPOMNIANI

Rest in peace. You are not forgotten.

In attendance were the township leader, a few Germans, and the Polish inhabitants of Miedzianka. A pastor also came from Cieplice, and in his sermon said they should join hands over the graves of Poles and Germans. In a short article on the event published later in *Schlesische Bergwacht*, Karl Heinz Friebe wrote, "I felt as though Christmas and Easter had come at the same time, on the same day."

But Germans aren't the only ones returning to Miedzianka. Occasionally, some of those who lived here after the war come too. Hanna Gębuś lives in Blachownia, near Częstochowa. She has three houses there—she lives in one with her husband and has left two for her daughters, though they have chosen to emigrate and currently have no plans to return.

"A stone from Miedzianka lies under each house," she says in a conspiratorial whisper. In Miedzianka, they occupied the building where Haenisch's pharmacy had been. She was the one who took the antlers of the deer old Mr. Ritter had shot out of the attic. She came back in the early nineties, and had trouble finding the place where her house used to be.

"I actually found it thanks to two oak trees growing in the backyard. We'd had a little bench between them, and if you stood on it, you could see Śnieżka Mountain."

There was no trace of the house, and only delicate marks on the trees from the bench. Even that one visit was too much for Hanna Gębuś. She never went back after that—she stays in touch with her former neighbors, and when they want to take her to Miedzianka, she does her best to politely, but firmly, refuse.

WAŁBRZYCH–WROCŁAW–KATOWICE

"Boyhood dreams, nothing more," says Bogdan Spiż modestly, pointing out his antique soda fountain standing in a dark cubbyhole. "Someday when I have some time I'll fix it up it and make sparkling lemonade again."

The room where the dusty soda fountain stands is in Katowice, and forms part of a large dance club where customers can order beer brewed before their very eyes. It's one of the most fashionable places in all of Silesia. The club belongs to Bogdan Spiż. His youngest sister Hania sometimes helps him run it.

Bogdan also owns a restaurant on the market square in Wrocław. It's run by his other sister, Barbara. Here, too, a person can sit down and order a beer that the waiter will pour into a mug straight from a large vat before bringing it to the table. For many tourists visiting Wrocław, Spiż's restaurant is a must-see. They often walk out weighed down with the mugs sold here on the side of the beer production. Each bears a distinctively stylized logo with the word *Spiż* in the middle. Then there's the mansion in Miłków, just south of Jelenia Góra, with banquet halls seating 180 people and a restaurant. Here, Bogdan Spiż does his best to relax, but he doesn't always manage to because there is constantly something to do.

Bogdan Spiż has made it big. By 1991, he was already on *Wprost* magazine's list of the one hundred wealthiest Poles, and two years later he was in thirteenth place. He started out with a single soda fountain and a little lemonade bottling plant founded back in the eighties in Legnica. Before that, he was director of the malt house in Ciechanowice and a brewmaster in Legnica. But all along he wanted to strike out on his own. When capitalism arrived in Poland, Bogdan decided to start following his dreams and become an entrepreneurial shark. He looks nothing like a shark, though—instead he's calm and quiet, people say he wouldn't harm a fly. He bakes sweet pastries known as angel wings for his employees. But when asked to think back to Miedzianka, he appears to lose himself in thought.

When he started doing well for himself, he thought of buying his parents a house in Wilków, near Legnica. He didn't want them to live in the yellow villa in the backwoods Miedzianka had become. Bogdan had already made a down payment on the house when he went to give his mother the good news. Helena didn't want to listen to him, she just kept saying that she would never leave Miedzianka and there was no way she was moving to Wilków. She didn't even come to look at the house.

"There would have been no sense arguing with my mother," Bogdan laughs. So the old Spiżes lived in Miedzianka until the end. They outlived the town. Stefan died in 1995. At the end of his life, his mind started to go—a few times, Helena found him wandering in his pajamas through the ruins of the brewery. She'd take him by the hand and lead him home. Then he would say:

"Don't worry, Helena, I'll just take one batch and I'll be right back to bed."

Bogdan Markowski, the friend of the Spiżes, remembers that in old age, Stefan Spiż would only read one single book over and over again: the novel *Homeless People* by Stefan Żeromski.

"When he got to the last page, he'd close it for a moment, then open it right up again and start reading from the beginning."

Helena Spiż died in 2000. Supposedly, to the end of her days, she smoked and made the best homemade liqueurs for miles around. The Spiżes are buried in two different cemeteries in Janowice. People say it's so they won't argue.

Barbara took her husband's name, Mudry, and is constantly on the road between Wałbrzych and Wrocław. She lives in the former, and runs Bogdan's restaurant on the square in the latter. Asked about Miedzianka, she puts her head in her hands.

"To count as a villa, a building has to have a fountain. We had one in the garden, right there in Miedzianka. And then it was all gone!"

It wasn't until the early nineties that she truly understood her father's anguish. At that time, she was living in Wałbrzych, right next to the Victoria mine. Mining had recently gone into decline across the region, and one pit after another was shuttered. Her husband was a mine worker in Victoria, and her father-in-law was director of the whole facility. When word came their mine would be closed too, both men cried like children. When Barbara Mudry walked her dog around the abandoned grounds of the mine, she felt the same pain her father must have felt.

"My husband's entire family was connected to Victoria, and that meant I was too. It was right out the window, you could hear it, you could feel it, it was what allowed us to live. Because of all that, I developed an affection for it. When they closed it down, I felt a tremendous sense of loss. My father went through the same thing in Miedzianka, but I was too young to understand—back then, it was the future that mattered to me. By the time I finally understood, I had already left it a little too long."

JELENIA GÓRA

In 1966, *Nowiny Jeleniogórskie* announced a writing contest called "My Dreams of the Year 2000." Over the course of a few weeks, the editors received dozens of submissions from the city's youngest citizens.

"The beautiful Zabobrze housing project is complete, it stands under a giant dome that shelters it from snow and rain. An underground tunnel a few miles long has been constructed to connect downtown Jelenia Góra with the center of Zabobrze. On the way into the fairy-tale land of the project, there is a huge carving of a deer standing above a waterfall."

WALDEK RUTKOWSKI

"We will have color TV in our apartments and there will always be running water. People will be better behaved and there will be no delinquents."

BASIA WIRSKA

"Special machines will be placed on the building which, at the push of a button, will dispense delicious candy and other small items. The phones in the telephone booths will be fitted with little screens. When having a conversation on one of these machines, we will be able to see the other person's face on the screen."

MARTA SAŁATA

"The stores will be well supplied with clothes, bed linen, and shoes of all sizes."

KRYSIA GAŁACH

"And that an apartment for four people will have three bedrooms, a large beautiful kitchen, and a tiled bathroom. That the elevators will go to every floor and we will have spacious balconies."

EWA CYMARA

Not all the dreams of these children from nearly a half-century ago have been fulfilled. While there really is no problem as far as vending machines or phones with screens are concerned, Zabobrze has not been covered with a glass dome, there is no tunnel connecting it to downtown, and the bridge over the train tracks is routinely jammed at rush hour. *Nowiny Jeleniogórskie* is still in print, and in early 2010 it called Zabobrze a "neighborhood of fear," where young thugs made off with old ladies' purses and broke into apartments. The editors of *Nowiny* were exaggerating—Zabobrze is actually a fairly sleepy housing project of mainly retirees. Crime here is no better or worse than anywhere else.

"Today, Miedzianka is in Zabobrze," laughs Barbara Majka, once the prettiest employee in the brewery.

If she knocked on any wall of her two-bedroom apartment, a neighbor from Miedzianka would answer her. In the apartment block at 45 Karłowicz Street, where the Majkas live, you can count the people not from the town on one hand. The rest are old friends—there are the Żureks, whose attic sang the loudest, there's Irena Wędzel, who didn't want to take the holy figures out of the ruins of the church. There's also Irena Barwicka, who cried with despair when she first saw Miedzianka. At number 43 lives Jadwiga Chutyrko, the last person to move out of the town. She was even on TV for the occasion—reporters came to ask how she could live without fearing the ceiling might collapse on her head. She said she lived just fine. In the next building along are the Szymczyks and the Mądreckis, as well as Czesław Plesiak, who, when asked about Miedzianka, stands silently in the middle of the room and merely shakes his head in resignation. Finally, Kazimierz Milcuszek, the last schoolmaster, lives at number 11. He has only gone to take a look at Miedzianka once—he went with his wife, but was unable to find his house and lost his enthusiasm. Janek Kluba lives one floor up on that same stairwell, and he goes there almost every week.

"I miss it terribly," he shyly admits.

They all keep one another's phone numbers in ancient notebooks ("With the cell phone I have a hard time finding them again, you know?"), they greet one another politely out on walks, and sometimes they sit down on a bench to exchange a few words. They know everything about one another: who has died, who is sick, who will soon be a grandfather. They ask each other not to share that information with anyone. Only a few mention Miedzianka, and then only rarely.

"Our memories of the town keep getting more beautiful as the years go by," they laugh. Because that's how human memory is—it sifts out the bad and only holds on to beautiful images.

There's no two ways about it: these days, Miedzianka is in Zabobrze, packed into four apartment buildings on Karłowicz Street and a few others on Paderewski, Elsner, and Różycki Streets. A Miedzianka of concrete slabs, on solid ground; a Miedzianka green once more, surrounded by trees and the shouts of children in the background. All this ten miles from the collapsing mountain, which is overgrown with bushes and grass. In the place where there had once been an entire town, the only evidence of its existence is a church standing unnaturally in the wilderness, a few abandoned tumbledown houses, and bricks you can trip on as you cross through the meadows.

It's easy to forget all this in Zabobrze. To conjure up the memories, you have to stand in line for the cash register at the grocery store on Monday, Wednesday, or Friday, and when asked "What kind of bread?" respond, as always:

"A loaf of Miroś's, please."

JANOWICE WIELKIE

There are still some who stayed nearby. They live nearly in the shadow of the mountain, though they almost never go up it. They have no desire to; it's out of their way—and they're a little afraid they might be stung by a memory surging forth after years of lying dormant.

Barbara Wójcik, who cheated death five times, lives to this day with her second husband on the outskirts of Janowice, where the road ducks under the old, German-built bridge and, meandering along the edge of the Bóbr, runs to Trzcińsko. It's the most beautiful road in the entire area. Their house is the last one in the village; it stands on a low hill, surrounded by vegetable gardens and beehives.

Before she buried her first husband, she beat him black and blue—not for revenge (he often hit her), but to keep him from dying. He was suffering from leukemia, and they were at a wedding when the end came: all of a sudden he collapsed to the ground. In a few moments, Barbara Wójcik was at his side, dealing him powerful smacks in the face.

"I was never exactly weak," she says modestly, "and once my mom told me the only thing you can do when someone is on the verge of death is hit them. He was a real bastard to me, but you don't just let someone die like that, so I had no choice. He didn't pass away until he was in the hospital, a few months later."

Now Wójcik lives in her house on the hill with Józek Chęciński. He'd tried to ask her out a few times, but she was never interested. He kept at it for so long she finally came around. "I wouldn't stop pestering her," admits Chęciński. "I always find if a woman is over two hundred pounds I fall in love with her."

Józef Chęciński is the stepson of Józef Ostrowski, the policeman who arrived in 1945 to bring order to Janowice.

"Dad and I would ride around on his motorcycle, and I saw everything that would end up in the papers later."

When asked to tell a story, Chęciński will often begin:

"There is one truth and one truth only..."

In the part of Janowice closest to Miedzianka—so-called "Old Janowice"—lives Stanisław Kopczyński, who used to smash Communists' faces in but wouldn't admit it, along with Staszek Gruszka, who didn't drink vodka and only worked in the mine for two years, which is why he's alive. On Zamkowa Street, there's also Karolina Burzawa, née Kolis. She's reluctant to talk about the mine. They, along with Baśka Wójcik, are literally the only miners from the Miedzianka uranium mine living in the area today. More lie in Janowice's two cemeteries, where others keep joining them. Many died of cancer, such as Franek Krupa, who as an old man had his larynx removed. As long as he lived he kept an eye on the mining damage. Once he'd been a miner, and after that he made sure the holes in the ground were quickly filled in. That was the task entrusted to him by the authorities at the copper mine in Legnica, which officially owned the ex-mining land in Miedzianka. Krupa had his work cut out for him, but he didn't complain, because he also felt an attachment to that pockmarked mountain. He never wanted to talk about the mine, and once his voice box had been taken out, he couldn't anymore. He only wrote whatever he wanted to communicate on little pieces of paper. His wife would read the notes out loud. That was how you had to communicate with Franek Krupa at the end of his life. He died in 2010.

A link between the high incidence of cancer among the mine workers and the conditions they endured was never proven. It was Stanisław Siuta, the director of the Janowice health center, who had raised the alarm that something grave might have been happening here.

"All over the region at that time, and especially in Janowice and Miedzianka, the prevalence of cancer was higher than elsewhere, mainly among relatively young people. I even called in specialists to investigate these cases, but we were unable to establish a broader pattern."

Today we know black lung—an occupational disease affecting all miners—took a much harsher toll in uranium mines, where it was radioactive black lung, at least for as long as the radioactive element was decaying in the dust the miners inhaled. It's difficult to determine how long that was, but for some it was sufficient to increase their susceptibility to cancer. After Communism fell in Poland, the Solidarity senator Andrzej Piesiak became interested in the fate of the R-1 mine workers, including those in Miedzianka. It was he who set up a parliamentary commission to determine what losses Poland had suffered due to the extraction of uranium for the Soviet Union. As they did so, the parliamentarians also investigated what became of the workers from R-1. Former miners came constantly to Senator Piesiak's office in Jelenia Góra to talk about their former working conditions. This testimony later served as evidence in claims for compensation and pensions. Few received anything—a large share of the R-1 medical documents had disappeared, and without them it was hard for the miners to prove that illnesses they contracted in old age were the direct result of working in the uranium mines.

Zdzisiek Jankowski also lives in Janowice. Now he is an older gentleman of almost sixty with prison tattoos, but back then he was a local hoodlum who pulled the sword out of Ueberschaer's tomb and stole the ball from the Lutheran church that was blown sky-high. When Zdzisiek Jankowski is asked about Miedzianka, he disappears for a moment into his apartment, and returns a little later with a school photo.

"This is me, and that's our teacher Mr. Milcuszek. See, I hadn't started getting in trouble yet."

Werka Butyńska lives right next door. She's still prone to swear when something catches her by surprise. She didn't stop smoking until recently. She hobbles on crutches around her sparkling-clean apartment in the back of Kluger's old hotel. At the mention of Stefan Spiż, she grins from ear to ear:

"He had a heart of gold."

Werka doesn't complain, she's comfortably off in her old age, and she's raised two sons and a daughter. The son she laid on sheepskin in the malt house now owns a construction company. When talking about him, Werka can't hold back her tears.

"It would have taken so little for neither of us to make it. My boy grew up strong as an oak. What a loss it would have been."

MIEDZIANKA

A couple of times Paweł Nowak found himself standing in the middle of the meadow, imagining the apartment buildings, the steep roads, the two church towers, the hubbub emanating from the windows of the tavern, the shouts of children racing out of the school, or the joyful cries of the stoneworkers from the quarry: all of it in German. Then he would open his eyes and see nothing now except clumps of greenery and trash by the roadside. Because Miedzianka is simply gone. Dozens of buildings, a mansion, old Glyschinsky's water-bottling plant, the church with the yellow facade—it's all vanished, destroyed, plundered, razed to the ground, trucked off, plowed under, collapsed into the ground.

Sometimes Paweł Nowak would see a car with German plates by the church. He even wanted to go up to them and tell them not to park there—only a few years ago the ground between the highway and the church caved in to a depth of about fifty feet, so far down that it was terrifying to gaze into the hole. It was a miracle the church survived. But Paweł has his own ideas about its future. Ever since trucks have started coming this way loaded with feldspar from the quarry in Karpniki, the church's days have seemed numbered:

"They make everything shake. You'll see our Miedzianka on TV again when our church falls into the ground."

Paweł says "our Miedzianka," although he himself lives in Janowice. Once his grandfather showed him a few postcards of the town that disappeared. He liked them, so he started poking through books and old documents. One day in the Jelenia Góra archive, someone tapped Paweł on the shoulder and said:

"You're interested in Kupferberg? She's the one you've got to meet."

"She" was Dora Puschmann.

She came from Jannowitz; in 1945 she was a teacher in Kupferberg's preschool. She was evacuated along with the children in the first wave, right after the Russians broke through the front on the way to Breslau. She returned nearly forty years later. What she saw inspired her to write her chronicle of Jannowitz, and then of Miedzianka as well, towns where she'd spent her youth but where she was unable to die. The first sentence of her Miedzianka chronicle reads: *Kupferberg ist verschwunden*—"Miedzianka has disappeared."

Dora Puschmann's chronicles were published in the eighties in the pages of *Schlesische Bergwacht*, focusing on people from these parts who were displaced after the Second World War. This is not reading material to bring both sides together. It is full of bitterness and sorrow, and occasionally even rage, about what happened. Dora Puschmann writes, "only a German plow is worthy of this land," that in fact all the evil the Germans experienced after the war was due to "drunken Poles." The Nazis only make sporadic appearances; the town seems almost perfectly isolated not only from the tumult of war, but also the ideology that unleashed that tumult. Sometimes in all this she also mixes up her facts—to her, Duke Bolko is Count von Bolz, and she writes Bolzenstein where it should say Bolczów Castle. She makes persistent use of the phrase "our homeland."

"In May 1987, I stood on Kreuzberg Mountain under the tall cross, and looked at the Giant Mountains and far into the

Silesian countryside. The houses I'd dreamed of in Fischbach, Neu Fischbach, and Waltersdorf were scattered among the blossoming meadows and trees, as though nothing had happened, as though humanity had not developed at all. [...] The cross was erected 156 years ago to defend the Falcon Mountains, and the valleys were spared the atrocities of war, but the expulsion had grievous effects for many. It is hard to say goodbye to this wonderful, beloved corner of our homeland."

Paweł Nowak never met Dora Puschmann personally, but they exchanged letters for a few years and she sent him dozens of photographs, postcards, and documents concerning Miedzianka and Janowice. Those who knew Dora Puschmann personally say she shunned meeting Poles, harboring deep resentment toward them. But she corresponded with Paweł nevertheless.

"I don't know why, maybe she felt I wasn't up to anything and just wanted to learn as much as possible," says Paweł. When she died, he decided to translate her chronicle and put it online. To this day he receives e-mails from people cursing him for it.

There's an old tree in Miedzianka that Paweł only shows a few people. You pass the brewery, then just after the bend in the road, turn off the highway onto the dirt road leading to one of the farms and stop by an inconspicuous, overgrown plum tree.

"I wanted the tree to be able to grow in peace," says Paweł. If you examine the trunk of the tree closely, you will definitely spot a tin plaque, placed so as to be invisible from the road. To see it, you have to wade into the nettles. On this plaque, which is no larger than a pack of cigarettes, someone has written:

ERINNER DIE LEUTE VON KUPFERBERG

"It means: 'Remember the people of Kupferberg,'" says Paweł. "This is how I imagine it: they've come here, they've looked around, and can only recognize this tree. Imagine: out of everything that was here, the houses, the churches, the restaurants, they only recognize one tree. Nothing more. So they put that here and left."

Paweł doesn't talk about this too often, but following him around Miedzianka, it's evident one question torments him constantly: if events had unfolded differently and the Germans had stayed here, would Miedzianka still exist? Of course, such a question can awaken the demons of the past. Besides, no one wants to hear a question like that, and nor do they want the answer to be "no." But this first question immediately begs another, equally important one, which torments the mind just as much: wouldn't the price of Miedzianka's survival have been too high? The retirees in Zabobrze don't ask themselves questions like this—instead, they occur in the mind of a brand-new father, an eternally overworked thirty-year-old, driving a chunky silver Opel Tigra with aluminum rims, which he doesn't park by the church because if he does, that Tigra of his might fall through the ground sometime.

HILDESHEIM

In 1999, Karl Heinz Friebe read in the paper about an old schoolteacher who was teaching German to Turkish children somewhere near Hildesheim. It was Gisela Franzky. Even today, when he speaks of her, his eyes go wide with emotion and his wife standing beside him smiles with embarrassment.

"Don't worry, darling, Gisela was my first love, but you're my second and last," Karl Heinz assures her, stroking her hand.

He and Gisela met the next spring at her house. She cooked a wonderful Silesian feast. They didn't know where to start, so Karl Heinz admitted how he had felt for her when he was a boy. Then they told one another stories of their little town that disappeared. Gisela wept.

JELENIA GÓRA–POZNAŃ 2010

EPILOGUE

I MIGHT HAVE JUST WANDERED around the remains of Miedzianka without even knowing what kind of history was hidden there if not for the considerable and painstaking help of a few people. This book would not have come about without Paweł Nowak from Janowice Wielkie, a great history buff and collector of old postcards. Without his factual assistance, sober perspective on certain subjects, and determination in putting me in touch with more people, I would not have written a single word. Thanks also to Bogdan Spiż and Barbara Mudry for their time, and Stanisław Tadrak for his invaluable help translating German texts.

Since *History of a Disappearance* was first published, I've been asked dozens of times why I wrote it. I tell myself and those who ask that I did it so I could feel something when I stood in that meadow. Because when I went there for the first time, I felt absolutely nothing. If I hadn't previously seen the archival photographs of beautiful Kupferberg, I would have passed through that place without paying it the slightest attention. And I don't suppose it's a good thing to be unaware of the disappearance of an entire town.

In mid-2013, two years after the first edition of *History of a Disappearance* was released in Poland, I went to see if it had actually done the trick. Somewhere past Strzegom, the GPS told us to turn off the main route. At first it was all right, but then more and more potholes started appearing in the road. It was getting dark when we passed an abandoned military post, and we had no idea where we were. I was looking for familiar shapes on the horizon, but at best I could only imagine them. There was nothing there I recognized.

And then came cool nightfall and Janowice. The cemetery, the bridge, the store, Kluger's old hotel where Werka Butyńska used to live. Past the train tracks, we turned left. When we stopped by the road next to the church, my knees were weak. We were walking through a meadow that had been the town square, it was windy, and I was teetering between euphoria and panic.

The next day we went there again. We went to see Ueberschaer's tomb and the plaque on the old plum tree. A considerable section of the bark had rotted and the plaque was only hanging on by a few scraps. It soon fell off and someone took it away.

After the book's release, deserted Miedzianka took on a life of its own. The local association worked with the township to put up informational signs, so now anyone can see what the town looked like when it still existed. The BWA art gallery in Jelenia Góra organized an exhibition of work by Polish and German artists who addressed the subject through heartbreaking paintings and photographs. Meanwhile, in 2014, the Copper Museum in Legnica published a wonderful historical monograph titled *Miedzianka. 700 lat dziejów górniczego miasta* (Miedzianka: the 700-year history of a mining town) by Marcin Makuch and Tomasz Stolarczyk. It makes a fantastic complement to my work.

The town has also made its presence known onstage. Since 2013, the Cyprian Kamil Norwid Theater in Jelenia Góra has been performing *History of a Disappearance* in repertory. Łukasz Cymerman adapted the book for the stage, and Łukasz Fijał directed the production.

Brewing will also return to Miedzianka: private investors have decided to build a small brewery there and return to the local tradition of beer making. As it turns out, what once seemed an absolute end was only a pause.

Now I have no need to go any longer. Miedzianka has disappeared, but it still remains.

SELECTED LITERATURE

Anon. "Dokąd wywożono polski uran? Ludzie odchodzą z poczuciem krzywdy." *Życie Warszawy* 132 (June 7, 1991).

Anon. "Geiger trzeszczał." *Życie Warszawy* 133 (June 5–7, 1991).

Anon. "Uran i sprawiedliwość." *Życie Warszawy* 81 (April 5, 1991).

Benz, Wolfgang. *Die Vertreibung der Deutschen aus dem Osten: Ursachen, Ereignisse, Folgen.* Frankfurt am Main: Fischer, 1995.

Bochnak, Władysław. "Ks. Jan Marcin Stulpe (1686–1753) i początki kultu Najświętszego Serca Pana Jezusa w diecezji wrocławskiej." *Wrocławskie Wiadomości Kościelne* 7–9 (1983).

Boćkowski, Daniel. *Niemcy w Polsce 1945–1950. Wybór dokumentów*, vol. 4. Warsaw: Wydawnictwo Neriton, 2001.

Bundesministerium für Vertriebene. *Dokumentation der Vertreibung der Deutschen OstMitteleuropa: Gesamtausgabe in 8 Bänden.* Munich: Deutscher Taschenbuch Verlag, 2004.

Chądzyński, Wojciech. *Wędrówki po Dolnym Śląsku i jego stolicy. Fakty, legendy, sensacje.* Wrocław: I BiS, 2006.

Chojnacki, Mieczysław. "Mokotowskie więzienie. Rozprawa – wyrok – pobyt w ogólnej celi śmierci," *Zeszyty WiN-u*, vol. 1 (1992): 28–61.

Chorowska, Małgorzata, Tomasz Dudziak, Krzysztof Jaworski, and Artur Kwaśniewski. *Zamki i dwory obronne w Sudetach. Tom II. Księstwo jaworskie.* Wrocław: Instytut Archeologii Uniwersytetu Wrocławskiego, 2009.

Czerner, Olgierd, and Arno Herzig, ed. *Das Tal der Schlösser und Gärten. Das Hirschberger Tal in Schlesien – ein gemeinsames Kulturerbe.* Berlin and Jelenia Góra: Gesellschaft für Interregionalen Kulturaustausch, 2003.

Czerwiński, Janusz, and Krzysztof R. Mazurski. *Sudety. Sudety Zachodnie: Góry i Pogórze Kaczawskie, Rudawy Janowickie, Kotlina Jeleniogórska i Karkonosze.* Warsaw: Sport i Turystyka, 1983.

Davies, Norman, and Roger Moorhouse. *Microcosm: Portrait of a Central European City.* London: PIMLICO, 2002.

Dobkiewiczowa, Kornelia. *Róże w błękitnym polu. Podania i opowieści o zamkach Dolnego Śląska.* Warsaw: Nasza Księgarnia, 1982.

Dolata, Bolesław. *Wyzwolenie Dolnego Śląska w 1945 roku.* Wrocław: Zakład Narodowy im. Ossolińskich, 1985.

Dziekoński, Tadeusz. *Wydobywanie i metalurgia kruszców na Dolnym Śląsku od XIII do połowy XX wieku.* Wrocław: Zakład Narodowy im. Ossolińskich, 1972.

Dziewit, Piotr. "Uranowi ludzie." *Panorama* 14 (1991).

Franzky, Georg. *Erinnerungen an Kupferberg.* Unpublished manuscript.

Gazeta Robotnicza. Annual 1969.

Gołębiowski, Bronisław, ed. *Tu jest nasza Ojczyzna. Z pamiętników mieszkańców Ziem Zachodnich i Północnych.* Poznań: Wydawnictwo Poznańskie, 1981.

Hirsch, Helga. *Die Rache der Opfer. Deutsche in polnischen Lagern 1944–1950.* Berlin: Rowohlt, 1998.

Janczak, Julian. *Spotkania z Duchem Gór. Sudeckie szkice historyczne.* Wrocław: Wieczór Wrocławia, 1991.

————, *Z tamtej strony historii czyli Wrocławskie i dolnośląskie legendy, podania, baśnie i niesamowite wydarzenia.* Wrocław: Wratislavia, 1993.

Januszewski, Józef and Włodzimierz Koszarski. *Skarby Ziemi Dolnośląskiej.* Wrocław: Zakład Narodowy im. Ossolińskich, 1979.

Jastrzębski, Włodzimierz, ed. *Ludność niemiecka na ziemiach polskich w latach 1939–1945 i jej powojenne losy.* Conference publication. Bydgoszcz: Wydaw Uczelniane WSP, 1995.

Jonca, Karol. "Francuscy i belgijscy więźniowie z akcji 'Noc i mgła' na Dolnym Śląsku." *Studia nad Faszyzmem i Zbrodniami Hitlerowskimi* 2 (1975).

Kapałczyński, Wojciech, and Piotr Napierała. *Zamki, pałace i dwory Kotliny Jeleniogórskiej.* Wrocław: Fundacja Doliny Pałaców i Ogrodów Kotliny Jeleniogórskiej, 2005.

Kersten, Krystyna, and Tomasz Szarota, ed. *Wieś polska 1939–1948. Materiały konkursowe.* Warsaw: Państwowe Wydawnictwo Naukowe, 1967.

Klementowski, Robert. "Wydział IX Departamentu IV MBP / Wydział IX 'K' WUBP we Wrocławiu z siedzibą w Kowarach (struktura, działalność, obsada personalna)." *Aparat Represji w Polsce Ludowej* 4 (2006): 79–126

————, "Skazani na uran. Kopalnie rudy uranu we wspomnieniach żołnierzy batalionów pracy." *Studia nad Faszyzmem i Zbrodniami Hitlerowskimi* 21 (2009): 293–307

————, "Uranowe mity. Kopalnictwo uranu w Polsce w społecznej świadomości." In *Gospodarka i społeczeństwo w czasach PRL-u*

(1944–1989), edited by Tomasz Głowiński, and Elżbieta Kościk, 133–150. Wrocław: Materiały konferencji naukowej, Polanica Zdrój, 21–23 IX, 2007.

Konieczny, Alfred. "Ewakuacja obozu koncentracyjnego Gross-Rosen w 1945." *Studia nad Faszyzmem i Zbrodniami Hitlerowskimi* 2 (1975): 16.

Kwaśniewski, Krzysztof. *Legendy i podania wrocławskie i dolnośląskie,* Poznań: Wydawnictwo Poznańskie, 2006.

Lippóczy, Piotr, and Tadeusz Walichnowski. *Przesiedlenie ludności niemieckiej z Polski po II wojnie światowej w świetle dokumentów.* Warsaw and Łódź. Państwowe Wydawnictwo Naukowe, 1982.

Nitschke, Bernadetta. *Wysiedlenie czy wypędzenie? Ludność niemiecka w Polsce 1945–1949.* Toruń: Adam Marszałek, 2000.

Majewski, Ryszard. *Dolny Śląsk 1945. Wyzwolenie,* Warsaw and Wrocław: Państwowe Wydawnictwo Naukowe, 1982.

Maroń, Jerzy. *Wojna trzydziestoletnia na Śląsku. Aspekty militarne.* Wrocław and Racibórz: WAW, 2008.

Mazurski, Krzysztof. "Likwidacja i rekultywacja Miedzianki." *Wierchy* 45 (1976).

Mistewicz, Eryk. "Uran ponad wszystko." *Reporter* 6 (1989).

Mońko, Michał. "Gułag Miedzianka." *Odra* 4, 1995: 33–39.

Nowiny Jeleniogórskie, 1959–1981.

Olczak, Mariusz. *Kampania 1813. Śląsk i Łużyce.* Warsaw: OPPIDUM, 2004.

Pasierb, Bronisław. *Migracja ludności niemieckiej z Dolnego Śląska w latach 1944–1947.* Wrocław: Zakład Narodowy im. Ossolińskich, 1969.

Primke, Robert, Maciej Szczerepa, and Wojciech Szczerepa. *Wojna w Dolinie Bobru. Bolesławiec–Lwówek Śląski–Jelenia Góra w 1945.* Jelenia Góra: Archiwul System, 2009.

Puschmann, Dora. *Chronik über Kupferberg*. Unpublished manuscript.

———, *Chronik über Jannowitz*. Unpublished manuscript.

Romanow, Zenon. *Ludność niemiecka na ziemiach zachodnich i północnych w latach 1945–1947*. Słupsk: WSP, 1972.

Schlesische Bergwacht. 1980–2010.

Springer, Filip. "I nikt tam nie wie, kim jestem." *Magazyn Turystyki Górskiej N.P.M.* 2 (2009).

———, "Nie ma miasteczka." *Polityka* 41 (2726) (October 10, 2009).

Staffa, Marek. *Słownik geografii turystycznej Sudetów. Rudawy Janowickie*. Wrocław: I-Bis, 1998.

Szoka, Henryk. "Miasto, które przestało istnieć – Miedzianka." *Karkonosze* 3/103 (1986).

Tęcza, Krzysztof. *Kamienne obiekty dawnego prawa na ziemi jeleniogórskiej*. Zgorzelec: Zukaj, 1992.

Urban, Thomas. *Der Verlust. Die Vertreibung der Deutschen und Polen im 20. Jahrhundert*. Munich: C.H. Beck, 2006.

Urbanek, Mariusz. "Blask uranu." *Przegląd Tygodniowy* 17 (April 28, 1991).

Wanderer im Riesengebirge. 8 / 1888, 7 / 1890, 9 / 1890, 2 / 1896, 1 / 1906, 5 / 1936.

Wąsacz, Józef. *Szlakiem wspomnień żołnierzy-górników z lat 1949–1959*. Wrocław: Biuro Tłumzczeń, 2002.

Wytyczak, Roman. "Podzwonne dla Miedzianki." *Wierchy* 40 (1972): 288–289.

Zdulski, Mirosław. *Instytucja totalna w monocentrycznym ładzie społecznym*. Zielona Góra: Rocznik Jeleniogórski, 1999.

———, *Źródła do dziejów kopalnictwa uranowego w Polsce*. Warsaw: DiG, 2000.

ABOUT THE AUTHOR

FILIP SPRINGER (born 1982) is a self-taught journalist who has been working as a reporter and photographer since 2006. His journalistic debut—*History of a Disappearance: The Forgotten Story of a Polish Town*—was shortlisted for the Ryszard Kapuściński Literary Reportage Prize in 2011 and was nominated for the Gdynia Literary Prize in 2012. He was also shortlisted for the Nike Literary Prize in 2012 and won the third annual Ryszard Kapuściński scholarship competition for young journalists in 2014.

ABOUT THE TRANSLATOR

SEAN GASPER BYE is a translator of Polish, French, and Russian literature. He has translated work by some of Poland's leading nonfiction writers, including Małgorzata Szejnert, Paweł Smoleński, and Lidia Ostałowska. An excerpt from his translation of *History of a Disappearance* won Asymptote's Close Approximations Prize in 2016. He lives in New York.